KARL FRIEDRICH SCHINKEL
'The English Journey'

KARL FRIEDRICH SCHINKEL
'The English Journey'
Journal of a Visit to France and Britain in 1826

edited by
David Bindman and Gottfried Riemann

translated by F. Gayna Walls

published for
The Paul Mellon Centre for Studies in British Art
by
Yale University Press
New Haven and London
1993

Designed by Sally Salvesen
Typeset in Linotron Bembo
by Best-set Typesetter Ltd, Hong Kong
Printed in Great Britain

Library of Congress Cataloging-in-Publication Data
Schinkel, Karl Friedrich, 1781–1841.
[Englische Reise. English]
The English journey: journal of a visit to France and Britain in
1826 / edited by David Bindman and Gottfried Riemann.
Includes bibliographical references and index.
ISBN 0-300-04117-9
1. Schinkel, Karl Friedrich, 1781–1841 – Journeys – France.
2. France – Description and travel – 1800–1918.   3. Schinkel,
Karl Friedrich, 1781–1841 – Journeys – England.
4. England – Description and travel – 1801–1900.
I. Bindman, David.   II. Riemann, Gottfried.   III. Title.
NA1088.S3A35   1993
720′.92 – dc20
[B]   93-18323   CIP

CONTENTS

PREFACE TO THE ENGLISH EDITION

The text which comprises the main part of this volume is taken from a small notebook of 75 hand written sides of text with many drawings all in Schinkel's hand, now in the possession of the Staatliche Museen Preussischer Kulturbesitz, in what was until 1990 the Sammlung der Zeichnungen of the Nationalgalerie of the German Democratic Republic in Berlin. In addition several letters written during the 1826 journey have been inserted in their appropriate place in the text, as have a number of separate drawings made on the same journey. The text was first published by Schinkel's son-in-law Alfred von Wolzogen in a three-volume compilation of Schinkel's writings entitled *Aus Schinkels Nachlass*, 1862–3 (reprinted without commentary, 1981). Wolzogen's text is wholly unsatisfactory: notes and even one word references to buildings were extended into full sentences, so that it became readable as continuous prose, but the terseness and immediacy of Schinkel's text was completely lost as well as some important references.

The new editing of the manuscript is entirely the work of Dr Gottfried Riemann, Curator in the Sammlung der Zeichnungen in the Berlin Nationalgalerie, and with his introduction and notes, it was first published in East Berlin in 1986 under the imprint of Henschelverlag, with the title, *Karl Friedrich Schinkel, Reise nach England Schottland und Paris im Jahre 1826*, edited with commentary by Gottfried Riemann, with an essay by David Bindman.

Schinkel's 'English Journey' had been the subject of Dr Riemann's thesis at Halle University in 1967, and he had the very difficult task of transcribing the text of the Journal itself, and relating it to Schinkel's own career as an architect and planner. My own involvement came rather late in the day. In 1981, on a visit to East Berlin I was given the unexpected opportunity, through my friend Dr Peter Betthausen, of seeing the original manuscript in the Nationalgalerie. I discovered that the publication of the manuscript had been delayed because Dr Riemann was unable to obtain permission to travel to Britain to identify many of the buildings and sites mentioned by Schinkel in the Journal, and to gather many of the photographs he needed. I offered to undertake this task, and I was also invited to write an essay for the publication looking at the Journal from the British point of view.

Dr Riemann's essay and footnotes, and the text of the Journal itself, have been translated by Dr F. Gayna Walls with additions by myself, but there are some changes to the structure of the book from the German edition. My own essay has been completely rewritten, and I have added new footnotes and enlarged a great many of the original ones. Some of the illustrations used in the German edition, mainly of familiar views, have been omitted, and instead all but a few of the illustrated pages in the Journal are reproduced. In addition I have been able to find a number of further illustrations of objects described by Schinkel since the German edition appeared. The aim has been to make the present volume more of a facsimile of the original manuscript, and many of the new illustrations in this volume relate to Schinkel's interests in technology. I have also taken into account the edition edited by Reinhard Wegner in the series *Karl Friedrich Schinkel: Lebenswerk*, published by Deutscher Kunstverlag in 1990, entitled *Die Reise nach Frankreich und England im Jahre 1826*.

D.B.

ACKNOWLEDGEMENTS

The English and the German editors would like to thank the following most warmly for their help with this edition: Jeremy Adler, Brian Allen, Patrick Baird, Peter Betthausen, P.J. Boughton, Lorne Campbell, Chris Ellmers, Celina Fox, Ian Gow, Francis Greenacre, Tom Gretton, Antony Griffiths, Mrs A. Heap, Ralph Hyde, Ian Jenkins, W.J. Jones, Emily Lane, Jane Legget, Michael Liversidge, Sheila O'Connell, J.M. Olive, Nicholas Penny, Alex Potts, Stephen Price, Catherine Reynolds, Nicolai Rubinstein, Francis Russell, Miss A.C. Snape, Jeremy Smith, Jeremy Taylor, L. Walrond, Christopher Wilson. Thanks are also due to Louise Govier, who compiled the index.

ILLUSTRATIONS

Unless otherwise indicated all works are by Schinkel and made on the 1826 journey. Words within inverted commas are inscribed by Schinkel himself in the *Journal* and refer to specific drawings in the volume.

ABBREVIATIONS

Braham, 1980
A. Braham, *The Architecture of the French Enlightenment*, London, 1980

Buildings of England
N. Pevsner, founding ed., *Buildings of England (Ireland, Scotland and Wales)*, Harmondsworth, 1951–

Collected Architectural Designs
Karl Friedrich Schinkel: Collected Architectural Designs, London, 1982

Colvin
H. Colvin, *A Biographical Dictionary of British Architects, 1600–1840*, London, 1978

Kalnein & Levey
W. Kalnein and M. Levey, *Art and Architecture of the 18th century in France*, Harmondsworth, 1972

OHT
C. Singer, E.J. Holmyard, A.R. Hall, T.I. Williams ed., *A History of Technology*, Vol. IV, *The Industrial Revolution*, Oxford, 1979

Snodin, 1991
M. Snodin, ed., *Karl Friedrich Schinkel: A Universal Man*, New Haven and London, 1991

Waagen
G.F. Waagen, *Treasures of Art in Great Britain*, 4 vols., 1854–7

Wegner
R. Wegner, *Karl Friedrich Schinkel: Lebenswerk, Die Reise nach Frankreich und England im Jahre 1826*, Berlin and Munich, 1990

1. Carl Begas, *Portrait of Schinkel*,
1826 chalk drawing. Architecten- und
Ingenieurverein, Berlin

C.B. f
1826.

The 1826 Journey and Its Place in Schinkel's Career

GOTTFRIED RIEMANN

When the forty-five year old Karl Friedrich Schinkel (plate 1), Privy Counsellor for Public Works and Professor of Architecture, set out from Berlin on 16 April 1826 on his journey to Paris and England, he had passed the midpoint of his life but by no means of his architectural career. As a member of the Public Works Commission he was in charge of all aspects of Prussian architecture. He was a member of the technical commission of the Ministry of Trade, and of the Senate of the Academy of Arts. He had designed and built the Neue Wache,[1] the Schauspielhaus,[2] and many other buildings in Berlin, and was working on the Museum am Lustgarten (Altes Museum).[3] He was inundated with commissions from the Court, aristocracy and citizens for buildings far and near. But the fundamental ideas which gave his later work its outstanding quality and were to have considerable influence, were, in many essentials, as yet unborn. A new impetus was necessary to give these ideas life, and to enable them to develop and mature: 'A highly interesting journey to Paris and through England and Scotland kept me away from Berlin this summer, I have experienced a great deal that was new to me', wrote Schinkel on 11 December 1826 to the painter Franz Catel in Rome. In fact his journey was to accomplish far more than its original purpose: it became a profoundly stimulating experience of unfamiliar cities, landscapes and architecture, art and history, and of the fascinating emergence of industrial society and mass culture in the two most highly developed countries in the world. Around 1825 Schinkel was concerned with architectural ideas and tasks which prompted him to investigate and exploit the changes effected by the industrial revolution.

He needed an external stimulus, however, to make the effort to see for himself the advanced social and economic conditions, new technology and new building materials in the countries where these were emerging most strongly, namely France and Britain.

The building of the Museum am Lustgarten in Berlin focused Schinkel's attention on the two great museums then undergoing transformation: the Louvre in Paris and the British Museum in London, both of which were to affect the plans for his own museum. Since 1823 he had been developing a successful architectural conception for the museum in theory, but on a practical level he was about to enter new territory, in which he would have to learn from the experience of others. He had seen the new Museo Pio Clementino in the Vatican in 1824, but it was equally important for him to see the wings of the Louvre, which had been converted to house the Napoleonic collections, and the new construction of the British Museum. He therefore requested King Friedrich Wilhelm III to allow him to visit Paris and London, and the cabinet order of 21 March 1826 instructed Schinkel 'to travel to Paris and London, there to take precise cognizance of the construction of the Museums with a view to the future erection of the Museum here in Berlin'.

Schinkel did in fact inspect the new museum buildings in Paris and London, and he was able to converse with the former's architects, but this was only one of many significant aspects of his journey, which became considerably wider in scope than originally planned. This was because he was accompanied by his friend and companion, Peter Christian Wilhelm Beuth (plate 2). Beuth had journeyed through England in 1823 and noted its turbulent economic and industrial development. As head of the Department of Trade and Industry in the Prussian Finance Ministry since 1814, he was eager to promote the cause of advanced technology in Prussian industry, for which British models in particular offered prototypes. The opportunity which came in 1826 for both Schinkel and Beuth to go to Britain was, therefore, welcome, and they also learned much from technological developments in France, especially during an extended stay in Paris. Schinkel's lively receptivity of mind and his universal interests, combined with Beuth's practical concerns, made the journey into an exciting exploration of the new worlds of modern architecture and industry, which Schinkel evidently found more compelling than the architecture of the past. This was already apparent during his stay in Paris, and in Britain, his main destination, he was most stirred by the engineers. He admired Rennie's and Telford's recent iron bridge constructions with their boldness of contour, the technological daring of the tunnel under the Thames begun by M.I. Brunel, and the docks, factories, market-halls, arcades and railway lines built by lesser-known architects and engineers. Machines themselves and their mechanical functions never ceased to interest him. If he had absorbed the great inheritance of European culture two years before, on his second Italian journey, he now experienced the incipient but already tangible existence of nineteenth-century technological progress.

The arrival of Schinkel and Beuth in Paris on 29 April 1826, after ten days of rapid travel, marked the beginning of a continuous round of sightseeing and meetings. This lasted over three weeks in Paris and more than two months in Britain, broken only by a six-day excursion to the highlands and islands of Scotland. When he returned to Berlin on 22 August, Schinkel brought back a wealth of impressions and a vivid documentary of his experiences, in the diary notes, letters and drawings which have come down to us – the unique testimony of one of the century's leading minds.

Schinkel's journey took place at a time of increasing German interest in British political and cultural life. The influence of English ideas and social forms had been evident since the mid-eighteenth century, falling on fertile ground in some German states. As in other countries on the continent, Picturesque landscape gardening and also Palladian and Gothic Revival architecture were seen as a liberation from Baroque and absolutist rigidity, and were taken up with increasing enthusiasm. An impressive early example of this is the design of Wörlitz Park with its two villas and other buildings scattered about the artificial landscape. The Anglophilia of Prince Leopold Friedrich Franz von Anhalt-Dessau had taken him and his architect Erdmannsdorff to England several times, and his emulation of English institutions extended to the administration and plan of his whole domain. The court of Hesse-Kassel was also influenced by English architecture, as the parks and buildings of Wilhelmshöhe near Kassel testify. English influences became noticeable again in Prussia around 1800, encouraged by the political ideas of Baron von Stein, whose efforts at reform were in part determined by English models. Schinkel's journey to France and England was thus by no means the first by a German architect.

The new architecture which England and France had produced within their very different social structures had been arousing interest since the end of the eighteenth century. Italy remained the traditional goal of educated travellers, but now it was facing the new challenges presented by the economic progress of capitalism and bourgeois liberalism. As early as 1763 and 1766 in England and 1766 in Paris, Erdmannsdorff had visited not only great houses and country seats but also factories, although his own subsequent buildings were still predominantly influenced by Adam and Chambers, and country-house architecture. Langhans came to England in 1775, Jussow visited Paris and England in 1786–87, and we know of visits to Paris and England by Gentz and Gilly. The travel journal kept by Gilly in 1797 of Paris under the Directory is devoted solely to new plans, especially of theatre buildings. On his way to England Gilly drew lighthouses and docks, and French and English country houses provided the underlying ideas for his designs. Schinkel reacted far more intensely to the novelty of the architecture which confronted him in Paris and England, and his written impressions are the most concrete and detailed that any architect had produced up to that time.

The young Schinkel had already visited Paris on the

2. *Allegory of Beuth riding Pegasus over a British industrial town*, 1837 watercolour. Inscribed in the bubbles: 'Gloria, Victoria'. Christmas present from Schinkel to Beuth in 1837: probably intended as a reminder of their 1826 journey. Formerly Schinkel Museum, Berlin (destroyed 1945)

way back from his first grand tour of Italy, but he had been more interested in the general atmosphere than in the architecture. On the other hand he had had some indirect experience of British architecture from his earliest years in Berlin, when Gothic architecture was becoming fashionable. Recent publications containing engravings of English Gothic were of particular interest to him, and he made copies of many of them. He perceived their character to be different from the north German Gothic with which he was most intimate, yet they were in harmony with his own architectural leanings: a tendency towards the horizontal, the two-dimensional quality, and functionalism. The innate character of the English style found an echo in his own search for form.

If we look for English influences in Schinkel's work before 1826, we can already point to the design of a mausoleum for Queen Luise in 1810.[4] Although direct borrowing would have been unlikely, the spatial effect seems to derive from English cathedral chancels. The stark linearity of the cast iron construction is also reminiscent of English neo-Gothic style. The plan for the construction of the Petrikirche in Berlin in 1814 is clearly influenced by English Gothic chapels, as are certain features in the designs from the same period for a memorial cathedral to the Wars of Liberation.[5] This is particularly clear in the domed section adjoining the nave, with its central pillar – one of Schinkel's most important architectural ideas – and the fan-vaulting which it supports, both inconceivable without the example of English chapter houses. English models also underlie the plans for the Gertraudenkirche in Spittelmarkt,[6] drawn up in 1819. In their interior design these reveal similarities to the early Gothic Temple Church in London, which is in turn an adaptation of the Church of the Holy Sepulchre in Jerusalem.

The *locus classicus*, however, of English influence in Schinkel's work before 1826 is surely to be found in the plans for the construction of the Friedrich-Werdersche-Kirche.[7] In the designs of 1824, which presented alternative Classical and Gothic proposals, Schinkel was already following the English pattern: English architects quite often offered Perpendicular and Classical versions of the same building for the client to choose. Crown Prince Friedrich Wilhelm (IV), who was involved in the building,

recommended English publications for Schinkel to consult. The whole structure shows the incorporation of ideas derived from Perpendicular chapels, which were characterized by an accentuation of the vertical and horizontal: slender columns and large tracery windows. Where the project was more modest and space more limited, the proportions were correspondingly condensed. Other features often adopted are the subdivision of space, a tendency towards the horizontal, twin-towered façades, centre windows and double doors. In the designs for Schloss Krzeszowice of 1823,[8] quite different English models can be discerned. In the interior especially, the influence of Palladian country houses can be clearly seen. The much-admired English furniture, known through imports, also inspired Schinkel at this time to imitation in his Berlin and Potsdam interiors. This is true of the Sternsaal[9] of the Crown Prince's apartment in the Berlin Royal Palace, in the living quarters of the New Pavilion in Charlottenburg, and the hall of the Potsdam Zivilkasino. Other types of work also point to English models, such as the Gothic buildings in his paintings and stage sets.

Some of the impetus behind Schinkel's journey must have come from Beuth's descriptions of the industrial parts of England. Beuth had already observed the elements that would decisively help Prussia's trade and industry, which had been developing rapidly since 1815. In a letter of July 1823, Beuth wrote to Schinkel from Manchester:

> It is only here, my friend, that the machinery and buildings can be found commensurate with the miracles of modern times – they are called factories. Such a barn of a place is eight or nine storeys high, up to forty windows long and usually four windows deep . . . A mass of such buildings stand in very high positions dominating the surrounding area; in addition a forest of even higher steam-engine chimneys, so like needles that one cannot comprehend how they stay up, present a wonderful sight from a distance, especially at night when the thousands of windows are brightly illuminated with gas light.

During his stay in Paris in 1804–5, Schinkel appears not to have made any architectural sketches. The information we have about this stay is contained in a letter to his guardian, Valentin Rose, where he claims that he 'was involuntarily tossed from one state of wonderment to another'. More than twenty years on, there is no sign of this; on the contrary, he records in detail a packed programme of visiting and sightseeing. The Louvre collections had already impressed him on his previous visit, but now his official programme included a close survey of the lay-out of the works of art in the completely refurbished wings. He made sketches of the antique section, identifying the works which excited him, and learning much to help him with the future exhibition of the Berlin collections. At the same time Schinkel's interest in new building types is evident. No Paris building is described in such detail as the new Bourse, particularly its construction. Concealed behind the temple façade and joists there were iron beams and fastenings, a significant achievement of contemporary civil engineering. Schinkel also took note of the arcades built around the Palais Royal after the 1789 Revolution, especially the roofs, in which iron and glass were combined in a new way. He was also interested in the ironwork dome with its glass-covered skylight on the relatively recently renovated Halle au Blé. In 1795 Friedrich Gilly had already taken an interest in the numerous Paris theatres, and Schinkel too, having just branched out in new directions in his plans for the Hamburg theatre, visited the important new ones. Apart from the above, he remarked on very few of the works of his Paris colleagues. One that he did note was the novel lay-out of the Chapelle Expiatoire, which he also sketched in detail. This was designed by Fontaine, who, with Percier, was for decades, in charge of official Paris architecture. Schinkel got to know both architects, visiting them on the very first day of his stay, but he seems to have been closest to Hittorff, whose architectural ideas were nearest to his own. These introductions to Paris notables were due to Alexander von Humboldt. Humboldt had lived in Paris since 1807 and was at the centre of a distinguished circle of scientists and artists. He also did Schinkel the great honour of introducing him into the Institut de France.

The great architecture of a city like Paris certainly appealed to Schinkel's highly-developed interest in his-torical buildings. In his main Gothic phase (1810–15) he had already made a study of Rheims Cathedral, and during the same period he had also made graphic reconstructions of Milan, Cologne and Strasburg Cathedrals. In Paris, however, it was not Notre Dame that interested him – he mentions it only briefly in the Journal – but the Abbey of St Denis, perhaps because the latter had been restored by Fontaine after the devastation of 1792. He also visited Baroque buildings like the Palais du Luxembourg, the Palais Royal – both extended and restored since 1800 and in part only recently completed – the Invalides and Val-de-Grâce. A visit to Versailles was of course obligatory. Because of his professional interest in centrally-planned projects, Schinkel paid particular attention to the Panthéon dome. His interest was aroused even more when he visited Saint-Philippe-du-Roule, the church which Friedrich Wilhelm III had wanted as a model for the building of the Nikolaikirche in Potsdam.[10] New optical spectacles and training institutions, as yet little known in Berlin, were potentially sources for imitation: the Diorama, the Georama, and the Conservatoire des Arts et des Métiers. The iron foundry and rolling mill at Charenton were also included in the programme, probably at Beuth's request. Schinkel's sketches of Paris show signs of cursoriness and haste: it seems that, because he was so close to the object of his journey, he could accept philosophically any omissions in his Paris sight-seeing.

On 26 May Schinkel took his first look around London, city of a million inhabitants. He was immediately confronted with its varied nature: present and past, art and technology, famous people and anonymous masses. He noted down his thoughts and opinions, fluctuating between warm approval and strong dislike. As in Paris, he soon turned his attention to the official reason for his visit, the new British Museum. Only one wing, the King's Library, had been completed by 1826, and many of the collections were still housed in temporary accommodation. On encountering the buildings of Robert Smirke, one of the leading architects of the British Greek revival, Schinkel directed his attention, albeit often critically, to the use of iron in ceilings and staircases, and it became clear that what was to fascinate him throughout the whole journey was the new technology and its successful constructional and practical application. Even in London he addressed himself as often as possible to the various feats of civil engineering and their technical execution: the bridges and the docks, the places of production and the machines themselves. He saw new construction problems overcome, sometimes in exemplary and sometimes in not quite so praiseworthy fashion.

Even before he visited the Museum, Schinkel went to inspect the new buildings in Regent's Park, an indication of the importance he attached to them. The elegant, sweeping terraces of John Nash and the incorporation of great stretches of parkland in one of the most expansive urban architectural concepts of the age, despite some hints of dismay at their lack of 'correctness', were, to an extent, compatible with Schinkel's own fundamental architectural and aesthetic ideas. Nash's adaptability and his light touch might have seemed more instructive to Schinkel than the original, uncompromising and intense work of John Soane.

The priority given by Beuth to observing industry, technology and contemporary life, an interest which was shared by Schinkel, and a shortage of time, led to a certain neglect of the historical architecture of London. Schinkel visited some famous buildings, and his interest in them was partly dictated by his own projects. This was particularly true of St Paul's Cathedral and its magnificent dome, which had implications for his work on the centrally-planned Nikolaikirche in Potsdam and the Berlin Cathedral. Schinkel sketched the ground plan, and twice drew the dome towering over the city. Another Baroque building which interested Schinkel was the Banqueting House, a part of the unfinished royal palace in Whitehall designed by Inigo Jones. In the architecture of Hampton Court Palace he found an impressive amalgamation of Renaissance and Baroque. London's medieval architecture was of minor interest to Schinkel. Apart from the Tower he mentions only a few buildings – Westminster Abbey, where he praises the Perpendicular Henry VII's Chapel, and the two great halls, Westminster Hall and Guildhall, which, with their large exposed timber roof trusses, attracted his interest in construction.

The route that Beuth and Schinkel took from London was determined by towns and locations of industrial and technological interest. Historical sites were subordinated to this priority. We know from an itinerary that Schinkel drew up before the journey, that he had expected to see more historic buildings than he in fact did. Schinkel's opinion on the character of the landscapes and towns transformed by industry is not consistent. He often responds favourably to landscapes with industrial elements, sometimes finding them picturesque or exotic. On the other hand he is horrified by the ugliness of the industrial towns with their amorphous mass of workers and their dwellings. The landscape around Dudley has a 'grandiose aspect of thousands of smoking obelisks'; Manchester, on the other hand, 'is a strange and terrible scene: enormous hulks of buildings, thrown up by foremen without any architectural thought, just the barest requirements, and built of red brick'. In Birmingham, the first purely industrial town he encountered, he stresses the ugliness of the buildings, where the only features among the mass of brick buildings are the 'pyramids and obelisks of the factory furnaces'. Most of the other industrial centres, such as Sheffield, Liverpool or Glasgow, receive similar cursory treatment. He describes in more detail the unplanned, hurriedly thrown up, clumsy crudity of Manchester, concentrating on the town centre where shops and factories coexisted, ignoring the crowded slums where thousands of workers were cooped up together.

Schinkel's main interest was in the factories themselves and their structure. His recorded impressions of these are probably the most detailed of all contemporary visitors to England. When he went to see the newly completed great ironworks of Wednesbury Oaks near Dudley, he produced a vivid sketch of these simple but well constructed industrial buildings, which reveals a constant concern with structure. The intensity of concentration with which he analyses, draws or describes the production process is sometimes astonishing. Exact descriptions of steam-engines, rolling mills and furnace complexes, supplemented by sketches, appear with detailed accounts of buildings, and roof-structures with iron joists and fastenings. Precise and succinct, they point to the fascination this traveller felt for the new technology and its applications.

Schinkel derived important insights from the interior

construction of factory buildings. In a textile factory near Stroud, he studied and drew a large open workshop with iron supports and barrel-vaulting, which, in its simple, clear structure, was both practical and elegant. Such examples employing a skeleton iron framework with brick walls and arches convinced him of the practical advantages of cast-iron supports, and their influence on his later designs is clear. He also learned much from buildings he saw in London and other ports: dock warehouses and market-halls were often simply constructed, lightly partitioned and minimally supported by cast-iron pillars and timber roof trusses.

The enormous technological innovation of cast iron, and its use in construction, had also featured in the architecture of the Royal Pavilion in Brighton, which Schinkel had special permission from the King to visit. The structural elements, the iron skeleton framework of the dome and the slender iron columns with their palm-leaf decoration, which divided the rooms both functionally and aesthetically, created a lasting impression on him. In Brighton he also encountered an early example of exposed glass-and-iron architecture: a glass dome, 'formerly intended as a greenhouse', but now used as a riding arena. Schinkel had already wanted to use exposed iron supports before he came to England, but it was their use in England that first gave him a real sense of the possibilities presented by their cheapness, ease of production and durability. More than architects it was engineers who were able to exploit the possibilities of iron and achieve an independence from the architects. Schinkel was one of the few architects of his generation to assimilate the new technology and to try to apply it to his own work. England offered a wealth of inspiration here, not only in terms of new building materials but also from the new aesthetic and spatial possibilities arising from their use.

An extraordinary variety of building projects attracted his attention: in Derby he visited the newly erected General Infirmary, a hospital famous for its innovations in comfort and hygiene. In Edinburgh he inspected the new gasworks, where the architect had been concerned to disguise in an archaising manner the function of the building, giving it a symmetry that makes it look like a country house.

In London, Brighton and North Wales Schinkel paid special attention to bridge construction. He was able to familiarize himself with some of the greatest achievements in this field, including Thomas Telford's bold iron suspension bridges: indeed the journey through Wales was undertaken specially to see them. The bridges spanning the estuaries at Conway and Anglesey are among the most impressive examples of early civil engineering, deriving their style not only from historical sources but also from the structural requirements of the particular situation. Schinkel saw the two bridges shortly after their completion and was profoundly impressed. Their significance for the future was not lost on him, and in 1828 he proposed that his drawings of them should be included in the *Verhandlungen des Vereins zur Beförderung des Gewerbfliesses in Preussen* (Transactions of the Society for the Promotion of Trade and Industry in Prussia), which Beuth edited. Telford was not only a bridge-builder of genius, he was also a pioneer in other fields. These include the canal aqueduct of Pont-y-Cysylltau which spans a wide river valley, and is constructed of cast iron troughs resting on stone supports. Schinkel also saw other great achievements in water transportation, like the canal in Manchester which crossed over and under streets, and the series of locks in the Crinan Canal in Scotland.

Schinkel also looked closely at buildings in which display was a major factor. The monarch, George IV, was increasingly concerned that the nation's buildings should present an opulence befitting a great empire. Schinkel was particularly alert to the use in public architecture of new technological achievements. In describing Nash's Brighton Pavilion he emphasizes the 'magnificence of the construction', and his description of the building is the fullest in the whole of the Journal.

The picturesqueness of the exotic elements of the building and their elegant flow of line and skilfully contrived modulations, impressed him as had Nash's Regent's Park buildings in London. Windsor Castle was also of particular interest because it had recently been extensively castellated in the medieval manner. Even so Schinkel was not enthusiastic in his assessment: 'The details are all mediocre'. Of the numerous grand castles and mansions he saw few were among the best examples, and even those he only saw by chance. Several castles and country seats, including Chiswick and Chatsworth, originally included in the itinerary had to be omitted for lack of time. The big manufacturers had palatial country mansions, which were included in the itinerary because of their owners: for example, Richard Arkwright's Willersley Castle and Benjamin Gott's Armley House. Of the more important contemporary mansions, only Eaton Hall near Chester, a building of extremely spacious proportions in the Gothic revival style, is accorded detailed critical comment: 'Unfortunately, for all its meticulous care this architecture is tedious'.

In Edinburgh the almost uniform classical plan of the New Town, begun in the eighteenth century and well advanced by 1826, proved a strong attraction for Schinkel, with his interest in town planning. Here, in more concentrated fashion than in London, was a contemporary architecture in which the finest examples of Greek revival in Britain could find a place. Though the new buildings excited Schinkel's critical interest, he was clearly dismayed by the uniformity of recent Classical buildings in provincial towns, whether they were churches or public buildings.

There was little opportunity to visit the great medieval cathedrals. Apart from his sight of Canterbury and the London cathedrals, Schinkel's only first-hand experience of English cathedral architecture was at York Minster, where he notes the 'beauty of proportion', and Durham. The itinerary had originally included Gloucester and Salisbury, but neither there nor in Peterborough, Wells, Lincoln or Exeter could he gratify the great interest in English medieval architecture with which he came to England. In the end everything had to be subordinated to industry. In the case of Kirkstall Abbey in Leeds, only in the interval between inspecting 'wonderful factory buildings with a 120 feet high chimney' and visiting the industrialist Gott, was there time to view the ruin of this Cistercian abbey, so celebrated in the art and literature of the English Romantics. In Oxford Schinkel sketched the university with its wealth of medieval and Gothic chapels and colleges, but, while he found it 'quite distinctive and opulent', he also complained of the 'very repetitive architecture'.

The extension of the journey to include Scotland had not at first been envisaged. In the handwritten itinerary, which was probably drawn up in London, the furthest north they were to travel was Leeds. Their stay in Scotland, with the journey round the Highlands and the boat-trip to the islands of Staffa and Iona, was a holiday. They needed some rest from their continual inspections of buildings, negotiations and conversations. They could now show a relaxed interest in the country and its inhabitants, as they trod the well-known trail to the 'Ossianic Islands', a particular goal for educated northern Europeans. We can gather from his vivid, detailed descriptions and the number of sketches he made, that the excursion reawakened something of Schinkel's youthful Romanticism.

Schinkel's concern to find a new architectural style in harmony with the tendencies of the age, one which would combine the experiences of the past with the principles of a new functionality, was already evident in the years preceding 1826. His architectural thinking was moving towards a basically ahistorical, forward-looking style. This change, chiefly theoretical, found confirmation in England, where Schinkel was inspired afresh. We can examine the significance of the journey for his work by seeing how he endeavoured to apply some of the ideas he had seen used in England. As a government official he had no opportunity to influence private industrial building, and he did not necessarily approve of all that he saw in the way of industrial building in England: indeed his experience was as much a warning as an inspiration.

The impetus given to Schinkel's work as a consequence of the 1826 journey can be observed at three levels: influence on basic structural and functional design; the absorption of certain characteristics of English Gothic, and the imitation of details. At the beginning of 1827 Schinkel drew up a plan for a bazaar (Kaufhaus)[11] to be sited next to the University in Unter den Linden. He was able to pursue his own ideas, and was prompted to take a decisive step in his architectural development. He had seen the Palais Royal with its rows of individual shops, and the new market-halls in Paris and London. The form of his building was, however, quite original and it marked the beginning of a new and bold phase of architectural activity which was to culminate in the Bauakademie.[12] The outer structure is completely determined by the interior frame of the building. This unity of interior and façade is the fundamental principle underlying Schinkel's later style. It is but a logical step from the Kaufhaus to the skeletal structure of the Bauakademie with its brick infilling. There is more than a suggestion here of English factory buildings, especially their large workshops with the iron supports and barrel vaulting. The new warehouses of the Berlin Packhof[13] constituted a further step in Schinkel's search for an integrated functional style. Fundamental alterations were made in 1829 to the first design of 1825. On the northern side of the Spree Island a group of warehouses and other utilitarian buildings were to be erected in close proximity to the Museum am Lustgarten. The Packhof warehouse with its five storeys was the dominant building of the group, and in its final form of 1829 it reveals the influence of English warehouses, especially those in London which Schinkel had inspected in detail. By gradually decreasing the storey height and the rows of round-arched windows, utilitarian architecture acquired an aesthetic value. Not only do the structural elements derive from English patterns; so also does the idea of barrel vaulting. The consistent application of the principle of 'radical abstraction' formulated by Schinkel himself in the drafts for his proposed architecture textbook (*Architektonisches Lehrbuch*),[14] which was based on the premise that the function of a building should determine its structural form, finds its best expression in the Bauakademie which was designed in collaboration with Beuth in 1831. Thus Schinkel was able to demonstrate in exemplary buildings his idea of appropriateness: 'Appropriateness of the division of space or plan; appropriateness of the construction or of the combination of materials in the light of the plan; appropriateness of the decoration or ornamentation'. The building is divided up by structural columns, so that the whole interior architecture is readable from outside. This concept of integration corresponds to the English industrial building of the time, which followed the principle of an iron skeleton structure with brick-wall infilling. Schinkel used only brick, however, as cast-iron pillars were still too costly in Prussia. While the English factories were purely utilitarian and functional and could not easily be seen at the time as architecture, Schinkel's particular achievement was to create what was undeniably architectural, while at the same time using new methods as a stylistic basis. Apart from the skeletal construction, the other important innovation was the use of brick in such a way that the fundamental structure of the building was revealed, also a consequence of his journey to England. He had already used brick in an innovatory way in 1825 in the Arkona Lighthouse and in 1828 in the Feilnerhaus,[15] and he was now able to develop and modify such ideas. If was above all through the use of brick and of prefabricated ornamentation that Schinkel arrived at the most logical and forward-looking architecture of his time. This was in effect an architecture beyond all tradition, combining Gothic wall-column construction with planar divisions and decorative elements derived from the Classical tradition, in a way that would have been unthinkable without a first-hand experience of English civil engineering. The innovatory trends in Schinkel's later work can also be seen in designs for a great new library[16] in 1835 which have survived in two versions. Apart from the round-arch style which articulates the façade in both designs, the inner structure of the large cube shape again indicates a derivation from English industrial architecture. The grid-type division into square compartments, created out of the penetration of the rows of supports, gives the building a solid geometric structure of the kind Schinkel would have seen in English factories. As in the Bauakademie there is barrel-vaulting on every floor.

Schinkel's work was also enriched by forms borrowed from English Gothic and neo-Gothic buildings. This is compatible with his efforts to achieve a style free from tradition, because his use of Gothic features was primarily functional. Even before the journey he was attracted to English Gothic, but after the 1826 journey he incorporated it in new ways. In his Gothic plan for a hunting lodge in the park of Schloss Glienicke,[17] the summer residence of Prince Karl, there are clear signs in this simple building, designed in 1827, of the influence of England. It is modelled on the style of an English country cottage, of the kind which even with its single storey and thatched roof reflects in a simplified way elements of English Gothic, with windows divided into two or more sections, and repeating small gables and chimneys. Details like the horizontal edges of doors and windows can be seen to derive from medieval college buildings Schinkel had seen in Oxford. The riding arena in the park of Prince Albrecht's Berlin palace, built in 1830, follows the English late Gothic pattern. The gable ends of this brick-built hall have wide Tudor tracery windows. The interior roof construction, consisting of longitudinal and transverse ribs, is very similar to the roof architecture of an English late Gothic hall. This simple building was probably a reduced version of a larger, more elaborate design in which Schinkel borrowed even more obviously from English late Gothic.

In the last decade of Schinkel's architectural activity, an English castellated style became dominant. This can be seen first in the plans for the lakeside house at Kurnik[18] near Poznan, which is in fact a complete reconstruction. He designed a regular structure with square corner-towers, the raised central element of which has large windows in three sections and turret-like, octagonal corner pillars. The central block is set back, and its window-frames, with their characteristic bracket shape, follow exactly the pattern of English late Gothic secular architecture. Thus, the design reflects variations of English late Gothic and eighteenth- or early nineteenth-century imitations, without any one specific model. In the case of Schloss Babelsberg[19] the client wanted Schinkel to use English Gothic forms for his designs. He had been commissioned to draw up the plans in 1833, and was asked to carry them out in the Anglophile country-house taste of Prince Wilhelm and Princess Augusta. By 1830 the English country-house style had become familiar in Europe, and especially in Berlin, through works such as Humphrey Repton's *Fragments on the theory and practice of landscape gardening, including some remarks on Grecian and Gothic architecture* (1816), J.B. Papworth's *Rural residences* (1818), and R. Luger's *Architectural sketches to cottages, rural dwellings and villas* (1815). These were, however, more favoured in dilettante circles, while Schinkel's ideas for Babelsberg were based on houses he had actually seen in England. The reconstruction of Windsor Castle in a castellated style had become a model for many German country houses, and it lurks in the background of Babelsberg.

Borrowings are also discernible in Schinkel's use of iron and in his interiors. Immediately after his return, he designed the conversion of Prince Karl's palace in the Wilhelmplatz,[20] in which he had the idea of using cast iron for the structural elements of the main staircase. This was the first such instance in Berlin, and was clearly based on Schinkel's knowledge of English staircase construction. The unusually tall iron columns supporting the flight of stairs are very similar to some in the Brighton Pavilion. Schinkel also used similar columns for the great staircase in Prince Albrecht's palace.[21] In Schinkel's extensive designs for interiors, decor and furnishings, the influence of late eighteenth-century English interior design is frequently visible. It is particularly noticeable in the furnishing and fittings of the palaces of Prince Karl and Prince Albrecht. A light and unostentatious classical decoration, derived from Pompeii and perfected by the Adam brothers, is certainly evident in some details of the decoration, but the effect of the whole and the relation of the various elements to each other, are Schinkel's own creation. Figured friezes, cameo-like pictures, decorated mirror frames, and the mirrors in the rounded alcoves of the rear wall in the marble hall of Albrecht's palace remind us of Adam in their light, integrated effect. The iron mullions dividing the glass doors of the library of Prince Karl's palace also give an English flavour to the interior decor. On 12 June 1826 in London, Schinkel wrote a detailed description of Lansdowne House and its interior, and it clearly became a model for the furnishing of Prince Karl's palace. On the same day he mentioned that he had been looking in a shop at carpets and fireplaces with the interior of the palace in mind. Many of Schinkel's discussions with London manufacturers, which are so often mentioned in the Journal, were concerned with ordering items for the interior of the building.

Schinkel's writing and drawings – succinct diary jottings, informative letters to his wife, Susanne, and quick pen and pencil sketches – stem from an artist who used writing and drawing only for immediate communication and recollection. In his daily jottings he simply notes down his thoughts and observations, his short sentences and sentence fragments producing a wealth of vivid impressions. The reader has before him the raw material or skeleton of a travel account. The writer did not have readers in mind, but the occasional difficulty of comprehension is compensated for by a particular charm. Behind the concise vividness of the descriptions and portrayals we can discern the sound judgement of the experienced architect and engineer, sensitive art connoisseur, sophisticated conversationalist, and romantic observer of landscape. The leaning towards the practical and concrete, together with a familiarity of tone, also characterizes his letters to Susanne. These usually summarize and reflect on a part of the journey in retrospect, occasionally amplifying the succession of observations with general comments.

The sketches scattered in between the jottings on the pages of the diary, and the freehand drawings he made on slips of paper, very few of which could be described as detailed, significantly amplify the text. The pen sketches accompanying the diary show mainly structural details of industrial buildings. Some are of whole buildings, and these can be extremely impressively depicted, as with the Manchester factories. Though the subjects are varied, all the drawings are clear and analytical. The sketches on separate slips of paper also convey an idea of Schinkel's multifarious interests. Their outlines portray a country-side drawn into rapid industrial change (The Potteries), new technological achievements (Menai Bridge), outstanding urban buildings (St Paul's Cathedral and the crescents in Bath), informal townscape (streets in Bath and Edinburgh), and views of the Scottish islands and coastline. Schinkel drew four panoramas from high points, a favourite genre of his. On his first Italian journey he had already drawn landscape and harbour views, and the second in 1824 also produced impressive examples of this kind. Around 1808–10, a series of geographical and historical panoramas was commissioned and executed. The panoramic prospect of town and landscape accorded with Schinkel's constant seeking for unity of art and nature, of building and landscape, and with the sensibility of the landscape painter which he never lost even though he gave up professional landscape painting early in his career. His four British panoramic views are of All Souls College and Oxford from the balustrade of the Radcliffe Library; a broad prospect of the town and ruined castle of Conway with the new iron bridge and its surroundings, and the two bird's-eye views of Edinburgh and its environs from the Nelson Monument and Arthur's Seat. The unique synthesis presented by Schinkel's text and drawings produced one of the most important legacies of the nineteenth century, left to us by a remarkable individual who by so presciently recognising the potential of the new industrial age was able to transform his own environment in otherwise unimaginable ways.

[1] Snodin, 1991, nos 42–4.
[2] Snodin, 1991, nos 46–7.
[3] Snodin, 1991, nos 48–56.
[4] Snodin, 1991, no. 16.
[5] Snodin, 1991, no. 21.
[6] Snodin, 1991, no. 102.
[7] Snodin, 1991, no. 103.
[8] *Collected Architectural Designs*, 49–54.
[9] Snodin, 1991, pl. 71.
[10] Snodin, 1991, 107–8.
[11] Snodin, 1991, nos 113–4.
[12] Snodin, 1991, 119–23.
[13] Snodin, 1991, no. 117.
[14] Snodin, 1991, nos 124–6.
[15] Snodin, 1991, nos 115–6.
[16] Snodin, 1991, no. 127.
[17] Snodin, 1991, nos 57–9.
[18] *Collected Architectural Designs*, 127–9.
[19] Snodin, 1991, nos 94–6.
[20] Snodin, 1991, no. 83.
[21] Snodin, 1991, pls. 77–8.

Schinkel and Britain in 1826

DAVID BINDMAN

Schinkel came to Britain as a high official of a Prussian state in the throes of modernisation, and his tour, which included a lengthy stay in Paris, was part of a long-standing Prussian concern to keep up with the latest developments in technologically more advanced countries. Architecture was only one of his interests on the journey, and he spent most of his time in Britain in the company of Peter Beuth,[1] who as Prussian finance minister and founding director of the Berlin technical school, was involved in a number of transactions from discreet industrial spying[2] to buying machine tools and flocks of sheep.

Schinkel was lucky to have had Beuth as a travelling companion, for he had been to industrial Britain before, and many of the most interesting visits to factories, workshops and private houses were clearly set up by Beuth. Beuth, for instance, had already visited the industrialist, Benjamin Gott, and had seen his house outside Leeds, designed by Robert Smirke, and his cotton mills. Schinkel often found himself to be an honoured guest, where other foreign visitors could only look from a distance.[3] Beuth was also a person of some wit, with a great interest in food, and a particular passion for turtle soup: he had written to Schinkel in 1823 complaining that England was a country of 40 religions but only two sauces.[4]

The Journal reveals Schinkel as a man of immense curiosity and learning, but also rather self-important and rank-conscious. He notes in the Journal and in a letter to his wife, Susanne, that he was only allowed in to the Brighton Pavilion because George IV himself, on hearing who Schinkel was, countermanded his Chamberlain's initial refusal.[5] From the statutory visit to Goethe in Weimar on his way to France, through Paris and London, and on his return through Germany he made a point of calling on those eminent in his fields of interest. In Paris he was received as a celebrity in his own right, and the part of the Journal which deals with his stay there is sprinkled with the names of eminent architects, painters and collectors. He was invited to present his work to the Institut, and he was out most nights at dinner parties or at theatres. In England, on the other hand, he had many fewer acquaintances, and he seems to have had no special entrée into the London architectural world; he called on Nash and Cockerell without meeting either of them.

With some notable exceptions, like the Brighton Pavilion, Schinkel was generally unresponsive towards modern British architecture, but full of spontaneous admiration for technological innovation, even in buildings he would not have recognised as architectural. His fascination with the new appears clearly in his accounts of the structures and productions of the advanced machine shops he was taken to by Beuth. We can follow his eye wandering upwards to the wood and iron beams and roof fastenings, and nothing in the Journal is more vivid than the quick sketches he jotted down of steam-powered trip hammers and other unfamiliar machines.

He was also, like every other German visitor of the period, awed into a feeling of provincialism by London. He was responsive, as were others, to the city's magnitude and the poetic effects of urban fog. He went to 'shows' like Bullock's Egyptian Hall and saw Tippoo's Tiger in East India House. As a reader of Shakespeare and Walter Scott he was on the look-out for traces of Britain's barbaric and mythical past. He visited and noted the Bloody Tower of the Princes in the Tower, and in

Edinburgh the room in Holyrood in which Rizzio was murdered, and, before Mendelssohn, who went in 1829, he took a boat trip with his German colleagues out to Fingal's Cave on Staffa, where they sang songs to the organ-like sounds of the waters rushing into the cave.

The Journal itself is a pocket book and *aide memoïre*, used to record things of interest in rapidly written notes or with small drawings, on the spot or after a day's sightseeing. Sometimes impressions are worked up more fully in his letters home, which are also included here with the text of the Journal. Opinions are often expressed pungently, and sometimes too cryptically to be easy to interpret; but this very spontaneity gives the Journal an unguarded quality. At the same time it means that the underlying assumptions of the text can often be inferred only with difficulty. Educated Germans tended to be more experienced in aesthetic debate than their equivalents in other countries, and were inclined to doubt whether something that was useful could also be beautiful. Schinkel has no space to reflect upon the issue in the Journal but only in exceptional cases, like the mill at King's Stanley near Stroud, does he praise factories or market halls without some reservations. He finds the great cotton mills of Manchester to be 'enormous hulks of buildings thrown up by foremen without any architectural thought',[6] and Liverpool's St John's Market is described as 'splendid' but he cannot forbear to remark that it is 'a pity that the exterior architecture is so bad'.[7]

It is obvious that Schinkel brought a great many assumptions with him to a country he had not visited before. To Prussians of his social background Britain represented on the one hand mechanical ingenuity, technological innovation and mass-production; on the other, especially if Scotland is taken into account, it was a country with a romantic history which left traces on the ancient architecture and the landscape, and upon the peoples themselves. As a prominent citizen of a state that was at the same time autocratic and meritocratic,[8] it was inevitable that he would find occasions for puzzlement and dismay in a country in which unrestrained capitalism and *ancien régime* social structures coexisted uneasily and untidily, as indeed they still do. Prussia under Friedrich Wilhelm III was liberal, in that it allowed the advance-

ment of someone like Schinkel to a high position in the bureaucracy, but the triumphalism of the plans for Berlin, in which Unter den Linden was to be a military parade route and the Royal Palace was to act visually and spatially as the pivot of all the functions of the state, reflects the political absolutism and fear of disorder which brought them into being[9] in the aftermath of the Congress of Vienna. Schinkel's Journal, as one might expect from someone who was both a courtier and a high offical of the Prussian state, reveals none of the admiration for British 'liberty' to be found in the travel accounts of liberals from abroad.

Like other foreign visitors to the industrial Midlands and North of England in the 1820s and later Schinkel took some relish in being shocked by Manchester, which was both the cradle of new technology and an object lesson in the dangers of the too-rapid accumulation of wealth. Like Johanna Schopenhauer,[10] the mother of the philosopher, who passed through Manchester in 1813, Schinkel was awe-struck at the sheer size of the cotton mills of Ancoats, and he made in addition detailed drawings of the canal system which crossed the river as an aqueduct and then passed under houses. By the 1820s visitors tended also to comment on Dantesque conditions in the factories, overcrowded smoke-blackened streets, and the civil disturbances which culminated in Peterloo, as indeed did British writers like Southey, whose horrific account of Manchester was published in 1808.[11] Manchester was seen as a violation of nature, a place in which the many were enslaved for the profit of the few and the sky was blotted out by smoke and dust.

In his account of Manchester Schinkel notes the soldiers sent to control civil disturbance, the distress of the Irish labourers, the threat of economic decline and the poor architecture of the factories, but he is also sensitive, as Beuth had been on his 1823 visit, to the city's sublimity: 'it is a strange and terrible scene', he comments, remarking that some of the mills of Ancoats are as big in area as the Royal Palace in Berlin but much taller. Such an observation reveals Schinkel's sense of decorum and his implicitly hierarchical conception of society: there is something unnatural to him in the idea of a factory constructed on a scale larger than a ruler's palace. Similarly his reservations about Nash's Regent's Park terraces stem from the pretentiousness implicit in their palatial grandeur. Their 'aristocratic', country-house façades act to disguise the fact that they are really row-houses for the bourgeoisie: 'palace-like buildings, which look at first sight like the dwellings of princes, but turn out to be nothing more than private houses joined together like a common terraced street'.[12] Such fastidiousness did not, however, dim his enthusiasm for the same architect's Brighton Pavilion, which he describes at unusual length in the Journal. One might expect the Pavilion's stylistic frivolity also to affront Schinkel's sense of decorum, but it could be seen as fitting to the Pavilion's purpose. As a pleasure-palace for a king it was implicitly licenced to present a contrast with more solemn buildings of state in the capital, and he would have had a close experience of the recreational buildings of Potsdam. For a servant of the Prussian state light-hearted architectural extravagance, as in Sans Souci and its surroundings, was accepted as appropriate for a king in a setting at a distance from the seat of power, but not for the town-houses of those of lesser rank.

Schinkel came to England at the specific request of the King of Prussia to examine the display of antique sculptures in the British Museum in connection with the installation of the new Museum am Lustgarten (now the Altes Museum), which Schinkel was erecting as part of the Royal Palace complex in the centre of Berlin. He also had a commission to buy furniture for the residence of Prince Karl of Prussia. The Museum am Lustgarten was to be a public museum for the citizens of Berlin but set up under royal command. Beuth's concern to import the latest high-quality manufacturing methods from abroad was also encouraged by the King, and the efforts to produce luxury goods can be seen as belonging to the courtly tradition of encouraging or financing porcelain and other kinds of ornamental ware. An interest in machine workshops and technical training was not necessarily a sign of political progressiveness; on the contrary, it could be a way of reinforcing royal, or, as in Napoleon's France, imperial paternalism. Schinkel spent as much time in Paris looking at the market halls and warehouses as he did the symbolic structures.

I have so far considered what Schinkel brought to Britain, but what sort of Britain confronted him in 1826? Certainly it was a country in the process of industrialisation, though it had by no means reached its apogee by 1826. At this point cotton was still the dominant industry, and it required concentration of labour, steam-power and large factories. The 1820s was a period of post-war slump, reflected in the closure of many of those factories and massive unemployment in the industrial areas. The country had also seen recently a substantial increase in population and the urbanisation associated with this increase led to a great deal of new building at all levels, as well as conspicuous overcrowding and poverty.

Schinkel remarked from the moment of his arrival upon the prosperity on the road from Dover to London, but the most striking signs of material progress were not necessarily a consequence of industrialisation. This visible prosperity was due as much to agricultural improvement, overseas trade and improved internal communications. As he travelled North from London Schinkel noted that prosperity increasingly was accompanied by poverty and signs of disorder, especially in the industrial areas of the Midlands, and that technological advance and wealth had been allowed to result in unruly growth which in turn led to conspicuous waste and vulgarity.

Instead of the organic public and political life and centralised government he had been part of in Berlin, and which to some extent he had observed in Restoration Paris, he found in England a public life appropriate to a consumer society, in which his own profession and all the arts tended to be governed by laws of supply and demand. Where we now find pleasure in Georgian and Regency buildings and schemes, Schinkel tended to see monotony, pretentiousness and shoddiness.[13] In Manchester he drew in the Journal a typical Georgian door as an example of 'The unfortunate door-architecture repeated here and many thousand times over in the whole of England'.[14] Bath is tedious (langweilig) because it is totally disorganised, with terraces following the hills upon which they are situated without focus or purpose, and the whole place lacks any kind of civic centre or ceremonial space. In the industrial context this monotony was synonymous with callousness, as in Birmingham's miserable red-brick houses, laid out in unvarying rows amid the discomforts and hazards of workshops and factories.

Schinkel uses the word *spekulation* to describe the building boom which had caused some 10,000 houses a year to be built in London in the 1820s, and to account for their hasty construction and extravagant design, free-wheeling treatment of the architectural orders and lack of concern to express their function in their façades. There is undoubtedly a connection between the speculative nature of much of London building in the early nineteenth century and the meretricious stylishness it often conveys. But from the perspective of some, if not all, British architects and their patrons such apparent lack of intellectual probity had the sanction of the past and was supported by theories of the Picturesque. The architectural picturesque as practised by Nash emphasizes the scenic effect of a building or buildings clustered in relation to each other and to the landscape. Each building might have an irregular plan, refer to one or more past styles at a time, or adopt a playful attitude towards functionality: the final result was to be a visual and associative unity rather than the symbolic and functional one primarily sought by Schinkel.

Such large schemes as Nash's Regent's Park/Regent Street development or Edinburgh New Town cannot be compared with Schinkel's own task of renewing and defining the historic centre of Berlin: power was too dispersed in Britain to allow for the unified transformation or symbolic organisation of the centre of a capital city. He met a number of architects, but found no equivalent to his own position as *Geheime Oberbaurat* or Privy Councillor for Public Works to the Prussian state. Though architects like John Nash, Sir John Soane and Sir Robert Smirke might have some official standing through connection to the Office of Works, in practice their commissions were almost always dependent on individual patronage, even where it was the King's own. The Prince Regent's and Nash's scheme for London was, in a sense, 'continental' in its ambition and its processional character, but the idea for a great double circus with a 'National Valhalla' in Regent's Park was thwarted by private interests and abandoned as financial reality entered in.[15] In any case Nash was obliged to use 'speculative' means to get the scheme going, since the Prince Regent had no control over the Treasury. Only in cities like Edinburgh and Liverpool could an individual architect approach an official position which might enable him to take a broad view of the related functions of the community's public buildings. In Edinburgh, perhaps the nearest there is in Britain to a planned city on the European model, the National Monument on Calton Hill remains today as it did when Schinkel saw it in process of construction: a group of stark and disembodied Doric columns, a mere reminder of the immense Acropolis of which they were to form a small part.[16]

John Nash was the British architect most comparable to Schinkel in national standing and influence, but Schinkel hints at a distaste for his vulgarity both as man and as architect. He called on Nash in his apartment in 14–16 Regent Street, and in the absence of the architect he was entertained at a small gathering by the latter's wife. Nash's apartment was well-known for the splendour of its appointments which Schinkel commemorated in a sketch in the Journal, but the latter's comment that Nash 'lives like a prince'[17] implies disapproval of an architect whose lack of propriety appeared to be reflected as much in his way of life as in his architecture.

Nash could not help but dominate Schinkel's perceptions of the new 'Metropolitan Improvements' in London because the plan to build a triumphal way through Regent Street, to unite first the Prince Regent's Carlton House, and after the Prince Regent became King George IV in 1820, Buckingham Palace, with the terraces and other buildings in Regent's Park to the north, was reaching completion by 1826. Almost all the terraces in Regent's Park had been finished, with the exception of perhaps the most palatial, Cumberland Terrace, which was not completed until 1827. Carlton House was due to be demolished in 1827 in favour of Buckingham Palace, where Schinkel apparently saw work in progress. Though he mentions Park Crescent just outside Regent's Park, it seems to have been the terraces within the park that provoked his disapproving remarks about the pretentiousness of London architecture in his letter to Susanne of 10 June.

Schinkel was also generally uncomprehending of the

eccentric achievement of John Soane. He admired the courtyard and triumphal entrance to the Bank of England but could not follow the architectural logic of the building, which he found to be *vieles Unnutze*, completely unfunctional. In fact he seems not to have gone inside. He was also a little put off by Soane's house in Lincoln's Inn Fields, which he described as bursting at the seams with every kind of antiquarian object all jumbled together, the very antithesis of the orderly and historical display he had in mind for the Museum am Lustgarten. Even so he could not fail to notice the ingenuity of the lighting which he notes comes from 'above and from the side'.

There are, however, hints of respect for Robert Smirke, who was the most technologically adept of British architects though not the most imaginative.[18] While Schinkel believed in 'correctness' and archaeological accuracy, he was concerned also to reconcile them with new technology. The new building for the British Museum had been commissioned from Smirke in 1823, the same year that Schinkel's plan for the Berlin Museum was approved. In 1826 it was far from finished, and Schinkel would have seen a confusion of half-demolished and half-completed structures, some of a temporary nature, as recorded in George Scharf's drawing of 1828 (see plate 37). On the left is Montague House, the late seventeenth-century building which housed the British Museum collections and which was progressively pulled down as Smirke's building reached completion, being finally removed in 1847. In the middle is the Townley Gallery, built in 1811 for the antiquities collection and a particular object of Schinkel's visit (this was also eventually demolished). To the right, still in an unfinished state, is the first phase of Smirke's new building, which was to house the King's library recently acquired by the nation. Smirke's Ionic front colonnade was not begun until after Schinkel's visit, and it used to be thought that he had been influenced by Schinkel's design for the Museum am Lustgarten; it is now clear, however,[19] that the colonnade was part of Smirke's original plan, and that both architects were almost certainly inspired by Durand's published proposal for an ideal museum.[20]

Schinkel's notes on the British Museum are confusingly cryptic, but the remarks on the 'Doric capitals simple fluting' must apply to the entrance to the Townley Gallery. The 'new building' must be the King's Library, which appears in a section drawing on page 19 of the Journal. After identifying its Greek prototype in the Erechtheum he notes what clearly interests him most: the use by Smirke of iron construction in the ceiling. He was probably still able to see the iron beams before they were encased in wood and made completely invisible (see George Scharf's later drawing, plate 40). He noted without enthusiasm the iron construction under the stone dressing of a staircase, which must be the north-east staircase at the end of the King's Library and not the more dramatic staircase to the left of the present main entrance which was not completed until much later. On a second visit to the Museum a few days later he made approving comments on the Townley Gallery as a showplace for antiquities: it confirmed his preference for small intimate rooms rather than grand displays, and he noted the effectiveness of overhead lighting.

Schinkel wrote approvingly of another building by Robert Smirke: Armley House, just outside Leeds, designed for the textile manufacturer Benjamin Gott.[21] Schinkel was certainly predisposed towards the house by the cordial welcome he received from Gott and his daughters, and he was impressed by the signs of cultivated life he found everywhere in it, but he also remarked favourably upon its commanding height over parkland, the beautiful stonework and the delicate Grecian portico looking over the view which had been laid out by Humphrey Repton to align itself both on one of Gott's mills and on the picturesque ruins of Kirkstall Abbey.[22] He must also have been aware, from talking to Gott, of the discreet use of ironwork in the house, especially as a support for the main staircase. Gott, then, exemplified something Schinkel rarely observed in Britain: technology at the service of a civilized life, without the bare functionalism or vulgarity he had noted in London and elsewhere.

If the English Picturesque, at least in an urban context, was lost on Schinkel he showed himself guardedly sympathetic to British attempts at the Greek Revival, though, like Smirke's British Museum, not all of its more adventurous monuments had been completed by the time of his visit. He even had words of approval for the Inwood brothers' pedantic St Pancras Church of 1819–

22, which is notable for its elements copied directly from different Athenian buildings. He was certainly critical of making the Temple of the Winds serve as a church tower, but does not note the endearingly absurd artificial stone caryatids on both sides of the church. He called on C.R. Cockerell, one of the younger generation of architects, who had brought an archaeological correctness to his buildings derived from study in Greece itself.[23] He showed the plans of the Museum am Lustgarten to the Earl of Aberdeen ('Athenian Aberdeen'), a famous traveller and archaeologist in Greece, and author of *An Enquiry into the principles of beauty in Grecian Architecture* (1822). Schinkel also remarked approvingly, though with some reservations, on the magnificent propylaea and the rustication of Chester Castle recently carried out by the local Greek Revival architect Thomas Harrison.[24]

The only city architect in Britain who might be compared professionally with Schinkel, even if on a very much smaller scale, was John Foster of Liverpool,[25] but a brief statement of his career only highlights the differences. Foster had inherited from his father of the same name the post of architect and surveyor to the Corporation of Liverpool at a salary of £1000 a year.[26] He was designer of a great range of buildings (though Schinkel attributes more to him than he was actually responsible for), but had none of Schinkel's powers or ability to plan a whole city centre with all its functions defined architecturally. Even so he designed churches in classical and Gothic modes that attracted Schinkel's respect, and he was also responsible for St John's Market, notable for using the most advanced forms of iron construction, though as we have seen, Schinkel was unimpressed by its façade. Schinkel also records a conversation he had with Foster (the only conversation with a fellow architect noted down on the whole journey) in which, like architects throughout the ages, they compared each-other's salaries!

It is scarcely surprising that London should dominate Schinkel's perception of the urban scene in Britain, but there can be no doubt that Edinburgh exerted a particular fascination, expressed not only in verbal descriptions but in some of his most expansive and highly-finished drawings, including a spectacular panorama (see plate 140). Edinburgh was well set up in the 1820s to provide

stimulation for both Schinkel's modern and antiquarian interests, and like all travellers of the period he was attentive to the stark contrasts presented by the New Town, with 'the magnificence, elegance and airiness' of its streets, and the Old Town, with its 'filthy cramped conditions' and 'coarse black dwellings', nestling under the Castle, which was, for the most part, by no means as old as Schinkel assumed it to be. At the same time he found it difficult to reconcile the scenic splendour of the view from Arthur's Seat and walks on Calton Hill, with the strangeness of seventeenth-century Scottish architecture represented by the Law Courts and Heriot's Hospital, and the traces (literally) of a bloody past in Holyrood.

Schinkel gives the impression in the Journal of being mentally unprepared for the sophistication of the new Scottish classicism, especially in the public buildings of Edinburgh. His responses can be oddly prosaic, and he exhibits no curiosity about the architects, whose names (except in the case of Burn) he does not record. He praises, without naming the architects, Robert Adam's University building for its magnificent stone and beautiful carving, and the sumptuousness of Playfair's Museum of Natural History within (he makes no comment on the ingenious use of iron in the dome[27]), but sees it condescendingly as 'more of an experiment than well-organized architectural endeavour', admiring details rather than the whole. William Stark's spectacular Upper Signet Library is characterized merely as having a 'good interior design', and is described briefly. Only one building in Edinburgh provokes real enthusiasm in the Journal: the Tanfield Gasworks, 'an excellent plant' which uses 'the most sophisticated construction methods'. Schinkel gives in the Journal a fairly detailed drawing showing the way the gas-holders have been contained most ingeniously inside what appear to be Scottish medieval towers, which act as corners of a vaguely Palladian-style edifice, and he also notes the iron construction of the roof. According to Schinkel, and the suggestion is to be found nowhere else, the plan was designed by, of all people, Sir Walter Scott (who was known to have been a Director of the Tanfield Gas Company), and William Burn was responsible for the construction.

The structural use of iron, especially in roof building, was the most important and distinctive technological development for a professional architect to observe in Britain, and Schinkel was extremely assiduous in noting it, not only in architect-designed buildings but also in factories and workshops.[28] Iron-frame construction had only recently emerged from its experimental phase by the time Schinkel arrived and his travels gave him a chance to see a remarkable number of the technological pioneers: he had already been attentive to French examples like the Bourse and the Halle au Blé. The use of iron by Smirke in the King's Library of the British Museum, by Playfair in Edinburgh University and by Nash in Brighton Pavilion represents the material's domestication and adaptation to works of architectural ambition, where it can play a structural part, but also, as in the last, a decorative one as well.

Iron-frame structures were originally developed in Britain to deal with the problem of fire in cotton mills which were especially susceptible to catching alight. The first person to tackle systematically the problem of making a mill genuinely fireproof by replacing the wooden supports by iron ones was William Strutt, the son of Jedediah Strutt the Derbyshire millowner.[29] In his Derby mill of 1792–3 Strutt eliminated exposed timber by means of a structure in which brick arches were supported by iron columns resting on brick floors; the beams were still timber but encased in plaster. This type of construction was repeated in the Belper West Mill of 1793–5, one of the cluster of mills at Belper to which Beuth and Schinkel were refused admission. Nonetheless Schinkel inspected the exterior of the Belper mills, and pronounced them 'the most beautiful in England', and was, no doubt, impressed by the size of the West Mill – still surviving – which measures 200 by 30 feet and rises to six storeys.

The breakthrough to a complete iron frame came with a flour mill of 1796–7 in Shrewsbury, which was owned partly by John Marshall, whose Leeds factory Schinkel was to see on his journey. The critical technical advance was made by a Shrewsbury man, Charles Bage, who first saw the possibility of making the complete frame out of iron. Bage was a friend and correspondent of Strutt and in 1803 he stayed in Belper to help him with the design of the North Mill, which remained the model for many later adaptations and represents the moment at which the

problem of the iron frame had effectively been solved. Refinements were to come, as Schinkel noted, such as making iron columns and beams into hollow tubes to double as drainpipes or hot-water pipes for heating. Most dramatically, the new iron-frame principle could allow the construction of very large structures like the great Manchester cotton mills which Beuth in 1823, and Schinkel on the 1826 journey, looked upon with such awe. Kennedy's Mill of 1805–7 in Great Ancoats Street measured 370 by 40 feet and was six storeys high, and the McConnel Mill round the corner in Union Street, of 1818, was notable in its day for having as many as eight storeys. The experiments of Strutt and Bage had made possible within a few years the construction of a fireproof mill which was, as Schinkel observed, taller than the Royal Palace in Berlin.

Though Schinkel was not at all approving of the aesthetic effect of Manchester factories, he was appreciative of the adaptibility of their principles. In Liverpool he comments very favourably on Foster's newly-erected St John's Market, despite his dislike of the exterior: it is described as a 'splendid covered market', and he notes that the iron columns act as water conduits, and that the size of the whole building is enormous, 400 feet long and 150 feet wide. It says much for Schinkel's and Beuth's assiduity that they inspected another notable early iron-frame building in the west of England on their return from Scotland. Though he does not name it, it is clear from Schinkel's drawing that the 'beautiful factory' he saw near Stroud, 'a fireproof building, extremely solid and better built than in Manchester', is the Stanley Mill at King's Stanley, built c.1812–13.[30] It was important technically for completely eliminating wood in its construction so that it was genuinely fireproof, and it was unusually elegant both inside and out. Particularly striking are the elaborately decorated capitals on the columns which in themselves represent an advance on the functionalism of iron-frame buildings by that date. The capitals extend into a series of rings at the top, which can be read as decoration but also support the power transmission system for the factory machines. As Dr Riemann notes, they appear to have directly influenced the iron columns in the entrance hall of Prince Albrecht's Palace in Berlin, which Schinkel designed after his return from England.[31]

Schinkel reveals in the Journal that some of the machine tool specialists he visited, like Maudslay in London and Winwood in Bristol, were in the habit of experimenting with the iron roof supports of their own workshops, and he has left precious records in detailed sketches made on his visits. He arrived at Maudslay's workshop only a few days after a new roof had collapsed in the process of installation, with some loss of life. Schinkel notes this fact, but nonetheless studied the structure of the roof in detail. There are signs of real warmth in the accounts in the Journal of encounters with these new British technological pioneers, and he records an animated conversation with Marc Isambard Brunel while inspecting the Thames Tunnel. He found their direct manners attractive and their ingenuity and versatility admirable, and his accounts of visits to their workshops tend to be without the barbs that mark some of his comments on architects.

Only one figure Schinkel encountered in Britain drew from him a response bordering on humility, and that was Thomas Telford. In travelling on what is now the A5 road from Anglesea to Shrewsbury he mused upon the fact that so many of the new roadworks and canals were due to that great engineer. He crossed the Conway Suspension Bridge nine days after it opened, and his detailed drawings of this and the Menai Bridge, and his remarks on these great structures are accompanied by exceptionally enthusiastic comments. He commented not only on the structure of the Conway Bridge but on the uniquely picturesque way it appears to emerge from the great medieval castle, as can be seen in the drawing he made from a nearby hill. His observations on the 'awe-inspiring' Menai Bridge are even more fulsome, and he noted the span to be 700 feet to reach across to Anglesea. Equally astonishing to him as an example of the use of iron was the canal aqueduct of Pont-y-Cysylltau near Llangollen, which was ninety feet high and had nineteen arches. 'All the work of Mr Telford', he remarked of Pont-y-Cysylltau, 'who has arranged his road construction in such a way that all his great works can be seen coming from the Menai Bridge'.

Schinkel also has much to say about the works of art and manufactured objects he saw on his visit, but his observations are rarely favourable. He visited the famous Birmingham foundry of Sir Edward Thomason and was appalled at the ugliness of a full-size bronze copy of the Warwick Vase which was proudly shown to him as one of the technological achievements of the age. He was even more dismissive of a life-size statue of the King being made in the same workshop: 'any baker could have done better with a piece of dough'. Sculpture, especially, seems to have disappointed him, and, though he visited the studio of Sir Richard Westmacott (perhaps to be able to report to his sculptor friends in Berlin), he was generally uncomplimentary about the works of the sculptor that he noted in his travels. He is particularly merciless, perhaps with reason, towards the group of *The Death of Nelson*, designed by M.C. Wyatt and executed in bronze by Westmacott, by the side of Liverpool Town Hall. Modern British painting he seems to have regarded as of limited interest: he dismissed an exhibition of water-colours at the Old Water-Colour Society as 'smears', and he was, like other German travellers,[32] offended by the painterly quality of much British landscape painting, expressing implicitly his own preference for the linearity of the German tradition. Yet he was alert to what he and other Germans thought was distinctive about British art: a sense of vigorous life, wit and realism, and mastery of 'low' genres. This he noted in Hogarth's *Marriage-à-la-Mode* and in Wilkie's *Blind Fiddler* (which he saw in the National Gallery, and which was, like many of Wilkie's paintings, already well-known in Germany),[33] and the only painting in the Royal Academy exhibition that he singled out was a genre scene by William Mulready.

The final impression given by the Journal is of Schinkel's purposefulness and preparedness. In areas where he had a particular interest, like that of iron-frame construction, he was able to see an unusually high proportion of all the innovative buildings to date. With Beuth he went to the most important machine shops in London like Bramah, Maudslay and Holtzapffel and Deyerlein, and he had a list of many of the leading British architects. He was able to inspect new docks, ironworks, gasworks, cotton mills, hospital sanitation, new tunnelling methods: there is very little of the new industrialisation that he did not see. Even so Schinkel does not emerge as just a technocrat. He was moved equally by the remains of the past, or traces of the past in the present.

He was capable, like other Germans, of seeing a certain romanticism in industrial views, hence the recurring image of the Midlands industrial landscape as Ancient Egypt, with chimneys and kilns as 'smoking obelisks'.[34]

Other visitors in the 1820s had looked at the industrial landscape of Britain, and the path to the 'Ossianic Isles' through the industrial North was a well-beaten one by 1826; but Schinkel stands out in engaging directly with the architectural and related social issues which arose from a country that could offer both new solutions to old problems and physical evidences of an ancient history, often, as he observed in Glasgow, in almost visible flight from new urban developments. Beyond his concern with the direct application of new technology to building lay the intractible problems of reconciling new methods with older building types like churches and palaces, or new building types with older forms. He also shows a prophetic sensitivity to the fragility of the wild landscape of the Scottish isles, noting the dangers to its sense of solitude implicit in the number of steamboats taking visitors out to them. In the Journal he appears to take relatively little interest in contemporary buildings, however impressive to our eyes, which did not employ new technology, and is all the more interested in those that do, though he is rarely uncritical. Schinkel came to Britain expecting to be more stirred by technology than architecture, and, given that people tend to find what they are looking for, we should not on reflection find it surprising that his Journal reveals a greater enthusiasm for the iron roof of Maudslay's workshop than for Soane's Bank of England or for Nash's Regent's Park terraces, nor that he found the Tanfield Gasworks to be more worthy of study than the great monuments of the Scottish Greek Revival.

[1] See *The Journal*, note 2.

[2] For Prussian industrial espionage in this period see K.D. Einbrodt and J. Roesler, *Die Industriespionage Preussens in England in den Jahren 1790–1850*, Berlin, 1962.

[3] See pp. 143–4.

[4] See A. von Wolzogen, *Aus Schinkels Nachlass*, Berlin, 1862–3, Vol. III, 139.

[5] See p. 108.

[6] See p. 176.

[7] See p. 179.

[8] See E.J. Feuchtwanger, *Prussia: Myth and Reality*, London, 1970, 139f.

[9] See H.G. Pundt, *Schinkel's Berlin*, Cambridge, MA, 1972, 106f.

[10] See L.D. Bagshaw ed., *Visitors to Manchester*, Manchester, 1986, 28.

[11] R. Southey, *Letters from England*, London, 1808, Vol. 2, 81–97.

[12] See p. 112.

[13] For Schinkel's dislike of picturesque and untidy development in his 1817 plan for Berlin, see Pundt, op. cit., 125.

[14] See p. 179.

[15] See John Summerson, *John Nash*, London, 1935 and 1980.

[16] See N. Allen ed., *Scottish Pioneers of the Greek Revival*, Edinburgh, 1984, 47f.

[17] See p. 87.

[18] For Smirke see articles by J. Mordaunt Crook in the following journals: *Transactions of the Newcomen Society*, 1965–6; *Country Life*, 1967, 846–8; *Architectural Review*, 1967, 208–10; *Journal of the London Society*, 1968, 381–2, and *Country Life Annual*, 1970, 102–5.

[19] See J. Mordaunt Crook, *The British Museum*, Harmondsworth, 1973, 113–19.

[20] Published in *Précis des leçons d'architecture*. See N. Pevsner, *A History of Building Types*, London, 1976, 126–7.

[21] For Gott see V.E.M. Lovell, *Benjamin Gott of Armley House*, Leeds, *Publications of the Thoresby Society*, n.d., Vol. LIX, part 2, no. 130, 177–221.

[22] See S. Daniels, 'Landscaping for a manufacturer: Repton's commission for Armley, 1809–10', *Journal of Historical Geography*, 7, 1981, 379–96.

[23] See D. Watkin, *The Life and Work of C.R. Cockerell*, 1974.

[24] See J. Mordaunt Crook, 'The Architecture of Thomas Harrison' in *Country Life*, 1971, 876–9, 944–7, 1088–91 and 1539.

[25] There is remarkably little modern literature on Foster. See J.A. Picton, *Memorials of Liverpool*, 1875.

[26] Colvin, under Foster, John.

[27] There are detailed drawings of the iron construction of the dome of this building in the University of Edinburgh Library.

[28] See A.W. Skempton and H.R. Johnson, 'The first iron frames' in *Architectural Review*, 1962, 175–86.

[29] H.R. Johnson and A.W. Skempton, 'William Strutt's Cotton Mills, 1793–1812', *Transactions of the Newcomen Society*, 1956, 179–201.

[30] For an illustration of the interior see D. Verey, *Gloucestershire: The Cotswolds*, pl. 90, *Buildings of England*.

[31] See Dr Riemann's Introduction, p. 10.

[32] See A. Potts, 'British Romantic Art through German Eyes', in W. Sauerländer ed., 'Sind Briten hier?', *Relations between British and Continental Art, 1680–1880*, Munich, 1981.

[33] See Potts, op. cit., 190–1.

[34] This perception was not new: Johann Caspar Escher, a Swiss textile manufacturer, had already compared Manchester to Egypt on his visit there in 1814: 'I could well have arrived in Egypt since so many factory chimneys . . . stretch up into the sky like obelisks'. L.D. Bradshaw ed., *Visitors to Manchester*, 1986, 26.

'THE ENGLISH JOURNEY'

From Berlin to Paris

LETTERS TO SUSANNE

Weimar, Monday 17 April 1826

Dearest Susanne. We arrived safely in Weimar at 2 p.m. today. I have just written to Herr von Goethe to ask if we might visit him this afternoon.[1] Beuth[2] is quite well, otherwise we would not have travelled through the night; we covered 34 miles.

In Zehlendorf we had to drive through a whole flock of sheep: a lucky omen. – My fur coat has been a godsend; it has been dreadfully cold. The ride is smooth and the coach very comfortable. Your Tokay was a success – Mamselle Beuth[3] only provided red wine; rather unfortunate as Beuth was expecting port. I am waiting to hear of your journey to Stettin and how you found everyone there, and hope you and the children are well.[4] I shall soon be sending letters to you via Gabain;[5] but I could not resist the pleasure of sending this first letter to you straight away.

We are now halfway to Frankfurt, so we shall be there in three days if we travel through most of each night. The moonlight is a great advantage in the late evening. As you can imagine, our discussions about the business of the journey are going fine – Beuth is very accommodating.

Regards to Wilhelm,[6] kiss the children for me, remember me to good old Tieck[7] etc. – best love from your loyal and devoted Schinkel.

[1] Schinkel's letter to Goethe (1749–1832) has been preserved in the Goethe-Schiller Archives in Weimar: 'Your Excellency would give Geheimer Oberfinanzrat Beuth and myself great pleasure if you would allow us to wait on you for a quarter of an hour this afternoon. We are journeying to Paris and London, and shall be in our travelling clothes. We should be grateful if you would be so kind as to stipulate a time. Your most humble and obedient servant, Schinkel. Weimar, 17 April 1826'.

[2] Peter Christian Wilhelm Beuth (1781–1853), Schinkel's friend: 1814 *Geheimer Oberfinanzrat* [Privy Counsellor for finance] in the department of trade and industry of the Prussian finance ministry, after 1817 known as the ministry of trade. 1819 director of the technical commission for industry. 1821 founder and first head of the Technische Gewerbeschule [technical school of industry]. He was also founder and chairman of the Verein zur Beförderung des Gewerbefleisses in Preussen [Organization for the Promotion of Trade and Industry in Prussia], whose transactions were published from 1822. 1821 member of the Prussian council of state. In 1823 he made his first journey to England.

[3] Beuth's sister, Elisabeth. Like Beuth she was unmarried, and kept house for him.

[4] During her husband's absences, Schinkel's wife Susanne stayed with her parents, sister and brother-in-law, Herr Kuhberg, a Stettin merchant.

[5] George Gabain (1763–1826), merchant, resident of Breite Strasse, Berlin, and a friend of Schinkel from youth. The letters to Susanne which Schinkel wrote on his journey were sent to Gabain's address.

[6] Wilhelm Berger (1790–1858), Schinkel's brother-in-law, who had worked with him in Berlin as an architect and building inspector since 1818. Schinkel's four children were Marie (born 1810), Susanne (born 1811), Karl Raphael (born 1813) and Elisabeth (born 1822).

[7] Christian Friedrich Tieck (1776–1851), sculptor, who worked in close association with Schinkel.

[8] Goethe recorded the visit of 17 April 1826 as follows: 'Towards evening Herren Schinkel and Beuth, journeying from Berlin to Paris and London. They brought architectural and other drawings with them. Conversed with me and Ottilie for an hour'. It was their fourth meeting. Schinkel had met Goethe in Weimar in 1816 (on his journey to Heidelberg and the Rhine), in 1820 (journey to Weimar and Jena with Tieck) and in 1824 (on his return from Italy). On the way to his last visits to spas in 1839 and 1840, Schinkel again went to Weimar, in connection with the interior decoration of the Goethe gallery in Weimar Palace.

[9] Ottilie von Goethe, nee Pogwisch (1796–1872), the wife of Goethe's son, August (1796–1872), who had kept house for her father-in-law since 1817.

[10] Schinkel had owned from youth drawings from the collection of Friedrich Gilly (1772–1800), whom he had always admired. Among these was a view of the Gotha castle of Friedenstein and its grounds, hence his familiarity with it.

[11] The ruins of the imperial palace of the Staufens and the thirteenth-century Marienkirche.

[12] A younger sister of Clemens von Brentano, Magdalena, known as Meline, had married Georg Friedrich von Guaita in 1810. Schinkel, a friend of Clemens, was also acquainted with their elder step-brother Franz, for whom he had designed a house in the Grosse Mainzer Strasse in Frankfurt in 1818.

[13] Karl Ferdinand Friedrich von Nagler (1770–1846), Prussian General Postmaster since 1823 and in 1824 Prussian envoy in the Frankfurt Parliament, was also a well-known art collector. His collection of prints, at that time the largest in Germany, achieved a special status on being acquired in 1835 by Friedrich Wilhelm III for the Royal Print Room.

Frankfurt am Main, 19 April 1826

Dearest Susanne. We went to see Herr von Goethe just after I sent you the letter from Weimar.[8] He was not very well, and also had a plaster over a boil on his chin. He had not received anyone for some days, and young Frau Goethe[9] told me that he would not have left his sickroom if it had not been for special guests. For the rest he talked very cheerfully to us for two hours. We were invited to spend the evening with young Frau Goethe, but declined since we would not have seen the old gentleman. We had a meal in our inn after a short walk in the park, and went to bed early.

We set off again early on Tuesday, stopped for one hour in Erfurt and another in Gotha.[10] In Gotha we climbed up to the terrace of the palace, which has a superb view, indeed the palace of Gotha[11] has the finest situation in all the duchies of Saxony. We drove on through the night via Eisenach, it was dreadfully cold, with alternate hail and rain during the day; the night was more settled but the cold increased. In Fulda early in the morning there was thick frost everywhere, but then the sun came out and we had wonderful weather. We saw the old things in Gelnhausen, had lunch there, and arrived in Frankfurt at 5 (plate 3). Here we had so much time to spare that we could walk round the town, where there has really been a great improvement. Grand houses and gardens everywhere, some of them very tasteful. Herr von Guaita's[12] house is almost the finest of them all. We returned extremely edified to our inn, 'zum Römischen Kaiser' (the Roman Emperor).

I'll finish writing to you, then we shall have supper and go to bed, as tomorrow we have the long stretch to Koblenz before us. On leaving our inn we immediately met Herr von Nagler in splendid full-dress equipage.[13]

We are both very well and want nothing more than to hear the same of you and the children. I shall give this letter to our servant; I hope it reaches you, as the post-office is closed and will not be open before we leave tomorrow morning.

Best wishes from Beuth, kiss the children and Wilhelm for me, and regards to all the friends of your loyal and devoted Schinkel.

3. J.F. Morgenstein, *View of Frankfurt am Main*, aquatint

4. J.C. von Lassaulx, *The Ruins of Stolzenfels Castle from the Rhine*, 1823, pen and wash

Trier, Friday 21 April 1826

Dearest Susanne. By 8 this evening we had covered 110 miles since 6 on Sunday morning, and even had 3 good nights' sleep. We are both very well indeed, and you would not recognize me now, for I am so sunburnt that I have become as black as a Moor, and so swollen all over with the heat that I look positively corpulent.

The stretch between Frankfurt and Koblenz was extraordinarily beautiful, and enhanced by the most splendid weather. From Frankfurt onwards and in the whole Rhine valley everything was in blossom, the green bursting forth everywhere. This time, with the coach roof down, I could really enjoy the fine view of the Rhine valley beyond Mainz near Ingelheim, which you will remember, and the Rhine valley itself. Prince Friedrich's castle Rheinfels, the first one after Bingen,[14] is in the process of being rebuilt according to my plans. But the Crown Prince's castle, Stolzenfels (plate 4), the largest of all and in the finest situation, has not been touched.[15] We arrived in Koblenz in the evening, and had a visit from De Lassaulx[16] and Clemens Brentano.[17] The latter is just the same as ever, but he was obsessed with his nun's story,[18] and I let him go on for a while in order to hear what it was all about. I will tell you more when I see you. You can imagine how much we talked about you. According to Brentano, De Lassaulx is in love with you, or at least he would be if he were not committed to an elevated destiny!

The whole of the journey from Koblenz to Trier, which we continued on Friday morning at 5 o'clock, has been extremely interesting, especially the first half from Koblenz, a route which you and I followed in the evening on our first journey together and did not enjoy very much. You miss the Eifel mountains, the Rhine and Mosel valleys, and since the road follows the contours of the mountains we found the vegetation here very undeveloped. It was only when we were approaching Trier that spring was again magnificently in evidence. In Trier several civic counsellors, acquaintances of Beuth, dined with us at the inn. Quednow[19] is away, so I shall just visit his wife briefly, so that we can see the antiquities tomorrow morning and be on our way to Mettlach by midday.

[14] This is the ruin of Vautzburg or Voigtsburg (fourteenth-century), situated to the north of Bingen. It had been acquired in 1823 for Prince Friedrich of Prussia, a nephew of Friedrich Wilhelm III. Schinkel, who had drawn the castle and its additions during his journey to the Rhine in 1816, was asked to provide plans for the rebuilding of the ruin, now known as Rheinstein, through the mediation of the Crown Prince. The building was put up in 1825–9, with alterations by the Koblenz building inspector De Lassaulx.

[15] Crown Prince Friedrich Wilhelm (IV) had been given the ruin by the town of Koblenz. The original plans of De Lassaulx, who had already started building work, were added to in 1823 by Schinkel, whose designs had been guided by the Crown Prince. New and altered plans were used as the basis of building work begun in 1836. It was only in 1842, after Schinkel's death, that the castle, a characteristic example of the Prussian Romantic Rhine type, was finished. See E. Brues, *Schinkel Lebenswerk: Die Rheinlande*, 1968, 129–53. For Schinkel's first design see Wegner, pl. 109.

[16] Johann Claudius de Lassaulx (1781–1842), architect, known to Schinkel from Berlin and also through the latter's first journey to the Rhine in 1816. Prussian regional building inspector in Koblenz.

[17] Poet (1778–1842) and friend of Schinkel's since 1809. After his conversion to Catholicism he had devoted himself since 1819 to his visions of the stigmatised nun Anna Katharina Emmerich. He lived in Koblenz from 1824 to 1827. In 1833 he published a volume on the subject of Katharina.

[18] A reference to Brentano's religious mysticism. See previous note.

[19] Architect (died 1836); he had been Government Building Adviser in Trier since 1816.

Trier, 22 April 1826

We are waiting for Bousson, a local official,[20] who is to guide us round the town. Beuth asks you to send him new shirts, because yesterday the brace-pin on the coach came loose and cut into his leather valise, badly damaging it. A new linchpin had to be fitted at the stop before Trier; he thinks that this should be paid for out of general funds. The damage is not so great, so I do not mind if that is what he wants.

Mettlach, 23 April 1826

We had a splendid morning for our walk.[21] First we inspected the Porta Nigra[22] (plate 5) inside and out, and climbed up to the top. A number of interesting antiquities have recently been found during excavations not far from the bridge, and are on show in the Porta Nigra along with others discovered earlier. The richly ornamented frieze of a projecting column is decorated with bas-reliefs of warriors from the time of Constantine. The setting of the pilasters and decorated friezes in a niche was particularly interesting. From the Porta Nigra we went to the cathedral,[23] and then to the fine Marienkirche[24] next to it, whose original design I admired once again. Bousson showed me the fine ornamentation of tall vine stems and leaves on the portals. Then we visited Madame Quednow for 5 minutes and looked at her husband's collection of antiquities.[25] A small bronze Laocoön in a version very different from the famous one (a boy in desperation flung across his father's knee), a small tomb vessel of dark reddish-brown glass, and some pretty mosaics, were the most impressive of the objects. From there we went on to the imperial palace[26] (plate 6). For the roof support you can still see a great arch with a span of about 70–74 ft, constructed of enormous flat bricks, 4 arches one above the other, with a separation of flat bricks between each layer. The mortar joints are very thick: between about 1¾ and 2 ins.

We then saw the baths,[27] which have for the most part been excavated; you can see from the exposed foundation walls that their dimensions are equal to those in Rome. The walls are massive, but their architecture is very intricate (almost Byzantine). Much of the

[20] Mentioned as a road construction engineer in Saarlautern and road construction inspector in Trier between 1820 and 1851.
[21] Schinkel is describing the previous day, 22 April, in Trier.
[22] Under Napoleon and since 1815 the Prussian government, the north gate of the Roman fortified town of Augusta Treverorum, a second-century construction, had been freed of most of its medieval additions (including the Simeons Kapelle). In 1822 the *porta* had been reopened as a town gate. During his stay in 1816, Schinkel had participated enthusiastically in the uncovering and restoration of the gate. Roman artefacts found nearby were exhibited inside, as depicted in a lithograph of 1824 by J.A. Ramboux. On a later visit in 1833 Schinkel made suggestions for the restoration of the exterior.
[23] St Peter's Cathedral, founded by Constantine but dating mainly from the eleventh to thirteenth centuries. Schinkel several times before and after 1826 offered advice on its interior decoration.
[24] Liebfrauenkirche. An unusual centrally-planned Gothic building (thirteenth century), and one of the earliest purely Gothic churches in Germany. Schinkel had already shown an interest in it and admired it in 1816 (see letter to Sulpice Boisserée of 3 September 1816, and sketches in the former Staatliche Museen zu Berlin; Brues, op. cit., 421–2).
[25] The *Baurat* [Building Advisor] Quednow had devoted himself to the preservation and examination of Roman finds, publishing a two-volume work in 1820: *Beschreibung der Altertümer von Trier und dessen Umgebungen aus der gallish-belgischen und der römischen Periode. [Description of the antiquities of Trier and environs from the Gallo Belgian and Roman periods].*
[26] This is the 'basilica', built as an Aula Palatina by Emperor Constantine, *c.*305. During the building of the Elector's palace in the seventeenth century it was partly dismantled, but later in 1844–56 Friedrich Wilhelm IV commissioned F.A. Stüler to reconstruct it 'in its original proportions and style' (Brues, op. cit., 414–7).
[27] The remains of the fourth-century imperial baths in Trier, though largely dismantled and built over, had been exposed and excavated since 1817, so that Schinkel was able to comment on their construction and technical design. They were scarcely less important than the Baths of Diocletian and Caracalla in Rome.

28 This was built *c*.100 as an earthwork, and there had been excavations on the site since 1816. Schinkel was able to note their progress on a later visit to Trier in 1833. It was smaller than the Colosseum (188 by 156 m), but about equal in size to the amphitheatre in Verona (138 by 109 m).

29 The stone piers date from the second century.

30 From 1819 to 1857 the former Jesuit and medieval Franciscan church was used as a Protestant parish church.

31 Johann Georg Wolff (1789–1861), architect and town-planner in Trier. Schinkel's critical remarks were perhaps directed mainly towards the palatial façade of the assembly room built in 1824/25 in the Trier Corn Market.

32 The ruins of this building, which was founded in the 10th century and destroyed in 1705, date from the Romanesque period.

33 The hermitage, the 'Klause von Kastel', is set upon a distinctive and long-settled rocky plateau overlooking the Saar valley, and in the Middle Ages a version of the Holy Sepulchre was built, and hermits looked after a later chapel, which had fallen into ruin by the end of the eighteenth century. In 1835, at the behest of the Prussian Crown Prince Friedrich Wilhelm (IV), seeking to reinforce the dynastic principle in the Prussian-occupied Rhineland, Schinkel designed a medieval-style chapel. This contained the tomb of the medieval chivalric hero King Johann von Böhmen [John of Bohemia], which was brought from the monastery of Mettlach, where it had ended up. Schinkel's visit in 1826 must have provided useful materials for his later design. For a full account of Schinkel's project see G. Metken, 'Das Grab des blinden Königs: Karl Friedrich Schinkels Kapelle für Johann von Böhmen', C. Beutler, P.-K. Schuster and M. Warnke, *Kunst um 1800 und die Folgen: Werner Hofmann zu Ehren*, Munich, 1988, 159–68.

34 The Benedictine abbey of Mettlach, designed by the Saxon architect Christian Kretzschmar, was built between 1728 and 1780 in an elaborate Baroque style.

35 The manufacturer Jean-François Boch-Buschmann (1782–1858) had built a stoneware factory in Mettlach in 1809. In 1841 it amalgamated with the firm of Villeroy in Wallerfangen (see note 37) to become Villeroy and Boch.

heating system still survives. The amphitheatre,[28] which we visited next, has also been extensively excavated. The arena is only 10 ft shorter than that of the Colosseum, but from the surviving traces of the outer encircling wall you can tell that the whole must have been larger. These buildings, amphitheatre, baths and imperial palace, appear to have originally formed a large unified complex erected by Constantine, Gratian and later emperors.[29] We had a brief look at the Mosel bridge with its ancient foundations, and then returned to the inn. On the way I looked at the interior of the Protestant church,[30] which was designed, not particularly well, by the planner Wolff,[31] who has also produced several over-ornate façades showing his lack of architectural understanding. After lunch we left for Mettlach at 1 o'clock.

On the way, at the second stop, we went to have a look at Kastel, half an hour's distance from the road. We had already passed Saarburg with an old ruined castle built originally by Caesar.[32] Here in Kastel the Romans had a *castrum* on a projecting plateau on the Mosel, formed of a magnificent mass of rock 1,000 ft above the water.[33] There is nothing Roman left apart from the great many coins found daily in the fields. In the Middle Ages a hermitage was established on the beautiful slope of the cliffs – an attractive place with all sorts of strange caves, steps, and a chapel etc, much visited by foreigners. We arrived towards dusk in Mettlach, a place consisting of a large monastery in the Jesuit style[34] around which, a short distance away, the dwellings of the factory-workers form a small village. Herr Buschmann,[35] a friend of Beuth's, bought this enormous building and set up a fine earthenware factory inside it (plate 7).

Metz, 25 April

I have not been able to write in my diary until today. We were very well received by Herr Buschmann, who has a charming wife, two nearly grown-up daughters and a little son. Everything in this house is very French, but Beuth made sure the party spoke in German. We had a very good supper and slept remarkably well in splendid beds in splendid rooms.

5. J. Saurborn, *The Porta Nigra in Trier*, lithograph

6. *The Basilica in Trier*, 1816, pen and pencil

7. Anonymous, *The pottery works at Mettlach*, lithograph

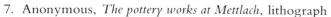

8. *Town house in Metz*, 1826, pencil

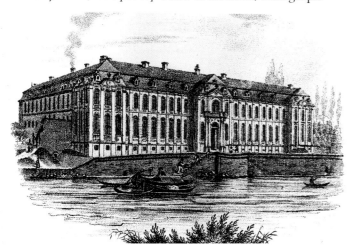

The next morning, 26 April [Schinkel means 23 April], we saw part of the factory, but not working as it was Sunday, so our hosts did not want to let us go before 9 o'clock the next morning, so that we could see it working. We spent the day in the garden and walking in the hills, and had a short boat-trip on the Saar. An old ruin,[36] octagonal, from Charlemagne's time, but with pointed arches added in the fourteenth century, stands in the garden right next to the large factory building;[37] they were going to pull it down, but we persuaded them not to. Beuth is always very amusing in company, and sometimes joins in the ladies' French conversation. An older lady finds this particularly enjoyable – a visitor who lives in Dresden and brought up her eldest daughter there, now visiting Mettlach with the daughter.

The next morning, 24 April [crossed out though it is the correct date], after our visit to the factory we continued on our way in pouring rain. We inspected the factory from 6 o'clock onwards. The kilns there are interesting and well thought out, easily operated from above, the air vents just beneath the roof, the kiln-doors of baked clay set in iron, which do not get too hot like those made only of iron. – A machine where a wire at regular intervals cuts the wedges of soft clay into pieces of varying sizes, which are then placed on the plate and bowl moulds to be worked. – Copper engraving on the earthenware.

Continuing on our journey, we saw a rolling mill near Dillingen, where large iron and copper panels were turned out between enormous sloping rollers; the rest of the large plant is very primitive. Not far from it there is another earthenware factory in Wallerfangen, which belongs to a Herr Villeroy; Beuth had announced his arrival for a day later, so we were not expected. Herr Villeroy had gone away for the day, and his elderly wife, like an old French noblewoman in manner, was most upset that her husband would not have an opportunity to see us, and that we were not going to stay the night at her house. The son-in-law showed us round the factory, which is very big and has a large output, but it is not as sophisticated as Herr Buschmann's.

We reached Saarbrücken towards evening; it was still pouring with rain. Here Beuth visited an old war-time comrade, Captain

[36] The 'Alte Turm' in Mettlach, built shortly before 1000 and altered in the fourteenth century. In 1838 the Prussian Crown Prince commissioned a cast-iron fountain with a statuette of King Johann von Böhmen from a design by Schinkel, to be erected in the surrounding park. This was in exchange for the king's sarcophagus which had been given to the Kastel hermitage (see note 33 and E. Brues, op. cit., 181–97).

[37] Built by Nicolas Villeroy (1759–1843) in 1789.

von Aschenbach. A big tall man, friendly and open, who lives in a barracks with his wife. We found him still limping from a hip injury incurred when his coach went over the side of a bridge. He complained that he had not been promoted since [18]13–15, and Beuth said he would mention him to General Witzleben.[38] The great bridge at Saarbrücken was closed. Marshal Marmont had blown up two of the stone arches during the retreat of [18]13–14.[39] They had been replaced by wooden supports, but they had become unsafe and had already been removed eight days before, when, by chance, Marshal Marmont, returning from a journey to Russia, wanted to cross back over the bridge, which he himself had destroyed. His coach and luggage had to wait a long time before a pontoon bridge was ready.

On 25 April we continued on to Metz. One stop after Saarbrücken, in the village of Forbach, we went through the French customs. When they discovered our status from the passports, they let us through without a search, for which we gladly paid a douceur of 5 francs. We arrived in Metz at 1 o'clock, had a meal straight away at the table d'hôte in the Hôtel de l'Europe with a number of Frenchmen, mostly officers of the old Napoleonic army, then went to view the cathedral inside and out.[40] A magnificent building in the finest medieval style, especially the choir and transepts, the gable of which holds a single enormous window of beautiful stained glass. A large antique free-standing vessel of porphyry, indifferently fashioned, is kept in the cathedral. The town is excellently situated on the Mosel, has 5 stone bridges, broad terraces and slopes, and on one of the hilltops there is the government palace and its garden.[41] From the terrace you look down on the green valleys and lovely gentle hills which surround the town. The roofs of the houses are flat, as in Italy, and everything is reminiscent of that country. Apart from other old churches the town contains many old houses with battlements and rows of windows which are only lightly supported (plate 8). They have begun building a large bishop's palace of yellow stone next to the portal of the cathedral;[42] this portal is modern, like the palace, as also is the large terrace with steps in the church square. Ridiculous notices are written everywhere in enormous letters on boards, and on walls. Amongst others, 'Hier

[38] Job Wilhelm Karl Ernst von Witzleben (1783–1837), General Adjutant of King Friedrich Wilhelm III since 1818, later (1833) Prussian Minister of War.
[39] Auguste-Fréderic-Louis Viesse de Marmont (1774–1852), one of Napoleon's commanders who had accompanied him during his retreat and subsequent defeat in 1813/14. He also held high office after 1815. He made the journey to Russia mentioned here in 1826 as King Louis XVIII's ambassador extraordinary on the occasion of the coronation of Tsar Nicholas I.
[40] Metz Cathedral, dating from the thirteenth to sixteenth centuries, is distinguished by its harmonious space and fine stained-glass windows.
[41] Schinkel possibly means the Town Hall designed by the architect J.-F. Blondel 1762–75 (see following note).
[42] The Bishop's Palace and Cathedral façade are both works of J.-F. Blondel, who was a pioneer of the new 'Enlightened' architecture of the 1760s, notable for its plainess, functionality and symmetry. The works that Schinkel noted are important forerunners of the architecture of the Napoleonic and Restoration periods he was to admire in Paris. See Kalnein and Levey, 1972, 300.

nimmt man jungen Deutschen in Wohnung und Kosten' [literally: Here we take young Germans in staying and tasting. 'Kost und Wohnung' means board and lodging] was written in German and two other languages on a house in the church square.

Because we failed to pick up our passports from the local police before 4 o'clock we have to spend 5 hours longer here; instead of leaving at 5 tomorrow we shall probably not get away until 10.

Wednesday, 26 April

We set off in bad weather after having to exchange our passports for French ones at the préfecture. We shall not get our own back until we get to Paris. About a mile from Metz we looked at a flour mill driven by a fire-powered machine.[43] When the owner realized that Beuth was an expert he was most pleasant and showed us round the whole mill, which had been ingeniously set up in the rooms of an old château. The position of the mill was also very picturesque. There were boats on the moat around it, in which the owner had travelled down the Mosel to Holland with his merchandise. He had a clever grinding-machine of his own invention. Beuth promised to send him some prints of recent improvements. From a small belvedere above the roof we could see fine hilly countryside around and the ruins of an ancient Roman aqueduct in the distance.

We reached Verdun by 3 o'clock, and had dinner in the 3 Moors [Inn]. I had a look at the cathedral,[44] which has an old groundplan but has been newly and badly altered. Why all the French sentries presented arms to me and the soldiers in the street saluted I do not know. At 6 o'clock we continued on, driving through the night to Châlons-sur-Marne.[45] An old cathedral there has fine windows; we looked at them at 5 in the morning, in pouring rain and freezing cold.

Thursday, 27 April

Another old church has got modern Gothic spires, very poorly done.[46] A few minor repairs had to be carried out on our coach at

[43] This is probably the so-called 'fire-air machine', a hot-air engine which had been used for the first time in 1807.

[44] Verdun Cathedral. The oldest parts, dating from the twelfth and thirteenth centuries, had been substantially renovated in the seventeenth century.

[45] The Cathedral of Saint-Etienne still has its original windows, dating from the thirteenth to sixteenth centuries when the cathedral was built.

[46] Of the four towers of Notre-Dame in Châlons, built in 1158–1322, the two over the façade have helm roofs which were added later.

the inn, then we continued on to Reims. Before we arrived in Châlons we stopped in a small village at 2–3 in the morning to have a look at the outside of the famous old church of St Marie d'Epine,[47] as far as was possible in the dark. This church is not large, but has some rich, intricate detail in the style of Reims Cathedral.

We arrived in Reims at midday, and the postillion drove us to a dirty inn we did not like from the outside. I looked at the rooms, which were just as dirty, so we drove to another, the Maison Rouge, where we were given a small, well furnished room, but when we lit a fire in the grate there was such a draught from the door, which did not fit the frame anywhere, that the table with our dinner had to be placed between the sumptuous beds, and we could only keep warm by having a constant blaze in the grate.

The magnificent cathedral[48] is, compared to other buildings, somewhat heavy in detail, but is distinguished by the wealth of stone-carving in the gable and portal windows, also the statues in the portals and buttresses. Inside, everything had been newly painted for the coronation,[49] the capitals a golden yellow. The gable in the portal is splendid from inside, where the stained glass in both the upper rose window and the lower portal window, also in an arched gallery separating the two, is magnificent, though somewhat overwhelmimg. The crossing in the Metz church was more beautiful. From the cathedral we walked across the Place Louis XV, whose bronze colossus with its huge allegorical figures set around the circular base was restored in very bad taste in the eighteenth century.[50] Around the square there are ordinary buildings of handsome yellow stone from the time of Louis XV, architecturally straightforward, but uninteresting in their proportions and detail.

We then inspected the very old church of St Rémi[51] which has been arbitrarily altered several times. The main façade is particularly interesting, with antique granite columns also found inside. In the cathedral we also saw an antique sarcophagus[52] with a lion hunt depicted on it, which is supposed to contain the relics of St Rémi. Everything was very dirty because of the rain; we walked round the town on the old wall to a late Roman triumphal arch.[53] It is set in the wall and copiously decorated (imitated in the drapery in the

[47] The church of Notre-Dame in L'Epine was built between the fourteenth and early sixteenth centuries.
[48] The building of Reims Cathedral, a site dating from the fourth century, was started in 1211. The chancel was finished by 1241, and the nave and transepts by 1300. The west towers were not completed until the fifteenth century. The extensive sculpture, especially that on the west façade, was finished in 1260.
[49] King Charles X (1757–1826), Louis XVIII's brother and successor, had been anointed and crowned in Reims Cathedral, the traditional place of coronation for French kings. Festive decorations were by Hittorff and Lecointe.
[50] Jean-Baptiste Pigalle's bronze statue of Louis XV, made between 1758 and 1765, had been destroyed in the Revolution, and only the figures at the base remained. In 1818 the sculptor Pierre Cartellier had made a copy of the statue.
[51] The church was founded as early as the sixth century. The western parts of the basilica were built *c.*1005–49 and the chancel *c.*1164–81.
[52] 'St Rémi's sarcophagus' is in fact Renaissance in origin.
[53] The Porte de Mars, a triumphal arch, was built in the fourth century. The reliefs in the arches depict the twelve months, Romulus and Remus, and Leda and the Swan.

cathedral). The triumphal arch has 8 columns and 3 three big arches, the latter decorated on the inside with bas-reliefs, all still being worked on with a drill, but badly.

Friday, 28 April

We set off at 8 o'clock in the morning and drove to Soissons, in weather alternating between snow-storm and sunshine. Here we had dinner and looked at the cathedral,[54] the portal of which has been ruined by the tasteless addition of 2 Tuscan columns and a pointed-arch filled in with angels' heads floating on clouds and sunbeams. From the town wall you can see the portal and towers of an old church of St Rémi,[55] built in somewhat coarse and muddled medieval style. In the evening we put up in Nanteuil, a small village, so that we should get to Paris in good time the next morning. Beuth had found no letters in Reims to tell us about our accommodation, and we did not know whether we would find anything straight away.

Saturday, 29 April

When we woke up next morning the roofs and fields were covered in snow and the air was raw. The sun gradually appeared, melting the snow but not banishing the cold. And so we approached Paris and the hill of Montmartre, and they shone welcomingly in the distance.

Paris

(Continuation of 29 April entry)

It was 10 o'clock when we arrived at the hotel, where Beuth had previously stayed, to find that Professor Kunth[56] had already booked rooms for us and had been there several times to inquire

[54] The cathedral of St Gervais and St Protais dates mainly from the early and mid-thirteenth century.
[55] Since there is no church of this name in Soissons, Schinkel must be referring to the abbey-church of St Jean des Vignes.
[56] Karl Sigismund Kunth (1788–1850), a botanist, was in Paris from 1813. He collaborated with Alexander von Humboldt and was in charge of the latter's botanical collection from America.

after us. We unpacked and washed. I bought a hat, as my old one had suffered on the journey, and an umbrella, and we set off for Herr von Humboldt's house.[57]

On the way we had a look at some of the glass-covered arcades,[58] which are most elegant and pleasing in construction, also the Palais Royal (plates 9 and 10).[59] Fortunately we found Herr von Humboldt and Kunth at home; they gave us a very friendly reception and immediately took us to the great Museum[60] and to the Egyptian collection of M. Passalacqua.[61] So it was not until 4 that we got to the restaurant in the Palais Royal; in the courtyard we had a splendid view of the lime avenue and fountain and lilac blossom, and ate a very good lunch. After the meal we went for a long walk with Herr Kunth down the Seine as far as Passy, where we could see the construction of the bridge by Navier.[62] It is to be a big chain suspension bridge; but the structures which are to hold the chains in position are unnecessarily thick and strong – to my mind a waste. Paris and its setting seemed incomparably more serene and beautiful than the first time I was here; it all seems far bigger and more magnificent as well.[63] – As we were tired out we went to bed early.

Paris, 6 o'clock Sunday morning, 30 April

Dearest Susanne. I enclose my diary with this; please keep it for me. I have thought of you and the children a thousand times, hoping you had a good journey to Stettin. This letter will probably reach you there. I am sure you will do your best to see that Karl[64] keeps up his studies, I particularly want him to progress well in Latin and French translation under private tuition. He can learn the grammar in more detail in school or at the academy, but he must practise fluent translating and translate extensively.

We shall probably stay here until 20 April [Schinkel means May], and I hope to have heard from you by then. My best regards to Karoline and Mother, and do what you can to support and comfort her in her misfortune.[65] I long to know how you and the children are getting on. I will have so little time here, since everything is so

[57] Alexander von Humboldt (1769–1859) lived in Paris from 1807 to 1827, after his journey to America (1799–1804). During this time he was mainly occupied with writing up the journey.
[58] After the Revolution some of the most important early Paris arcades were built near the Palais Royal, which served as models for the later construction of arcades.
[59] Originally built (1634–9) for Cardinal Richelieu, it became the residence of Louis XIV's brother, the duc d'Orléans and his family. Under the duc de Chartres, later duc d'Orléans and Philippe Egalité, the park of the private palace was enclosed within a continuous arcade of lettable buildings, designed by the architect Victor Louis and begun in 1781, and the park became a popular promenade ground, a kind of Paris Vauxhall (Braham, 1980, 156–7). Louis Philippe commissioned Fontaine to restore and further extend the palace (1818–30).
[60] The Louvre.
[61] Joseph Passalacqua (1797–1865), Egyptologist, whose important collection of Egyptian antiquities was acquired for the Royal Collection in Berlin by Friedrich Wilhelm III in 1828. Passalacqua became the first Director of the Egyptian Museum in Berlin.
[62] Louis-Marie-Henri Navier (1785–1836), engineer and pioneer of structural engineering. In 1824 he had begun building a bridge across the Seine with a 155 metre span, along the axis of the Hôtel des Invalides. It was demolished in 1826, because the foundations had sunk.
[63] Schinkel had already visited Paris on his return from his Italian journey (1803–5). He did not record that visit in detail, so we have no impressions or even the length of his stay, which was between December 1804 and March 1805. In two letters to Berlin, to David Gilly and Valentin Rose, he made some remarks on the Halle au Blé and a brief comment on the city. In a third letter, from Italy, to the Cabinet Minister Count Haugwitz, Schinkel asked (unsuccessfully) for 'financial support from the state to allow him to stay in France, even for only six months'. See G. Riemann (ed.), *Karl Friedrich Schinkel: Reisen nach Italien, Tagebucher, Briefe, Zeichnungen, Aquarelle*, Berlin 1979, 124–5.
[64] Schinkel's son Karl Raphael, born in 1813.
[65] Schinkel's sister-in-law Karoline's husband, the merchant Kuhberg of Stettin, had died shortly before.

9. Gavard, eng. Salathé, *The Palais Royal, Paris*, aquatint

10. C. Gilio, eng. J.H. Martens, *A gallery in the Palais Royal*, 1832, engraving

spread out, that I shall only be able to write very briefly. Today we visit our ambassador, Herr von Werther,[66] then we shall go with Herr von Humboldt to see Quatremère de Quincy,[67] Percier, Fontaine,[68] etc. I must hurry now to take this letter to the post, which is a long way away. Farewell, dear heart, and think of your Schinkel.

THE JOURNAL

Paris, Sunday, 30 April 1826

Invalides cathedral [*sic*].[69] – Iron steamship (Le Commerce de Paris), which goes to Le Havre. – Ambassador Herr von Werther not at home. – Herr von Humboldt, fine view from his window. – Percier. Fontaine. – Quatremère de Quincy. – Gérard.[70] Ill, studio with splendid pictures, portraits, Battle of Austerlitz. – Sculpture Gallery.[71] – lunch at Grignon.[72] – Théâtre Feydeau,[73] good seats. (La Vieille Coradin; aujourd'hui Judis.[74])

Monday, 1 May

Percier, Fontaine. Went through the whole of the Louvre. The construction works,[75] access to the great gallery by staircase and over the central portal. – Café Turque – boulevards[76] – abattoir de Ménilmontant – Bouverie slaughterhouse[77] – Cimetière du Père-Lachaise,[78] monuments, fine view of Paris, plantation of cypresses, *arbor vitae*, etc., road leading up to it where stonemasons keep a supply of monuments for sale, as do smiths the railings, and gardeners the plants. – Dinner at 8 in the evening in the Palais

66 Wilhelm Baron von Werther (1772–1859). From 1837 to 1841 Prussian Foreign Minister. He was ambassador in Paris from 1824 to 1837.
67 Antoine-Chrysostome Quatremère de Quincy (1755–1849). Art theorist, from 1815 director in charge of arts and monuments, from 1816 Secretary of the Académie des Beaux-Arts, and sometime general director of museums. His publications include: *Dictionnaire historique d'architecture*, 1785–1825; *Essai sur la nature, le but et les moyens de l'imitation dans les beaux-arts*, 1823.

68 Charles Percier (1764–1838), architect, and Pierre-François-Léonard Fontaine (1762–1853), architect. They worked in collaboration from 1794, and were the first to develop the Empire style as Napoleon's official architects and interior designers. Their most important projects were: the Arc du Carrousel, 1806–8, and the Rue de Rivoli, 1802 onwards. They also made designs for a palace for the King of Rome, the Palais de Chaillot. (Braham, 1980, 257–8). They produced publications on the history of

architecture, their main work being *Choix des plus célèbres maisons de plaisance de Rome et des environs*, 1809–13. Schinkel met them several times in Paris; in 1827 after his return to Berlin he sent them a large drawing, a copy of an earlier drawing by himself, of the Taormina Theatre (now Potsdam-Sanssouci, Aquarellsammlung).
69 The church of the Invalides, commissioned by Louis XIV and built (1680–91) by Jules Hardouin-Mansart. Like St Paul's Cathedral in London of the same period, it derives from St Peter's in Rome. The Invalides clearly influenced Schinkel's thoughts on centrally planned structures, especially for the domed church in Potsdam which was on his mind during this period.
70 François-Pascal, Baron Gérard (1770–1837). Pupil of David and painter of portraits and historical scenes. He had been official portrait painter under Napoleon, and continued under the restored Bourbons. The painting of the battle of Austerlitz (1811) which Schinkel mentions is one of a series of monumental historical paintings produced for Napoleon, later removed to Versailles.
71 In the Louvre.
72 Well-known restaurant, until 1838 in the Rue Neuve des Petits-Champs.
73 Former name of the Opéra Comique, built 1789–91 by Jacques-Guillaume Legrand (1753–1809) and Jacques Molinos in the Rue Feydeau. The architects were also responsible for the celebrated first dome of the Halle au Blé (see note 104 and Braham, 1980, 110).
74 Name of a play and perhaps that of an actor: not identified.
75 Under Napoleon the former royal palace had been extended and converted into a museum by Percier and Fontaine. After 1815 the south-west and adjacent parts of the sixteenth/seventeenth century building (Cour Carrée) were altered and rebuilt by Fontaine. When fragments of the Parthenon frieze were acquired in 1818, and the *Venus de Milo* in 1820, the collection of antiquities was reorganized. Fontaine built a sumptuous stairway between the Cour Carrée and the Grande Galerie.
76 'Les Grands Boulevards' had been built at the time of Louis XIV, when the fortification walls had been demolished.
77 The largest slaughterhouse in early nineteenth-century Paris.
78 Cemetery on land surrounding a country seat belonging to the La Chaise brothers, in the suburb of Ménilmontant, laid out by Brongniart, the architect of the Bourse (see note 144).

Royal. – markets (Marché) Halle du Temple[79] – Les grandes Halles. – Place and Fontaine des Innocents[80] – Place de Grève.[81]

Tuesday, 2 May

Café Porte St Denis. – Went to St Denis with M. Blanc, Dessinateur des Machines. Superb mill buildings with gardens. church of St Denis[82] (plate 11) outside and in, high proportions with the outside in old style, round arches in the tower section, the inside very spacious, handsome style. Pillars beneath the towers and an organ loft form a pleasing entrance. An old zodiac is attached to the doors in the outer portal. Monuments of Dagobert, Francis I and other kings, finely made. The gallery and the high altar, newly built, and a [illegible] balustrade 4 ft high of green marble, with a bronze railing, were closed off.

Excursion to St Ouen,[83] where an auction was being held of unusual rams from every country, on the estate of the comtesse Cayla[84] (the previous king's mistress). – Big fat Abyssinian ram, wild, colossal. Large garden with a most tasteful country house and splendid view of the banks and hills of the Seine, and a small, picturesque dairy farm. The sale was in the yard of the dairy farm. The whole auction was a sham, the animals were all sold back to their owners, the bidding started at 1,400 francs. Pennants with the name of each animal.

The comtesse herself sat there in distinguished company, most of the people there were extremely fashionable. They just want to show that the upper classes have done something for industry.

The house was open to the buying public; it is very tasteful, wall-hangings painted by Gérard and a large picture of the former king working in his library, very stylish as in everything he produces.

Visited M. Ternaux,[85] the richest factory-owner in France, orator in the Chambre des Deputés; he owns the former royal palace and garden in St Ouen, magnificent position on the Seine, combination of English features and old French garden lay-out. Building with double silos to keep corn airtight. His dissertation on silos.[86] His

[79] First significant precursor of later market halls. It comprised four blocks of six adjoining sheds with passages running through them. It was built in 1811 and demolished in 1863.

[80] Built originally in 1548–9 by Jean Goujon as a three-sided tribune, it was moved and re-erected in the centre of the Place des Innocents and a fourth face was added by Augustin Pajou.

[81] The square in front of the Hôtel de Ville.

[82] The famous abbey, whose west front and chancel are seen as the beginning of Gothic architecture in France. It was built in the twelfth and thirteenth centuries, and until the sixteenth century was the burial place of the kings of France (from Saint Louis to Henry II). After the devastation of 1792, in which the fine interior was substantially damaged, Napoleon ordered it to be restored. Schinkel's remark 'the gallery and the high altar, newly built' refers to the restoration.

[83] This château, built in 1660 by Lepautre, was occupied by Louis XVIII from 1817 to 1823.

[84] Zoé Talon, Comtesse du Cayla (1784–1850), Louis XVIII's favourite, lived mainly in St Ouen, in a small house on the site of Lepautre's château, designed by Hittorf and Huvé, and decorated internally by Gérard and Fontaine (Hautecoeur, 1955, vol. 6, 9–10 and fig. 6).

[85] Guillaume-Louis Ternaux (1763–1833), cloth manufacturer, an important French industrialist. His château was designed in 1743 for the Prince Rohan-Soubise (Hautecoeur, 1950, vol. 3, 130–1 and figs. 100–1).

[86] *Mémoire sur la Conservation des Grains dans les Silos*, 1824.

11. *St Denis from the north west*, pencil

12. *Journal*, p. 2, (top) nameplate on estate of Comtesse Cayla, St-Ouen, (middle) canopy on the outside of the Théâtre Favart, Paris

goats and fine rams are far more impressive than those of comtesse Cayla.

Returned to Paris round the back of Montmartre. – Favart Theatre[87] from the outside, bronze windows and pilasters behind the portico, covered ways under metal roofs, half for carriages, half for pedestrians (plate 12). – Midday with Prévost in the Palais Royal. – Walk, Library, Favart Theatre, Théâtre de l'Opéra,[88] Venetian, not bad, boulevards, Place Vendôme, column,[89] where we had a look at all kinds of shops; the magnificent little steam-driven machine that produces chocolate in a large shop-window, the setting looks like a little temple of polished steel, with the capitals of the columns, pediments and structural parts all painted in gold.

Wednesday, 3 May

On our way to fetch Herr Kunth, we went to see the preparations for the jubilee celebrations in the Place Louis XVI.[90] Tuileries Gardens,[91] magnificent lilac, wide paths, the lawns enclosed by box trees, flowers, wonderful terraces with arbours and clusters of tall trees, blue haze over the city. – Visited Herr von Werther. – M. Delafontaine,[92] bronzes, old cellar under the workshop in an old chapel. – Herr Gau[93] not at home. – Church of St Germain des Près.[94] – St Sulpice from outside[95] (plate 13), fine portico below, with arches on the second row of columns on the second story. Inside, fresco in one of the chapels, by pupils of Gérard,[96] good. – Fish and vegetable market. Large blinds to close off the arcades, almost useless: uncovered they allow in air, then the light comes through most strongly. Palais Luxembourg,[97] garden, wonderful great square enclosed by terraces and avenues of tall trees, adorned with marble statues, lawns, lilacs, roses, flowers, pools. View of the Observatoire[98] at the other end. Magnificent view of the

[87] Salle Favart was the former name of the Théâtre des Italiens.
[88] The version seen by Schinkel was built 1820/ 21 by François Debret in the Rue Le Peletier, to replace earlier opera houses. It was destroyed by fire in 1873.
[89] In the square designed by Mansard in 1699 as the Place Louis-le-Grand, 'La Colonne de la Grande Armée', or 'Vendôme Column', was erected 1806–10 to replace the equestrian statue of Louis XIV which had been destroyed in 1792.
[90] Even before the Revolution there had been a plan to demolish the Bastille and put in its place a square with a statue of Louis XVI, but the idea had not been realized. The square which was built in 1803 was named Place Louis XVI after the return of the Bourbons, and every year their restoration was celebrated there. Schinkel is referring to preparations for this.
[91] Park created by Le Nôtre from 1664, with sculptures added in the eighteenth century, to the west of the Tuileries palace. The palace was built for the most part at the end of the sixteenth century for Catherine de Medici and was rebuilt and extended several times. It was destroyed in 1871.
[92] Pierre-Maximilien Delafontaine (died 1860), bronze-caster and engraver.
[93] Franz Christian Gau (1790–1853), architect and archaeologist originally from Cologne. Like Hittorff he lived in Paris from 1810, then from 1815 to 1821 in Rome (on a Prussian grant) with visits to Greece and the Middle East. After his return to Paris he designed public buildings (Bank of France, hospitals). From 1826 he held the office of government architect. He published works on Egyptian architecture.
[94] Of particular importance for its early Gothic twelfth-century chancel. The restoration begun in 1821, following the damage caused during the Revolution, is not mentioned by Schinkel.
[95] The building was begun in 1646, and the façade mentioned by Schinkel was built 1733–66 by Jean-Nicolas Servandoni. The portico has Doric, the upper story Ionic columns. Servandoni was responsible for the first two storeys of the façade and began on the towers, but ten years after his death in 1766, Chalgrin took on the completion, working on the interior with de Wailly (Braham, 1980, 135–6).
[96] The interiors of the chapels in St Sulpice were designed by Chalgrin and de Wailly and date from the years before 1789, when work on them was interrupted.
[97] The building was designed by Salomon de Brosse as a residence for Marie de Medici. It was begun in 1615 and completed in 1631. The spacious layout of the park mentioned by Schinkel was designed by Chalgrin, who had been imprisoned in the Palace under the Terror.
[98] Built 1667–72, after a design by Claude Perrault.

13. L. Geoffroy, *St Sulpice*, engraving

14. H. Courvoisier, eng. Guiguet, *Interior of the Halle au Blé*,
engraving

15. *Journal*, p. 3, detail of iron construction of roof of the
Halle au Blé

[99] See note 180.

[100] The Ecole de Chirurgie, one of the most celebrated eighteenth century buildings in Paris, was built 1769–74 from a design by Jacques Gondouin. Schinkel seems not to have gone inside, in which case he must be referring to the street façade. The upper story rests unusually upon Ionic columns and there is no projecting portico, but a kind of lodge which provides an entry into the courtyard (see Braham, 1980, 138–43).

[101] Built during the reign of Henri IV (1578–1607), whose equestrian statue in the middle of the bridge is not mentioned by Schinkel.

[102] Charles X (1824–30).

[103] See note 180.

[104] The Halle au Blé was, like the Ecole de Chirurgie, one of the most notable buildings of the recent past in Paris. Its fame rested on its remarkable dome, which was built first in timber and then with iron. The building was first put up in 1762–6 by Nicolas Le Camus de Mézières as one of the first new market halls, and as a corn exchange to regularize the distribution of essential foodstuffs. It was arranged as a circular gallery around a courtyard, with a double staircase, noted with approval by Schinkel. With the increase in business a dome to cover the courtyard was proposed. Because the gallery was not designed to be load-bearing an exceptionally light dome had to be made, and this was designed by J.-G. Legrand and Jacques Molinos, basically of timber planks with glazed panels and iron in the lantern, spanning a diameter of 150 ft. It was remarkably successful and notably elegant, but eventually burned down in 1802. It was then replaced with what Schinkel actually saw in 1811–13, an iron dome with a large glazed skylight, designed by François-Joseph Belanger. This remarkable work was the first modern iron and glass dome, and owed something at least to his knowledge of the English use of iron, though iron was generally used at that time in England in quite a different way structurally, as Schinkel was soon to observe. Schinkel had seen the importance of the Halle au Blé on his first visit to Paris in 1804 (see note 63).

[105] Sergius Prince Dolgoruki (1768–1829) was Russian ambassador in Paris in 1826.

[106] Heinrich Julius Klaproth (1783–1835), orientalist, originally from Berlin, Professor of Asiatic Languages in Paris from 1816.

[107] Karl Benedikt Hase (1780–1864), philologist and historian, in Paris from 1801, librarian from 1805, from 1816 Professor of Paleography and Greek, from 1825 member of the Académie des Inscriptions.

Panthéon[99] at the end of an avenue of tall overhanging trees. Chocolate. Ecole de Médecine,[100] simple, beautiful architecture. Fountain in a Doric hall opposite. – Pont Neuf.[101] Procession of the King[102] from Notre Dame;[103] enormous number of clergy and court attendants, all on foot. – Halle au Blé[104] (plate 14), iron construction 120 ft in diameter, interior diameter 36 ft, beautiful simple combination of materials. The copper panels are not joined to the iron grill. Vertical bars composed of 3 cast iron rods, horizontal bars of wrought iron (plate 15). Vertical bars 2½ to 1 ft in width, the iron 3 ins thick, the grill sections about 1 ft square. Everything rests on a rib below. (Floor cement in the gutter, small cracks.) Fine stone construction interspersed with brick, the double staircase excellently constructed.

Changed shoes at home. Then to Café de la Rotonde in the Palais Royal, where Herr Kunth met us to take us to the country to see Prince Dolgoruki[105] in Courbevoie, with Herr von Humboldt in a hired coach. Grand dinner: Klaproth,[106] Herr Hase[107] librarian, Herr Steuben[108] painter, Herr Mark, doctor to the duc d' Orléans, Frau von Knoblauch and her son. – Journey back in a similar coach. – In the evening to Gérard, he saw us alone in his room as he is still ill, interesting company downstairs: M. Huyot[109] artist, antiquarian; Pacho[110] (Cyrenaïque); Hittorff;[111] Thibaut[112] architect; Millingen;[113]

[108] Karl von (Charles de) Steuben (1788–1856), painter of German and Russian origins who became a pupil of Prudhon and Gérard and settled in Paris where he had some reputation as a painter of portraits, battle scenes and historical subjects.

[109] Jean-Nicolas Huyot (1780–1840), architect, in Italy from 1807 to 1813, carried out archaeological work in Asia Minor and Egypt from 1817 to 1821. Apart from original designs, he also devised conjectural reconstructions of ancient buildings.

[110] Jean-Raimond Pacho (1794–1829), painter; worked in Egypt and North Africa from 1822–5. Published *Relation d'un voyage dans la Marmarique et la Cyrénaïque* (1824–9), 4 volumes.

[111] Jakob Ignaz Hittorff (1792–1867), architect, originally from Cologne, resident in Paris from 1810, pupil of Percier and Belanger. Worked

with the latter on the Halle au Blé (see note 104). 'Architecte du Roi pour les fêtes et cérémonies', together with Lecointe, from 1818. Travelled to Germany in 1821, when he met Schinkel. Designed the rebuilding of the Théâtre des Italiens (see note 168) in 1825. Most of his architectural work was done after 1826. Schinkel was influenced by his ideas on the original colours of the exteriors of ancient temples (published in 1830 under the title *L'Architecture polychrome chez les Grecs*), for example in the later designs for the Acropolis and Orianda. In 1857 he wrote the not uncritical *Notice historique de Charles-Frédéric Schinkel* for the Institut de France.

[112] Jean-Thomas Thibaut (1757–1826), architect, pupil of Boullée. In 1818 he became a member of the Institut de France and Professor of Perspective at the Ecole des Beaux-Arts.

[113] James Millingen (1774–1845), English antiquarian and numismatist.

Madame Gérard and Mamselle Godefroi. – Home at 1 o'clock, accompanied by Hittorff.

Thursday, 4 May

In the morning a short walk round the Bourse[114] (plates 16 and 17) (20 columns down the long sides, 14 along the short sides). – Herr von Humboldt called to take us to see M. Raoul-Rochette,[115] who is in charge of inscriptions at the Library; he showed us the inscription collection, and the zodiac from the Temple of Dendera (Tentyra).[116] – Afterwards walked with Beuth to Ste Madeleine (plate 18).[117] Large, beautiful building, simple, no windows behind the columns, 8 columns in the frontispiece, the columns composed of many sections, the capitals rough-hewn, the doorway with several outer mouldings. – The Chapelle Expiatoire[118] from outside in the Rue d'Anjou. – Boulevards in festival. Georama,[119] superb construction of the spiral staircase and globe base, the globe 40 ft in diameter. – (Transparent arabesques in the ceiling for lighting.) – Diorama,[120] horribly crowded. 3 displays: an Anglo-Saxon cloister, set against a view of mountains in the receding mist etc.; a Gothic cloister against a beautiful sunlight and floating clouds, natural effect on the ground, pine-trees, leaves playing in the shimmering light, wooden bridge, mossy stones etc.; a view of Paris, serene landscape, impressive sky. – Expensive dinner in the Rocher de Cancaille, large amount of fish. – Théâtre Porte St Martin:[121] *Joco*[122] (Mazurier) and before that three other plays of no consequence.

Friday, 5 May

Herr von Humboldt took me to see Count Forbin,[123] Director of the Museum. His paintings: landscape of a château belonging to his family in the South of France on the Mediterranean; a Spanish prison scene, much use of light effect, little actual drawing; view of Jerusalem. Pictures by Grenet [Granet],[124] kitchen with figures, good style. – Went with Herr von Humboldt to see Cailleux, Secretary of the Museum, marble from the Pyrenees, conversation. – Museum with statues and pictures. – Visited Hittorff. Sicilian

[114] See note 144.

[115] Désiré-Raoul Rochette, known as Raoul-Rochette (1790–1854), archaeologist and historian, became a member of the Académie des Inscriptions in 1816 and curator of the medal collection of the Royal Library in 1819.

[116] The Hathor temple in Dendera, main temple of the Upper Egyptian city, was one of the best preserved in Egypt (first century BC). Parts of the ceiling painting, of signs of the zodiac, had been removed in 1820 and later exhibited in the Louvre.

[117] This building, originally designed by Pierre Contant d'Ivry, was commissioned in 1763, but only reached its final form in the early nineteenth century. It was redesigned under Napoleon in a more severe style in 1806 by Pierre Vignon, as a Temple of Victory 'aux Soldats de la Grande Armée', and in 1816 the same architect was commissioned to transform it into a church, which, when Schinkel saw it, was still unfinished. The severity of the building and the extensive use of columns had an obvious appeal to Schinkel. It was not until 1842 that the building was finally completed by Vignon's successor Huvé.

[118] See note 196.

[119] In 1826 Delanglard opened a 'Georama', constructed and given that name by him, in the Rue de la Paix. This was a globe, over 30 metres in circumference, which could be entered and observed from the inside, by means of filtered lighting.

[120] In 1822 Daguerre, later inventor of photography and also a designer of stage-sets, opened the first diorama in the Rue Samson, where translucent paintings of up to 20 metres in width could be viewed.

[121] This building had been restored by François Debret in 1818.

[122] Probably the title of a play by Claude-Louis-Marie, Marquis de Rochefort (1790–1871).

[123] Louis-Nicolas-Philippe-Auguste, comte de Forbin (1777–1841), after a military career became a landscape painter and pupil of David. From 1816 Director of the Royal Museums, member of the Académie. He was responsible for acquiring Gericault's *Raft of the Medusa* for the Louvre. Granet (see following note) often painted the figures in his landscapes.

[124] François-Marius Granet (1775–1849), one of the most famous artists of the day, particularly for his medieval interiors.

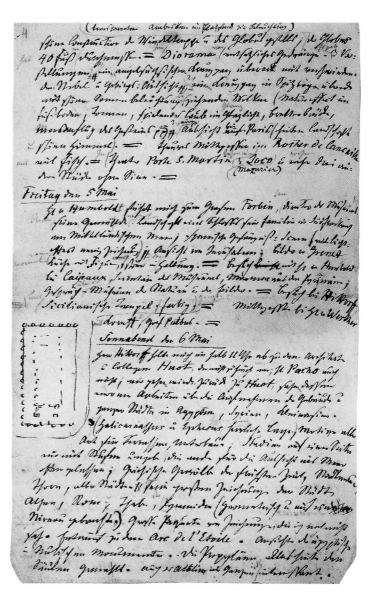

16. Gavard, eng. P. Legrand, *La Bourse* designed by Brongniart, steel engraving

17. C. Gilio, eng. J.H. Martens, *Interior of the Bourse*, engraving

18. Gavard, *La Madeleine*, steel engraving

19. *Journal*, p. 4, groundplan of model of an antique Sicilian temple in the house of the architect Hittorf

temple, colourful (plate 19)[125] – Dinner at Herr von Werther's house, Koreff,[126] Count Putbus.[127]

Saturday, 6 May

Herr Hittorff called at half past 10 to take me to see his colleague the architect Huyot,[128] who was not at home. Neither was M. Pacho, so we went back to Huyot and saw his extensive studies of buildings and whole cities in Egypt, Syria, Asia Minor, Halicarnassus and Ephesus, magnificent position, all kinds of motifs for terraces, foundations, stadia surrounded by nothing but steps on one side, with the other side left open to the sea; Greek vaults of the earliest period, city walls, gates, old towns. Grand drawings by himself of Athens, Rome, Thebes, pyramids (geometric and two-dimensional). Huge piles of drawings which I have not yet seen. Design for the Arc de l'Etoile. Views of Egyptian and Nubian monuments. The propylaea, everything painted behind the columns. The studio itself was also interesting.

Herr von Humboldt introduced me at the Institut[129] at 2. Quatremère de Quincy, the President, had me sit next to him, and he read a treatise on the importance of symmetry and harmony for Vitruvius.[130] After the meeting my design portfolios were presented,[131] and I and Herr von Humboldt spoke about them. M. Debret[132] was asked to produce a report on them for the Institut; Percier was very friendly, I thanked him meanwhile, together with Fontaine, for sending me the sketch of the rooms displaying sculpture in the Louvre, which the Comte de Clarac[133] is publishing. They had also enclosed their plan for the restoration of the whole of the Louvre,[134] and for the Palace of the King of Rome[135] and its surroundings. – We fetched Beuth to take him to dinner, and afterwards went to the Théâtre des Variétés, Brunet and Potier acted in short pieces. – At home I found a letter and invitation from Madame Spontini[136] which I am unable to accept.

Sunday, 7 May

Wrote to Madame Spontini. The painter Müller[137] and brother-in-law. Several scholars.

[125] See note 111 and Hittorf's treatise *Recueil des Mouments de Ségeste et de Sélinonte*, Paris, 1870.
[126] Johann Ferdinand Koreff (1783–1851), doctor and writer, originally from Berlin where he was a colleague of Hardenberg. In Paris 1804–13 and from 1820 onwards.
[127] Count Wilhelm Malte von Putbus (1783–1854), who built himself a new town residence in its own grounds from 1810 onwards. In 1838 Schinkel advised on the extension of Putbus's hunting lodge at Granitz on the island of Rügen, through the addition of a central tower. It was designed by Schinkel's old friend Steinmeyer and became a prominent landmark. Schinkel met Putbus again in London.
[128] See note 109 and Wegner, 99, note 9.
[129] The Institut de France (in the former Collège des Quatre Nations, see note 173). Schinkel had been elected an 'Associé étranger' of the Académie des Beaux-Arts, part of the Institut, in 1823.
[130] In Vitruvius's aesthetics – expounded mainly in Book I of *De architectura* – particular emphasis is laid on the concepts of symmetry and proportion.
[131] Schinkel had been publishing his *Sammlung Architectonischer Entwürfe* since 1819, in separate parts. They contained his main designs with engravings and commentaries. By 1826 ten instalments had appeared (by 1840 28 had been published, with 174 plates).
[132] François Debret (1777–1850), architect, pupil of Percier and Fontaine, in 1815 Paris City Architect, designer of theatre buildings in particular, for instance the Théâtre de l'Opéra (see note 88).
[133] Charles-Othon-Frédéric-Jean-Baptiste, comte de Clarac (1777–1846), archaeologist and Conservateur du Musée des Antiques du Louvre. His publications included a series of engravings entitled *Musée de sculpture antique et moderne*, which first began to appear in 1826. See obituary in *Revue Archéologique*, 1846, 754–6.
[134] See note 75 and Wegner, 99, note 11.
[135] The only son of Napoleon I, the Duke of Reichstadt (1811–32), bore the title King of Rome from birth. For Percier and Fontaine's designs for the Palais de Chaillot see Braham, 1980, 258, pl. 350 and H.-J. Hassengier, *Das Palais du Roi de Rome auf dem Hügel von Chaillot*, Frankfurt, 1983.
[136] The wife of Gasparo Spontini, who had been general director of music in Berlin since 1819.
[137] Charles-François Muller (1789–1855), painter of portraits and historical scenes, pupil of David, and regular exhibitor at the Salon.

20. *Journal*, p. 5, (lower middle) wall cabinets in Château of St Cloud inscr.: 'a. Mirror b. clothes cabinet.' (bottom) ironwork around a window at Château Bellevue

Drove to St Cloud.[138] Versailles. On the way, country houses. St Cloud, beautiful avenues, chestnuts, elms, magnificent position and view. Beautiful ceilings inside the castle – green and gold decoration on chocolate background, delicate white bas-reliefs on soft blue-grey background. – Bathroom with mirror, the bath with green cloth and yellow fastenings. – Cabinet with soft lilac background and delicate white stucco ornamentation (plate 20), yellow furniture with borders worked in red and green, arabesques on a blue background in gold, beautiful mid-tint.

Not much of interest in the gallery. – In the rest of the state rooms a profusion of poor-quality new things. – Picture of the King by Vernet[139] with a white horse, the horse pawing the ground, somewhat crudely done. – The sofas have seat cushions a foot high. – Vestibule with bas-reliefs on the walls, neatly done but in poor style. – Marble floor. – Garden, Lantern of Demosthenes[140] on the terrace, view of Paris, Seine, 2 bridges, island, Meudon etc. – Breakfast in St Cloud. Walk to Meudon. The village of Bellevue, pretty little country houses of various kinds and in different positions. – A terrace projecting far out from the hillside. The houses are small at the top, the windows have only one pane. Latticework. The roofs of the stables are often decorated in the style of tents (plate 21).

Soon after this village one climbs the terrace of the Meudon château,[141] which seems too enormous for its setting, but has a magnificent view over Paris and its environs. The terrace is walled for a length of 2,000 ft, at some points to a height of 80–100 ft, and behind the terrace plateau, which is about 200 ft wide, there is a second terrace set against the wooded hill of the same length but about 30 ft high. The château is insignificant, without side-wings, but a large earthwork at the edge of the terrace suggests that the building was originally meant to be more extensive. – We returned to the park of St Cloud, where our coach was waiting. – Rain and the long distance made our drive less pleasant than it could have been. – The porcelain factory of Sèvres[142] is conveniently situated on the way to Versailles.

Arrival at Versailles,[143] very extensive buildings, something like Potsdam. – The palace interior. The chapel is quite pleasing inside,

[138] This palace had been built in 1676/7 for Philippe d'Orléans by Antoine Lepautre, who also designed the Gardens, and it was later added to and altered by Jules Hardouin-Mansart. It became Napoleon's main residence and was renovated in a full Empire style by Percier and Fontaine, to which Schinkel's description refers. (The building was destroyed in 1870/71.) Schinkel also comments on the park, designed by Le Nôtre.
[139] Horace Vernet (1789–1833), painter of military and historical scenes. The King referred to is probably Charles X.
[140] This is an imitation of the 'Lysicrates monument' in Athens, built in St Cloud in 1800–1802, also known as the 'Lantern of Demosthenes'. After its portrayal in Stuart and Revett's *Antiquities of Athens*, 1762, numerous imitations were made cf. for example the Inwoods' St Pancras Church (plate 30) For Schinkel's version at Schloss Glienicke see J. Sievers, *Schinkels Lebenswerk: Bauten für den Prinzen Carl von Preussen*, 1942, 112.
[141] This is the Château Neuf in Meudon, which Jules Hardouin-Mansart built for Louis XIV's son between 1706 and 1709. (Most of it was destroyed in 1870/71). For an illustration see Wegner, 100, fig. 14. It was perhaps the ruins of the old palace, burnt down in 1804, which Schinkel mistook for a 'large construction layout'.
[142] The famous factory, founded in Vincennes in 1738, had been in Sèvres since 1756.
[143] This palace, built for the most part between 1663 and 1686 by Louis Le Vau, Jules Hardouin-Mansart and Charles Lebrun, was intended for Louis XIV's magnificent court. The court chapel dates from 1699–1710. By 'gallery' Schinkel means the 'Galerie des Glaces' or Hall of Mirrors. Le Nôtre devised the layout of the park in 1663. The Grand Trianon and Petit Trianon palaces within the park are not mentioned by Schinkel.

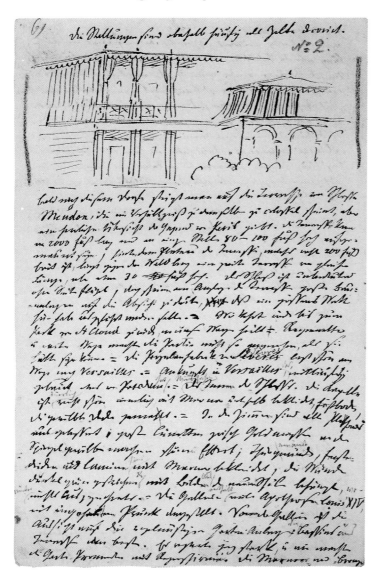

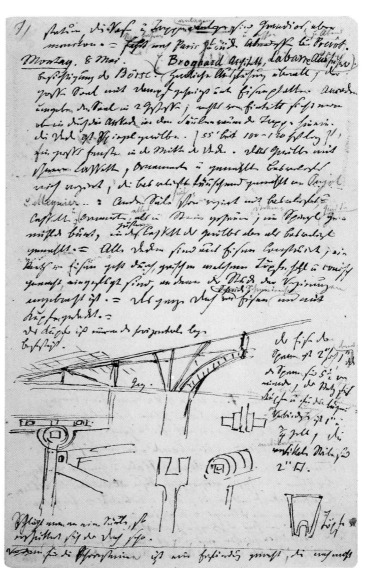

21. *Journal*, p. 6, stable buildings in Bellevue

22. *Journal*, p. 7, details of the iron construction of the roof of the Bourse

with a marble floor and painted vaulted ceiling. – In the rooms all
the ceilings have been restored, large lunettes between a mass of
gold on the mirror arches create a superb effect, door and window
frames and fireplaces clad with marble, the walls painted dark green
and hung with pictures of the modern school, nothing particularly
memorable. – The gallery, many grand apotheoses of Louis XIV.
The view of the regular garden lay-out, pools and terrace, is most
impressive from the gallery. It was raining hard, and we walked
round the garden under an umbrella. The marble and bronze
statues, vases and flights of steps are grandiose but monotonous. –
Went back to Paris, supper with Prévost.

Monday, 8 May

Went round the Bourse. Designed by Brongniart,[144] built by
Labarre. Magnificent construction work everywhere, the great hall
heated by steam under iron plates. Arcades around the hall on two
storeys; to the right of the entrance one sees through the arcades
above into the columned area of the staircase. The ceiling is a glazed
vault. (55 ft wide, 100–120 ft long.) A large window in the centre of
the ceiling. The vault is richly decorated with heavy coffering,
ornamentation and painted bas-reliefs, the illusion of relief cleverly
produced by Pujol and Meynier.[145] Other rooms finely decorated
with bas-reliefs and coffering, ornamentation in imitation of stone,
colourful painting in the glass, in the larger coffers of the vault
above, the illusion of bas-reliefs. – All the ceilings are constructed
of iron, there is a continuous network of iron into which hollow,
conical jars have been integrated and to which the stucco
ornamentation is attached (plate 22). The whole roof of wrought
iron is covered with copper. – The copper is fixed to the horizontal
bars only. The iron rods are 2 ins wide and 1 in. thick, and 5½ ins
apart, there is 1¾ ins space for the copper and the connecting rods,
the vertical bars are 2 ins wide. If you strike a supporting pillar the
roof shudders. A new invention has been used for the chimneys,
made of copper, which has not yet been tested.

    With Herr von Humboldt to Count Pourtalès,[146] Place
Vendôme, his magnificent collection. Antique objects: head of

[144] In 1808 Théodore Brongniart, commissioned
by Napoleon, began this building as a
rectangular 'Temple de l'Argent' girded round
by Corinthian columns, following Vespasian's
Temple in Rome. Building was interrupted in
1814, but continued 1821–7 under Eloi de
Labarre. No other building is described in
Schinkel's Journal in such detail as the Paris
Bourse. This is probably because it combined a
certain austerity with the extensive use of
columns, and employed the latest methods of
contemporary engineering, especially in the use
of iron and glass, though less dramatically than
in the Halle au Blé (see note 104 and the
exhibition catalogue *Alexandre-Théodore
Brongniart, 1739–1813*, Paris, Musée Carnavalet,
1986, 117–92).
[145] Alexandre Denis Abel de Pujol (1787–1861),
pupil of David, painter of portraits and
historical scenes, and Charles Meynier (1768–
1832), painter of historical scenes. Both were
among the most highly thought of painters of
their day. They decorated the interior of the
Bourse with series of pictures in grisaille.
[146] Member of a Neuchâtel family, most of
whom worked for the Prussian state. The
collection of antiques was described in T.
Panofka, *Antiques du Cabinet du Comte de
Pourtalès-Gorgier*, Paris, 1834. The gallery
apparently remained in existence until 1862,
when it began to be sold (See sale catalogues: La
Galerie Pourtalès Tableaux, antiques etc. Paris,
1862. Dept. of Prints and Drawings, British
Museum; and Count Pourtalès-borgier . . . Cat.
des objets d'art . . . Medailles, Tableaux. Paris
1865. BL7805.bb.2.) Wegner reproduces what
must be the 'small female figurine [in]
terracotta' from a lithograph (Wegner, 102,
fig. 18).

[147] Schinkel may be referring to the sculptor Jacques Biot, active at the end of the seventeenth century.

[148] Cornelis Engebrechtsz, or Engelbrechtsz (1468–1533).

[149] Hans Memling (*c.*1433–94).

[150] In the manner of Barend van Orley (*c.*1492–1542).

[151] Monastery of Petits-Augustins, founded in 1608 and dissolved in 1790. From 1791 to 1816 it housed the Musée des Monuments Français, where important works of art and architectural fragments were saved from destruction during the Revolution. After the dissolution, and dispersal of the contents, some important works remained there, for instance the columned portico of the central section of the château of Anet (Philibert de l'Orme, 1547–52), the façade of the château of Gaillon (1501–10), and the attic from the south wing of the Louvre (Jean Goujon, *c.*1500). This is the 'old architecture' to which Schinkel refers. The Ecole des Beaux-Arts has been housed in the former monastery since 1820.

[152] Begun 1645 by François Mansart, in the following year the project was taken over by Jacques Lemercier following Mansart's plan. The dome is the third highest in Paris after the Invalides and the Panthéon (A. Boinet, *Les Eglises Parisiennes*, II, Paris, 1962, 258). Like the Panthéon (see note 153), this important centrally-planned building attracted Schinkel's particular interest, since at the time he was contemplating projects for domed buildings (the Cathedral in Berlin; churches in the suburbs of Berlin; Nicolaikirche, Potsdam).

[153] Originally the Church of St Geneviève conceived by Jacques-Germain Soufflot in 1755, it was transformed in 1791, shortly after its completion, into the Panthéon Français, to contain the ashes of 'les Grands Hommes de la Patrie'. Quatremère de Quincy (see note 67) was charged with the conversion, and after his imprisonment under Robespierre, the Panthéon became the resting place of Marat and Rousseau. Under Napoleon it combined church and Panthéon, but with the restoration of Louis XVIII it reverted to being the Church of St Geneviève in 1816, and in 1822, after the removal of the tombs of Voltaire and Rousseau from the main body of the church, it was reconsecrated, remaining a church until 1830. As one of the grandest domed and centrally-planned churches in Paris it would have been of particular interest to Schinkel, though he expresses some disappointment in it.

[154] The exterior of the Palais de Justice –

Apollo – Greek vase found near Marathon. – Lucius Verus, Marcus Aurelius and their teacher Andronicus Atticus, found together near Marathon. – Head of a beautiful heroic female, the hair lying neatly at the back without a knot. Other fine heads, female with delicate curls. Bas-reliefs, 4 horses pulling a quadriga. Bull with Europa. Lead bowl, richly decorated, by Biot.[147] Bronze hind found in Sybaris. 4 small bronzes, a priestess, Jupiter and a little bull and another statue, found in Besançon, the most delicate thing I have ever seen. Large bronze vase: superb piece, magnificently carved ornamentation. A small female figurine, terracotta, wonderful flowing movement, she sits cross-legged, has a little mirror on one knee and is plaiting her hair behind with both hands. Beautiful candelabra on a stand, very slender legs, light and delicate. Alabaster bowl and receptacles for medicines, [found] near Athens. Large ancient Greek vase with a representation of Actium. A pig's head incorporated into a fine vase. A helmet with a brim similar to those in Naples, greaves. A man and a woman carved in wood, excellent. Portraits, Bas-reliefs, Dürer period, pictures [by] Carlo Dolci, very beautiful woman, reading, irridescent colour, yellow, bluish red. Harmonious portraits by Sebastiano del Piombo, Andrea del Sarto's wife, blue gown. – 2 pictures by Engelbrechtsen[148] (Hämling[149] and Orleyish[150]), 2 animal studies by Hondius, better than Snyders. – Murillo, female figure with chalice and old heads down in the background, undefined, deathly and imitative. – Claude Lorrain.

Old architecture in the Petits-Augustins,[151] a fountain with fine heads on the ledges between the water-spouts. – Luxembourg Garden, chocolate. – Val-de-Grâce church,[152] fine building, barrel vaulting decorated with large bas-reliefs, also the triangles of the pendentives. – Panthéon,[153] dome with decorative mouldings everywhere, even in the peristyle, errors of proportion, many oval cupolas with poor coffering, much that seems flimsy. Palais de Justice.[154] – Baths. Julius Cavour. Rue de la Hargue. – Home with

Schinkel appears to have seen only this – was dominated by the façade, rebuilt after a fire in 1776 by J.-D. Antoine and others. The parts of the medieval royal palace remaining within the building and the Gothic Ste-Chapelle were apparently not visited by Schinkel.

Beuth, dinner at Prévost's. Evening walk round the streets to look at the shops. Home, tired out.

Tuesday, 9 May

M. Erard,[155] Madame Spontini's uncle, called to take us to his country house to see his gallery. Excellent pictures by the two Ostades, Teniers, Ruisdael, Steen, Pynacker, Moucheron and others. A magnificent Giulio Romano, Jupiter's birth on the island, Venus by Correggio from the Orléans gallery, [St] Thomas by Correggio, which seemed doubtful to me, several pictures [by] Claude Lorrain, Albani from Galerie Sta Croce in Rome.

Breakfast. Return in his equipage, then to the Conservatoire des Arts et Métiers.[156] Conversation with M. Christian the Director. We took a hackney-coach with M. Blanc to Charenton, where we saw the large factory belonging to Aron Memby,[157] from Horseley Works near Birmingham. He came with 500 Englishmen and built an enormous factory for the production of steam-engines, and for iron-casting and rolling. The rollers are driven by steam-engines of 300 horsepower. Hammers (pig-iron casting in sheds). Here the pig-iron is [extracted] in a puddling or reverberating furnace with hearth and vault. The molten metal remains inside without the addition of coal. In this furnace the pig-iron is stirred under certain conditions, and sprayed with water; it is turned until it all separates out like sand, then it coagulates again into a mass. This mass is pounded into a square beneath an extremely powerful hammer, then heated until it is red-hot and rolled again. Great skill is necessary for this. The workers are almost naked, and have enormous strength. If the iron is below standard, it is put through the process again. The metal is again melted in a refining-furnace; it then runs out and is doused with water so that it cracks easily; the pieces are then reheated and placed under the great hammer.

Back to Paris, to No. 17 Rue Bourbon. At Trentel and Wurtz's I took 2 copies of my design album on Herr Wittich's[158] account for the Institut and for Herr Humboldt. Then we drove home, and went to the Palais for dinner. – After eating, the architect Debret from the Institut came to visit me. He has to give a verbal report on

[155] Sebastian Erard, officially Erhard (1752–1831), piano-maker and manufacturer, possessed a large collection of paintings at his country seat of La Muette near Passy.
[156] See note 198.
[157] The factory was founded in 1819 by Aaron Manby from Birmingham. It was the most important source of cast and rolled iron products in Paris and the surrounding area.
[158] Ludwig Wilhelm Wittich (died 1832), publisher and engraver in Berlin. He published Schinkel's *Sammlung Architectonischer Entwürfe* and his *Dekorationen auf den Königlichen Hoftheatern.*

my album, so I went through all my designs with him.

Wednesday, 10 May

With Herr von Humboldt to the Comte de Clarac[159] at 11; we had to pay for the viewing of his works in advance. Fine casts of bronze statues, an heroic figure 8 ins high, the most magnificent thing you could imagine, other fine objects in terracotta (seated figure), Greek vases. – Library. Herr Hase gave us an account of the collection. – Cameos, mounted and with handles, in glass cases. – The bookcases have ornamental lattice doors. The folios are secured halfway up with iron clips which can be locked. – Engravings in books, the most notable examples hung framed and behind glass, representatives from all schools.

Walked to M. Pacho, who has a highly interesting collection of Cyrenian antiquities. A combination of Doric and Egyptian elements is predominant; almost exclusively burial monuments, many carved in rock, some constructed. Two pointed arches with Greek archivolts and keystone, very remarkable. – Thierry's papier-mâché ornamental workshop, No. 4 Rue de Sèvres, very clean and pleasant. A pilaster capital, Corinthian-Florentine, 15 ins high, 1 ft wide, 3 ins thick, 8 francs; a small complete capital, 5 ins high, 4 ins square, 10–12 sous. – We had a meal at Prévost's and then went to the opera: *Cortez*[160] and *Chasse de Henri IV*,[161] good production. Mamsell Cinthie's[162] interpretation of the part of Amazili was highly enjoyable. The orchestra was straightforward and precise. Good scenery. – We should have gone to see Gérard afterwards but it finished too late, 12 o'clock.

Thursday, 11 May

In the morning visited Herr von Humboldt, I took Gérard's album back and gave one to Herr von Humboldt. – Then visited Fontaine, where there was a crowd of people. – Promenade on this beautiful morning to the Tuileries Gardens, wonderful air, lilacs and flowers, magnificent groves of trees with statues in front. – Then to the Museum, plan of the sculpture gallery with the positions of the

[159] See note 133.
[160] The opera *Ferdinand Cortez* by Gasparo Spontini, first performed in Paris in 1809. Schinkel had designed the set for a Berlin production of the opera in 1818.
[161] Charles Collé's comedy *La partie de chasse de Henri IV* (1774).
[162] Laure Cinthie Montalant (born 1801), singer, at the Paris Opera since 1825. She sang the role of Amazili in *Ferdinand Cortez* (see note 160).

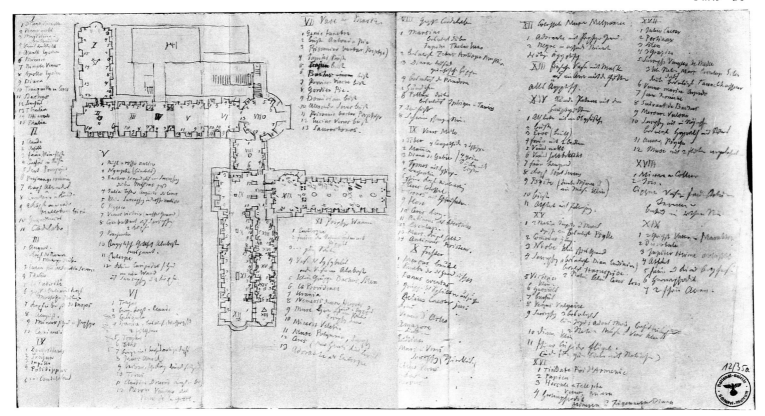

23. Plan of the display of antiquities in the Louvre, 1826,
pencil 194 × 351 mm

[163] Schinkel is referring to his outline plan of the new arrangement of the Louvre (see note 75).

[164] Nicolas-Jean de Dieu Soult (1769–1851), army commander and later politician. He was one of Napoleon's marshals in the Spanish campaign (1808–13), and acquired at that time a great collection of Spanish paintings, many of which ended up in the Louvre.

[165] Jean-Auguste-Dominique Ingres (1780–1867), painter, pupil of David from 1806 to 1824 in Rome, member of the Institut de France from 1826, later director of the French Academy in Rome. One of the greatest artists of the age, and a notably conservative figure in the face of the new Romantic generation of painters like Delacroix. His presence at the dinner is a sign of the well-established circles in which Schinkel mixed in Paris.

[166] This is probably Antoine-Marie Peyre (1770–1843), architect, a pupil of Boullée and teacher of Percier and Fontaine. He was involved in the remodelling of the Hôtel de Salm as the Palace of the Légion d'Honneur under Napoleon.

[167] François Debret (1777–1850) (see note 132) was one of the architects who with Fontaine (see note 68) and Viollet-le-Duc were responsible for the restoration of the Abbey of St Denis (see note 82), over many years. He also worked on the Arc de Triomphe de l'Etoile.

[168] The Théâtre de l'Odéon, formerly the Comédie-Française, was begun in 1778 and opened in 1782. It was designed by Marie-Joseph Peyre (1730–85) and Charles de Wailly (1730–98). After a fire in 1808 the building was altered by Chalgrin who lowered the roof but otherwise generally adhered to the original exterior. In 1818 it was again damaged by fire (restored by Provost), and the side-arches over the neighbouring streets were removed in 1822.

[169] A tragedy by Pierre Corneille (1606–84), written in 1640.

[170] An opera by Giacomo Meyerbeer (1791–1864) written in 1820.

[171] The Chapelle Expiatoire was the first important building of the Restoration, and it was commissioned by Louis XVIII to commemorate his brother Louis XVI and Marie Antoinette who had been executed in 1793. It was begun by Fontaine in 1816 and completed 1824. It was sited over the cemetery of St Madeleine, where Louis XVI and Marie-Antoinette had been buried after their execution (Hautecoeur, 1955, vol. 6, 12–17).

main statues marked (plate 23).[163] – Picture gallery, Italian masters.

Walked to Marshal Soult's[164] to see his Spanish pictures, were made very welcome, saw his magnificent paintings. The masters in his collection: Alonso Cano, the Spanish Raphael, his portraits penetrating, his other figures cold (his portrait is reminiscent of Titian, Raphael and Boltraffio), 3 epochs of Murillo, (of which) the second is the finest (French-Venetian-Dutch). – Morales, old (like Albrecht Dürer-Venetian), suffering and tragic character. Erida[?], Navarrete (Caravaggesque), Juan de Juanes (like bronze). The schools of Valencia, Madrid, Seville.

To Werther's, but he was not at home. – Dinner at Hittorff's. His modern Sicilian drawings. House and church motifs. Dinner guests were: Percier, Humboldt, Thibaut, Ingres,[165] Pere,[166] his father-in-law with wife and her father, Madame Hittorff. In the evening another lady from Hamburg, Jewish.

Friday, 12 May

In the morning visited Debret,[167] who had my album on his desk and was in the process of writing the report for the Institute. He showed us several drawings of stained glass for St Denis church. – Fruitless call at the house of Herr Arnoldy, who is away in the country. – To the Museum, via the Tuileries Gardens and the Quai Malaquais. Herr Goldschmidt in the museum. – Dinner, then Odeon Theatre,[168] where we saw *Les Horaces et les Curaces* by Corneille,[169] and *Margarethe d'Anjou* by Meyerbeer.[170] Indifferent music, burning forest at the end.

Saturday, 13 May

Early in the morning, the interior of the Chapelle Expiatoire (plates 24 and 25),[171] Rue d'Anjou, original plan. Forecourt, propylaea, like a monumental tomb, chambers on both sides, whose barrel vaults form the roof from the outside but closed off inside by a flat ceiling of iron and hollow vases. Raised courtyard to the side enclosed by the catacomb-like overhanging upper vault of the lower-level ambulatories. The chapel in the background, you climb

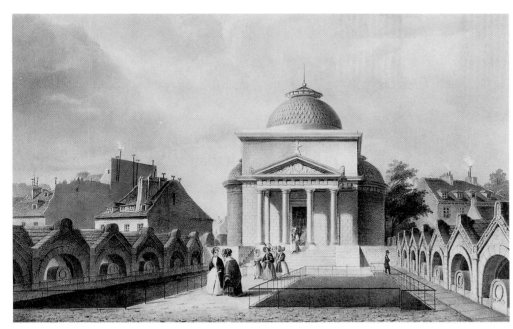

24. J.B. Arnout, *La Chapelle Expiatoire de Louis XVI*, 1836, colour lithograph

25. *Two sketches of the Chapelle Expiatoire*, 1826, pen and pencil

steps up to the Tuscan peristyle of 4 columns. Doric cornice, the lower edge of the hanging part richly decorated with flat consoles and ornamentation, which continue into the frontispiece. The chapel itself is round, with 3 round semi-domes next to it, behind the altars of the two side apses one descends into the crypt and the ambulatories.

M. Debret took me to the Théâtre de l'Opéra;[172] everything in wood and plaster, pleasant entrance-halls. A handsome foyer stretching the length of the façade with 2 balconies covered with deal board, which is quite hard-wearing but has cracks everywhere. Very good system of air circulation. Along the passageway to the boxes there is a series of air-vents which open out between the support beams of the boxes behind the ornamentation, directing the air towards the chandelier opening which has an attachment forcing the air out on to the roof. The difference in air temperature between outside and in is a constant 2 degrees. – Very good heating by means of steam, which rises in small pipes, condenses in broad iron containers standing in the various rooms, and is thus returned to the boiler. The proscenium arch is solid, with iron support above and below, and the forestage is fitted with an iron framework filled in with stucco and small pieces of stone. Behind, an hôtel is used for administration; it has a beautiful courtyard. – A large amount of machinery above the flies, drums and winches in the middle. Under the stage so much space that whole backdrops can be let down. Proscenium 46 ft wide, stage is 90 ft deep.

Collection of architectural models [at the College des] Quatre-Nations,[173] excellent plaster models of Greek monuments, also Roman, Indian, Egyptian etc. – Meeting in the Institut, lecture by the director of the Royal Music[174] on the need for the coordination of ballet movement with musical rhythms. – Théâtre Français:[175] Britannicus.[176] Talma.[177] played Nero, Herr Wolff[178] and his wife in the theatre.

Sunday, 14 May

Unwell (diarrhoea), I stayed in, wrote to Princess Wilhelm,[179] sent 3 gold bottles, 7 francs each, 21 francs altogether, to Berlin. – I

[172] See note 88.
[173] The former Collège des Quatre-Nations, a late seventeenth-century building, was the home of the Institut de France, founded by Napoleon in 1805. It comprised, as it does today, the Académie Française, the Académie des Inscriptions et Belles-Lettres, the Académie des Sciences, the Académie des Sciences morales et politiques and the Académie des Beaux-Arts. The last contained a collection of architectural models made under the direction of L.F. Cassas (see Wegner, 107, note 22 and fig. 24).
[174] This is presumably Luigi Cherubini (1760–1842), who was Director of Royal Music from 1816.
[175] Built 1786–90 by Victor Louis, near the Palais Royal, known as the Théâtre Français since 1799. Well-known for the use of iron roof-trusses (see Braham, 1980, 254).
[176] Tragedy by Racine.
[177] François-Joseph Talma (1763–1826), actor.
[178] Pius Alexander Wolff (1782–1828) and his wife Amalie, née Malcomi (1783–1851), actors, who after working as court actors in Weimar, spent some years (from 1816) acting in Berlin.
[179] Anna Maria, wife of Prince Wilhelm of Prussia (1783–1851), third son of King Friedrich Wilhelm II. Schinkel executed plans for the rebuilding of Fischbach palace in Silesia, which had been acquired by Prince Wilhelm in 1822.

went out at 4 o'clock, saw Notre-Dame,[180] then I sat on the terrace of the Tuileries in the Place du Louvre, watched the fountains and the crowds out for their Sunday walk. – When I got back in the evening Hittorff was there; he had heard that I was not well and had come to visit. Until 10.

Monday, 15 May

Cash transaction at Rothschild's,[181] took out a note for 400 thalers which I cashed in silver at the Bank of Paris. – St Geneviève[182] with Gros's painting in the dome representing St Geneviève; Clovis and his wife, Charlemagne and his wife, St Louis and his wife, and Louis XVIII and his wife, all being blessed by the saint. Louis XVI is on a higher level in the sky. It is all brightly coloured, no facial expression, but technically skilful. – Visited other churches.

Went to see Gérard, who talked at length about the wrong direction art was taking in France, how it was all decoration, no serious art, much was produced but little of any worth. His suggestion for the Museum was that the walls should be in a rich ox-blood colour rather than the mid-tone of grey-green[183] – Tuileries Gardens. – Dinner with Herr Blanc at Prévost's. – Ambigu-Comique theatre,[184] one amusing play, one tragi-comedy, both well acted, we enjoyed them.

Tuesday, 16 May

Hittorff picked us up early in his cabriolet, we saw St Philippe du Roule,[185] which our king had particularly liked (plates 26 and 27). – The new houses in the suburb of Roule and Sablonville; the street sellers have already spoilt the area with their markets. – Mont Calvaire,[186] a church by Huyot, strange capitals. Fine bas-reliefs on the tympanum, 5 figures. Christ with raised head not particularly

Restoration. The painting on the domed ceiling by Antoine-Jean Gros, originally commissioned by Napoleon in 1811, underwent a metamorphosis. It began as part of Napoleon's attempt to reconcile the church's history as the church of St Geneviève with its more recent role as a monument to the great men of France. It depicts the apotheosis of St Geneviève, and on the advice of Vivant Denon, French rulers were shown in homage to her. These were Clovis and Clotilde, Charlemagne and Hildegarde, and St Louis and Marguerite, to which were added the Emperor Napoleon with the Empress Marie-Louise, holding their son, the King of Rome. Under the Restoration Gros was obliged to make changes to the iconography, substituting Louis XVIII and the Duchess of Angoulême for the Imperial couple, and adding in Louis XVI, Marie Antoinette and the Dauphin above St Louis (to illustrate the Abbé Edgeworth's famous cry on the scaffold: 'Louis, fils de Saint Louis montez au ciel'.), as royal martyrs. The painting was inaugurated in November 1824 by Charles X who conferred on Gros a barony. (See G. Auguier in *Le Panthéon: Symbole des révolutions*, exhib. cat., Hôtel de Sully, 1989, 248–51.)

[183] At the time Schinkel was preoccupied with the interior decoration of the new Museum am Lustgarten in Berlin (built 1824–30). The official reason for his journey to Paris and London was in fact to seek new ideas for this project. Gérard's advice about the colour of the walls (oxblood) was followed by Schinkel.

[184] Théâtre de l'Ambigu, built by Célerier in 1769, in the Quartier du Temple. Burnt down in 1827, and rebuilt by Hittorff and Lecointe in 1829, it was demolished in 1965.

[185] Designed *c*.1768 and finished by 1774 by Jean-François-Thérèse Chalgrin, who completed St Sulpice begun by his master Servandoni (see note 95). St Philippe-du-Roule was the most famous of the basilican churches to come into fashion in the 1760s, and it retained its reputation into the nineteenth century (Braham, 1980, 128–9). King Friedrich Wilhelm III, who saw the church on visits to Paris in 1814 and 1817, regarded it as a potential model for the Nikolaikirche in Potsdam. In response Schinkel produced basilican plans which eventually, in collaboration with the Crown Prince, resulted in an acceptable design for the church.

[186] This is Mont Valérien, where Huyot (see note 109) planned the layout of a cemetery for the Mission de France in 1826. The building was abandoned after the July revolution of 1830 (see Wegner, 108 and fig. 26).

---

[180] Built from 1163 to the end of the thirteenth century. Schinkel would have seen Notre-Dame after the damage caused under the Revolution and before the restorations of Viollet-le-Duc.
[181] The Paris house (founded 1812) of the famous international banking family, directed by James Rothschild (1792–1868).
[182] Schinkel calls the building the Panthéon on 8 May (see note 153), but here uses the name by which it was known in 1826 under the

26. *Journal*, p. 14, (left) St Philippe-du-Roule, plan, section and façade, (centre and right) Mont Calvaire, façade and two plans

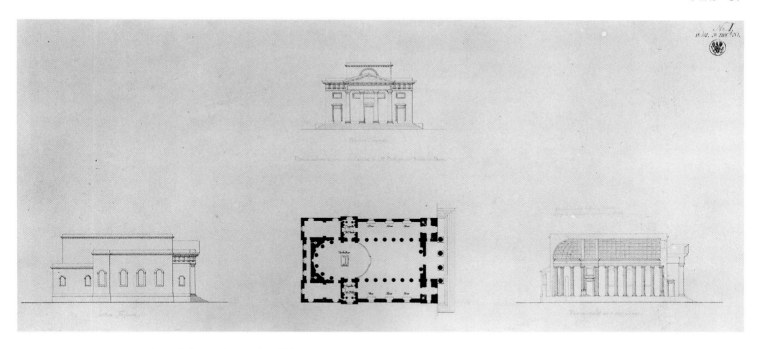

27. *Plan and elevations of St Philippe-du-Roule*, 1826, pen

good unfortunately; he is risen from the dead, the warriors draw back in terror on both sides. The poor quality of the building is due to lack of funds. There is as yet no nave at all. Fine situation of the hill, view of Paris, steps, aqueduct, Marly.[187] Breakfast in a beautiful inn. – House in Choiseul, Gouvier, Erechtheium, Pandrosium, sun temple of Palmyra, Rue de l'Etoile. – Models of the Arc de l'Etoile, Huyot's magnificent coffering,[188] good architectural details in general. –

Palais Luxembourg,[189] the architect, Provost,[190] reveals talent. The design of the church is innovative (basilica), with the emphasis on stained glass and mural painting. – Gold chamber[191] for the Livre des Pairs [Book of Peers] very skilfully put together from old paintings, bright colours on gold background, superb pilasters, the frieze has a white background with dark blue arabesque figures upon it. There are as yet no wall-coverings. – Luxembourg Gallery, modern masters, mere display – outside Massacre of the Innocents by [Chamartin?, followed by illegible words] on the children, and another by Heim,[192] Guidoish. – Madonna by Ingres. – Stairs straight up to the Chambre des Pairs [House of Peers], Ionic, handsome. Chambre des Pairs semicircular, velvet, beautiful chairs. – Archives kept under the roof, windows made of translucent taffeta.

Book-dealer Bancs. – Arcade in Rue St Denis, light and practical. – Room displaying interior decoration. – To Hittorff for dinner, pleasant family. – Théâtre des Italiens[193] in Hittorff's box, shortened version of Don Juan.[194] – Interior of the auditorium very impressive, tasteful and good craftsmanship. – Two rows of boxes, unsupported. A gallery with one row in front of the circle. Proscenium box, red velvet balustrades with gold at the front of all the circles, not particularly attractive. The top gallery is almost a round continuation of the proscenium, but is there filled out with pictures. – Curtain handsome on the whole, figures hovering on a green background, arabesques on the folds, large braid trimmings below. – Ceiling divided by gold candelabra, between which gods and goddesses in their temples are depicted. Vestibule or foyer very rich, the frieze beautifully decorated in colour on a white background.

[187] The château of **Marly-le-Roi** had been built between 1679 and 1690 for Louis XIV to the north west of Versailles. It was destroyed in 1806. 'Gouvier' is probably the French archaeologist **M.G.F.A.** de Choiseul Gouffier (see Wegner, 108).

[188] See note 109. The Arc de Triomphe de l'Etoile at the top of the Champs Elysées. Essentially the design of Chalgrin under Napoleon, the design passed to several other hands after the architect's death in 1811. Huyot had picked it up again in 1823, but it was not finished until 1836, having undergone a number of further alterations.

[189] The seventeenth-century Palais du Luxembourg (see note 91) was used as the seat of the Senate from 1800, and during the following years underwent a series of alterations by Chalgrin. There had been a picture gallery in the building from 1750 to 1780, which was reopened, to Chalgrin's design, in 1804 and used from 1818 to house contemporary art.

[190] Jean-Louis Provost (1781–1850), architect, pupil of Percier, from 1820 engaged on the rebuilding of the Palais du Luxembourg.

[191] The 'Salle du Livre d'Or', with ceiling paintings glorifying Marie de'Medici and medallions with allegorical female portraits. The Peers were privileged members of the aristocracy under the Restoration.

[192] François-Joseph Heim (1787–1865), painter, pupil of Vincent, from 1825 member of the Institut.

[193] Built in 1825 by Hittorff and Lecointe, who converted an older building. It was destroyed by fire in 1838 (Wegner, 110, note 26).

[194] We do not know whether this was Molière's (1665) or Goldoni's version (1736).

Wednesday, 17 May

Herr von Humboldt took us to see the minister Pasquier,[195] where we [saw] the cast of the head, without a nose, of a huge statue of Diana.[196] The fragment was found in Arles, not far from where the Venus d'Arles was found,[197] and which is on display there in the museum. This piece must be the most beautiful thing to survive from antiquity (Greek). – In the Conservatoire des Arts et Métiers[198] we saw a large collection of bad and mediocre models and machines, displayed in some of the enormous rooms of the former Convent of St Martin, for the most part dated and valueless.

In the exhibition for the Greeks[199] [i.e. in support of Greek independence] which we visited, Horace Vernet's picture of Mazeppa from Lord Byron[200] (beautiful horses but too gaudily coloured). – A picture of a scene from the Massacre of the Innocents simply executed by Cogniet:[201] a woman with her child presses herself into a corner in terror, forming the whole of the foreground (dark blue skirt, brown jacket); in the background a fleeing mother with two other children comes rushing towards the foreground; away in the distance you can see the massacre itself, in little figures. – Boilly,[202] a minor master [*Kleinmeister*], many figures, in fine harmonious colours, portraits have a most natural expression, very cleanly done; mannered landscape – Two landscapes in the style of Ruisdael, very bold (by Van Os).[203] Comte de Forbin's pictures.[204] – Afterwards we drove to Prince Dolgoruki in Courbevoie for dinner, and had a meal there with Klaproth, Hase, Steuben, Leo, Kunth. – Frau von Knoblauch sent her regards to all in Berlin.

[195] Etienne-Denis Pasquier (1767–1862), Foreign Minister (1819–21), then in the Chambre des Pairs, later its president and Chancellor of France.
[196] This is probably the fragment of the statue of a young goddess, the so-called *Livia* in the Musée Lapidaire in Arles.
[197] This statue was discovered in 1651 and formed part of the decoration of the Roman theatre in Arles. It is now in the Louvre.
[198] The training centre for technology and industry, founded in 1795 under the Directory, also contained a collection of machines, apparatus and models, which was later extended and converted into the Musée National des Techniques. After 1798 the Conservatoire was housed in the former monastery of St Martin des Champs, built in the twelfth and thirteenth centuries, one of the main Cluniac priories (See Wegner, 110–11, note 27).
[199] The exhibition Schinkel saw was the famous one 'au profit des Grecs', held at the Lebrun Gallery, 4 rue du Gros-Chenet, between 17 May 1826 and 19 November of the same year. This was the period of the long drawn-out siege of Missolonghi, when Greek independence became a great liberal cause in France as well as elsewhere. The paintings were mainly lent by prominent liberals, and it was meant to point up the indifference of the French government towards the Greeks. Many of the best-known artists of the day exhibited, and there was a group of paintings by the recently deceased Jacques-Louis David. With these, and a strong representation by Horace Vernet and Baron Gros, there was a decided 1789 Revolutionary and Bonapartist air to the exhibition, and many of the most famous paintings of Napoleon were brought out for the exhibition. It is interesting, though not unexpected, that Schinkel should have ignored all the most notable and spectacular paintings on display: as a Prussian he might have found the deification of Napoleon hard to cope with, though he was on cordial terms with Baron Gros, and indeed with the Emperor's architects. (All the information about the exhibition is taken from N. Athanassoglou-Kallmyer, *French Images from the Greek War of Independence, 1821–1830*, New Haven and London, 1989, 39–41, and appendix 2.)
[200] No. 189 *Mazeppa, sujet tiré d'une nouvelle de Lord Byron. (Ce tableau appartient à M. Duchesnet).*
[201] Leon Cogniet (1794–1880), painter of portraits and historical scenes, pupil of Guérin. The painting was no. 28 *Une scène du Massacre des Innocents.*
[202] Louis-Léopold Boilly (1761–1845), portrait and genre painter. There were two paintings by Boilly: 13. *Rejouissance publique aux Champs-Elysées*, and 14. *Le public au salon du Louvre, regardant le Tableau du Sacre* [by David].
[203] G.J.J. Van Os (1782–1861), flower and landscape painter, who worked at Sèvres. There were three paintings by him in the exhibition: 185 and 186 *Paysage; interieur de la forêt de Compiègne*, 87 *Paysage.*
[204] The Comte de Forbin (see note 123) exhibited 5 paintings (nos. 69–73), four of which were landscapes.

Paris, Wednesday, 17 May 1826

(To Susanne)

I received your first letter safely, also your second of 1 May from Stettin, and I was very pleased to hear of your safe journey, even though the situation for you all in Stettin, especially your own, is not very pleasant and you have very little reason to rejoice. But I'm sure you are a great comfort to your mother, and this must surely help you to feel better. I cannot add any further suggestions to your sensible arrangements for carrying on our children's education, especially Karl's. I have absolute confidence in all that you do in this respect.

I simply would not have the space to tell you all about my stay in Paris, and will save it until I see you. But there is so much to see, and time passes so quickly that I don't know where it goes to. The architects here have been overwhelmingly hospitable; I was introduced to the Institut and attended a few meetings; they are giving a paper in the Institut on my buildings. Herr Hittorff has been most friendly; he has married into a most agreeable family, and we have spent some very enjoyable hours with them; his work is highly interesting and painstaking. – Baron Werther, our ambassador, has also been anxious to be of use to us, I met Koreff, Klaproth, and Count Putbus at his house. A few days ago we saw the actor Wolff and his wife in the Théâtre Français, Madame is very keen on Talma but I cannot take to that style. Hittorff's Théâtre des Italiens is without doubt the finest; we watched a shortened version of Don Juan from his box.

Paris is a beautiful city with splendid surroundings, one notices it more and more the longer one stays. Don't be offended if this letter is short, dearest Susanne; I always go to bed late, tired out with the day's work, and when I get up in the morning at half past 6, domestic business and visits take up all my time until 9 o'clock so that there are very few minutes left for writing. By 9 o'clock at the latest we have to be on our way, otherwise we can't get through the day's work; everything has to be arranged in advance, all the people we want to see have to be informed beforehand; so that not a minute is to be lost everything has to be exactly timed.

Our departure is set for next Sunday, 21 May; I won't be writing to you again until I get to London. The journey will take at the most 6 days, so that we shall be in London on the 27th or the 28th, then I'll write again immediately.

Kiss our children warmly for me, and give my best wishes to Mother and Karoline, Wilhelm will presumably learn from you that I am well, best wishes to him. Think often of your loving Schinkel.

Thursday, 18 May

Went to fetch Kunth at 9 o'clock, and drove to the part of town called Le Marais (plate 28), which was formerly the most aristocratic quarter, hence the many old hôtels with forecourts. In one of these is the workshop of the skilled bronze-founder, Crozatier,[205] who casts the biggest and most complicated statues in such a way that no extra chiselling is needed. Very few and exact joins, great elegance and inexpensiveness are his excellent qualities. The fine antique vase from the Villa Albani, now in the Paris Museum, extraordinarily beautiful, without chiselling [*ciselure*], a splendid patina, altogether perfect. 2 vases for 3,500 francs. (Rue de l'Arc Royal, appt. no. 6), a lifesize bust 500 francs, a Laocoön group 18,000 francs, chiselled, the old way (figure 7 ft high, 1,800 lb, 10,000 francs), statue of Louis XIV, depôt Calvados (12½ ft high, 4,500 lb), vase (by) Benvenuto Cellini in the Museo, 450 francs, Hercules with the serpent by Bosio[206] comprising 3 pieces (9 ft [illegible word], 1,600 lb, 17,000 francs), Louis [X]VI under construction, will be 18 ft high.

The Halle aux Vins,[207] a complex of storehouses, cellars below, warehouses above with roof lighting. The cellars project out, forming large terraces, where inclined planes lead out. The carts drive up there with the barrels, and there is a simple device for lowering them from the vehicles (plate 29).

Jardin des Plantes,[208] animals in the open, cages with four-legged animals, birds, minerals, shells, butterflies etc. – Hill with fine view. – Breakfast in the garden. Parts of the garden made available for research by botanists, who can also pick flowers. Elephants etc.

[205] Charles Crozatier, Sculptor and bronze-caster (1795–1855). Many of the great bronze statues of the time were cast in his foundry, including Napoleon on the Vendôme Column and the quadriga on the Arc du Carrousel.
[206] François-Joseph Bosio (1769–1845), sculptor. 'Le Canova français', he flourished under both Napoleon and the Restoration, being responsible for many of the largest (and dullest) monuments of the period.
[207] The huge Paris wine warehouse by the quai Saint-Bernard was begun 1811 at Napoleon's behest by the architect Gauché (illustrated in Wegner, 111, fig. 29).
[208] The Jardin Royal des herbes médicales, begun in 1635 and greatly extended until 1788 under the direction of Buffon, was converted into the Musée national d'histoire naturelle during the Revolution, when a zoo was also added.

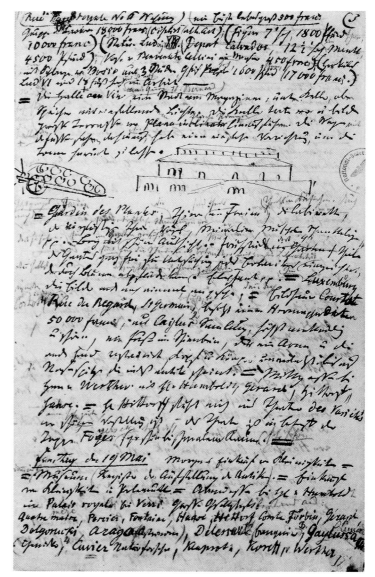

28. *View in Paris*, possibly the Marais, 1826, pencil

29. *Journal*, p. 17, view of the Halle aux Vins, Quai St Bernard of 1808, with a wagon for carrying barrels on the left

– Luxembourg, looked at the pictures again. – Sculptor Cortot,[209] Rue du Regard, St Germain, owns a hermaphrodite, 50,000 francs, from Caylus's[210] collection, fascinating and beautiful, one leg only to the shin, one arm and the other hand restored, head and trunk undamaged apart from the point of the nose, which does not appear to be antique. – Dinner at Herr von Werther's with Herr von Humboldt, Gérard, Hittorff, Hase. – Herr Hittorff took me to the Théâtre des Variétés,[211] where there was a very good performance, considering the restricted space; the theatre is very fine, especially the foyer and stairway.

Friday, 19 May

Small purchases in the morning. – Museum, register of the inventory of antiques. – Small purchases in mother-of-pearl. – Supper with Herr von Humboldt in the Palais Royal at Verri's ['Veuve Véry']. Large gathering: Quatremère, Percier, Fontaine, Hase, Hittorff, Comte Forbin, Gérard, Dolgoruki, Arago,[212] astronomer, Delessert,[213] banker, Gay-Lussac,[214] chemist, Cuvier,[215] natural scientist, Klaproth, Koreff, Werther.

Saturday, 20 May

Farewell visits to Hittorff, Werther, Percier and Fontaine. Palais Royal, Karl's watch, small purchases, Rue Vivienne. Packing.

Sunday, 21 May

Kunth's visit, left Paris at 9 o'clock, fine weather, pleasant countryside, evening in Beauvais, procession, cathedral.[216]

Monday, 22 May

Evening in Abbeville, in Constant's[217] country seat. Night.

Tuesday, 23 May

Evening in Calais. M. Dessin's very pleasant inn.

[209] Jean-Pierre Cortot (1787–1843), a notably academic sculptor and professor at the Ecole des Beaux-Arts, who carried out some important projects of the Restoration period.
[210] The comte de Caylus (1692–1765), archaeologist and collector of antiquities in Italy and Greece, author of: *Recueil d'antiquités égyptiennes, étrusques, grecques, romaines et gaules*, Paris 1752–67, 4 volumes.
[211] Built by Jacques Célerier (1742–1814) in 1807, the theatre was on the Boulevard Montmartre.
[212] Dominique-François Arago (1786–1853), physicist.
[213] Benjamin Baron Delessert (1773–1847), banker and manufacturer, collector and patron of the arts and sciences.
[214] Louis-Joseph Gay-Lussac (1778–1850), chemist and physicist. Worked with Alexander von Humboldt after 1804.
[215] George, baron de Cuvier (1769–1832), natural scientist and biologist.
[216] Built, with interruptions, between 1227 and the sixteenth century. It was unfinished, and is notable for the great height of the chancel and crossing.
[217] Benjamin Constant de Rebecque (1767–1830), politician and author. He spent most of his last years in seclusion in the country.

1 Dover
2 Canterbury
3 London
4 Greenwich
5 Brighton
6 Windsor
7 Eton
8 Oxford
9 Warwick
10 Birmingham
11 Dudley
12 Stafford
13 Newcastle/L.
14 Etruria
15 Matlock
16 Cromford
17 Belper
18 Derby
19 Leicester
20 M. Mowbray
21 Nottingham
22 Chesterfield
23 Sheffield
24 Leeds
25 York
26 Durham
27 Newcastle/T.
28 Edinburgh
29 Lanark
30 Glasgow
31 Dumbarton
32 Inveraray
33 Oban
34 Tobermory
35 Staffa
36 Iona
37 Carlisle
38 Lancaster
39 Preston
40 Manchester
41 Warington
42 Liverpool
43 Chester
44 Conway
45 Bangor
46 Shrewsbury
47 Coalbrookdale
48 Tewkesbury
49 Cheltenham
50 Stroud
51 Bristol
52 Bath

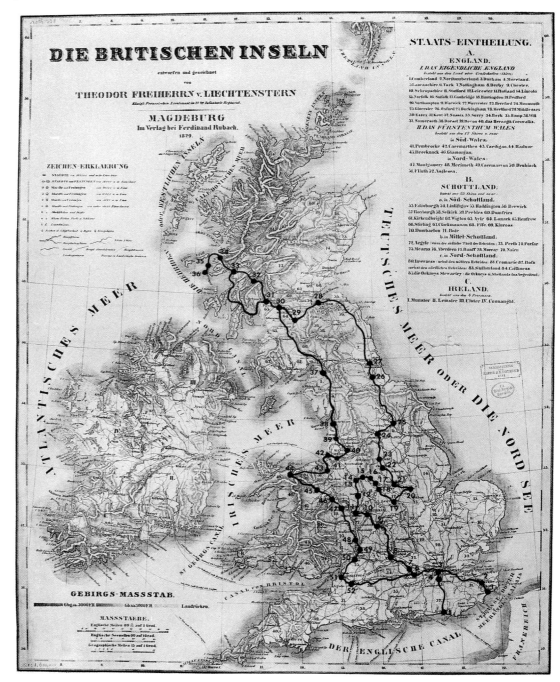

30. Theodor Freiherr von Liechtenstern, *Map of the British Isles*, 1829

London, Friday, 26 May

My dearest Susanne. Until now fortune has smiled on me as much as on my Italian journey: I received all your letters directed to Paris, and also the last one via Count Danckelmann in London, and was profoundly happy to hear of everyone's good health.

Unfortunately you seem to find yourself in sad circumstances, over which an uncertain future has pulled a disturbing veil. Karoline's plan to live with Wilhelm is in my opinion quite impracticable. Wilhelm's life would be unbearably disrupted, and it would be of no advantage to her, for her character cannot be changed and will always give cause for concern. Since you cannot avoid sounding out Wilhelm, under pressure from Karoline, this may be the opportunity for him to reconsider his decision, so that Karoline's scheme would fall apart of its own accord. Let us wait and hope for the best, since it is not in our power to intervene. I bought some presents for the children in Paris; and for Karl, if he is a good boy, a handsome little silver watch, which I used on the journey myself and have found keeps good time so far. Tell him, dearest Susanne.

Now a few words about my journey: we left Paris at 9 on Sunday morning, 21 May, in good weather. The beautiful spring green and blossom have stayed on an unusually long time, because it's not yet hot; this makes our journey particularly pleasant. We arrived in Beauvais in the evening, where there was a big church procession, which is always a strange affair in France. You have no idea where this crowd of priests suddenly comes from; many women followed on behind; I also received the blessing of the bishop. After viewing the cathedral and the old walls of the town we went to bed. The countryside is pleasantly hilly and cultivated. On Monday 22 May we drove as far as M. Constant's little farm near Abbeville, where we spent the night. They are decent people, who have, it seems, made every sort of mistake in settling here: the region and climate leave much to be desired, the yield from the farm must be very poor. M. Constant and his daughter have rheumatism from the sea winds; and as Protestants they are not looked on with favour here and have much to fear.

On Tuesday 23 May we arrived in Calais, a dreadful town in dreadful surroundings by the sea. We put up at a large inn owned by M. Dessin, furnished in the English style; we arranged with a captain to make the crossing to Dover in the steamboat His Majesty's Steam Packet Spitfire. The boat is very comfortable and clean. There were at least 50 people of different nationalities and sexes on the boat, the weather was moderately good, and the voyage was so calm and pleasant that I was not seasick at all during the three hours' crossing, though Beuth was. In fact, though I had to shut my eyes to avoid feeling the effects of the movement, the trip cured me of a slight problem with my digestive system which I had recently had in Paris. In Dover the cure was completed by the English porter beer, which does me good. (plate 30)

London

(Continuation of the letter to Susanne of 26 May)

When we arrived in Dover we went for a walk on the cliffs, where there is an old castle;[218] there is a fine view from there over the sea and the cliffs of the English coast which are a few hundred feet high and covered with grass at the top. One's first impression of England is welcoming and pleasant. All the establishments in the towns and villages and in the country are small but superbly kept, pleasant and clean. Every country cottage has at the very least shining bright window-panes, with white curtains behind. If you look inside you see that even if the table is only cobbled together out of rough planks and is on makeshift legs, a clean tablecloth is spread on it and tea, bread, butter, eggs and meat are served. In the country houses you see all the daughters of the house at the window in their finery when the stage-coaches drive past.

At 9 o'clock the next morning we drove in such a coach to London; it was extremely elegant, 4 beautiful horses pulled it in the finest harness just like the English ambassador's in Berlin, and it

[218] Dover Castle is chiefly twelfth and thirteenth centuries.

was driven by a huge great coachman sitting up on a box. The man looked like a fine gentlemen, he wore many bright scarves, a handsome hat, thigh-boots, an elegant black under-coat and a large beige overcoat. Every two miles we changed horses, by turns greys, chestnuts, bays, and blacks. The countryside is a lovely green, full of trees and like one enormous park. Beyond Canterbury, where we saw the cathedral, one has a magnificent view over the Thames valley; there is so much variety on the journey to London that you do not notice that you are already in the suburbs.

We found very good accommodation in St Paul's Coffeehouse, Count Danckelmann was there and gave me your letter, and gave us an invitation to supper with Ambassador Herr von Maltzahn[219] at 8 that same evening. We had covered the 60 or 70 English miles[220] from Dover to London by 6 in the evening. This morning, Friday, I'm happy to be able to write to you, but I have to stop now as we are once again in a great hurry and I am just about to go out with my companions.

Farewell, dearest Susanne. You will hear from me again soon. My best regards to everyone. Your ever-faithful Schinkel.

Wednesday, 24 May

Embarcation on the steamboat and 3 hour crossing to Dover. View from Dover Castle, comfortable inn, English priest from Rome with the little son of Lord . . . and another gentleman.

Thursday, 25 May

Journey with the above-mentioned in the stage-coach to London, lovely green countryside, variety, many trees, parks, country mansions, small cottages, everything small and pretty and clean. Magnificent harness and handling of the stage-coach. The distance from Dover to London of . . . miles was covered between 8 o'clock in the morning and 6 o'clock in the evening. Canterbury, cathedral, region overlooking the Thames valley, ships, Woolwich, Greenwich, in London to St Paul's Coffeehouse, Count

[219] Boguslav Hellmuth Baron von Maltzahn, Prussian ambassador in London in 1826.
[220] In fact the distance is only 42 miles.

31. T.H. Shepherd, *East Side of Park Crescent, Regent's Park*, from *London in the Nineteenth Century*, pub. 1827

32. T.H. Shepherd, *East Side of Park Square, and Diorama, Regent's Park*, from *London in the Nineteenth Century*, pub. 1827

33. John Linnell after Van Eyck, *A wing of the Ghent altarpiece*, from the copy in the Aders collection mentioned by Schinkel, engraving, 1826. Private collection, London

Danckelmann. In the evening to Baron von Maltzahn, supper at 8 o'clock, with Willisen,[221] Count Putbus,[222] Yorck,[223] Lottum.[224]

Friday, 26 May

Wrote letters to Berlin, sent them to Count Lottum. 100 pounds from Rothschild,[225] with Count Danckelmann. – Visited Solly,[226] his invitation for Saturday evening. – Went to Regent's Crescent (plate 31),[227] park, new lay-out, palatial buildings; Panorama,[228] Rotunda – Diorama[229] (plate 32). – Iron railings, heavy, Lincoln's Inn,[230] old lawcourts – machines – signs [illegible words] – Madame Aders's[231] pictures by Hämling[Memling], copies of van Eyck[232] (plate 33), not as red as those of M. Coxie,[233] but the landscape less detailed. Madame Aders's own copies. – Christ with crown of thorns Rogier van der Weyden,[234] (van) Eyck's madonna with architecture.[235] – St Pancras church[236] (plate 34), Pandrosium,

[221] Karl Wilhelm von Willisen (1790–1879), major on the Prussian general staff, later general.

[222] Wilhelm Malte, Count von Putbus, whom Schinkel had met in Paris (see note 127).

[223] Ludwig, Count Yorck von Wartenburg (1805–1865), son of Fieldmarshal Ludwig David Hans, Count von Wartenburg, later member of the Prussian upper chamber.

[224] Friedrich, Count von Wylich und Lottum (1796–1847), senior official in the Prussian embassy in London in 1826. On 26 May 1826 he wrote from London: '. . .we had lunch at Maltzahn's, in the company of Count Danckelmann and Privy Counsellors Beuth and Schinkel, who have just arrived in London. Tomorrow I intend to visit the British Museum with Herr Schinkel . . .' (see also note 242).

[225] In 1813 Nathan Mayer Rothschild (1777– 1836) had moved the English branch of the international banking house from Manchester, where he had first set it up in 1798, to London.

[226] Edward Solly (died 1846), merchant. His important collection of paintings had been acquired for the Berlin Museum in 1821 by Friedrich Wilhelm III. For an account of Solly as a collector, see F. Herrmann, 'Who was Solly?', *Connoisseur*, April 1967, May 1967, July 1967, September 1967, and September 1968.

[227] The layout of new buildings round Regent's Park had been planned and carried through by John Nash (see page 116) from 1812 onwards. Park Crescent, which Schinkel noted in particular, was the semicircular, colonnaded entry to the Park and the surrounding terraces. By 1826 the layout – one of the most important integrated architectural compositions of the nineteenth century – was largely complete (see J. Summerson, *John Nash*, London, 1935 and 1980).

[228] The Panorama in Regent's Park, known as the 'Colosseum', was begun in 1824 by Decimus Burton, who used the Roman Pantheon as a model. It was still under construction in 1826. The entrepreneur and draughtsman Thomas Hornor, who had directed the building work, opened it in 1829 with a giant panorama. This had taken many years to complete, and showed London as seen from the lantern of St Paul's Cathedral (see R. Hyde, *Panoramania!*, London, 1988, ch. 2, 79–96).

[229] In 1823 Daguerre's brother-in-law John Arrowsmith opened a branch of the former's Paris Diorama (see note 120) in Park Square just across the Marylebone Rd from Park Crescent. It was designed by John Nash, Augustus Charles Pugin and the engineer James Morgan (see R. Hyde, *Panoramania!*, London, 1988, 110–20).

[230] A seat of the legal profession in London, it was extended from the fifteenth century onwards, and by Schinkel's time had become a picturesque architectural ensemble.

[231] Karl (Charles) Aders possessed a collection of paintings, mainly by Flemish and German masters (auctioned in 1835). His wife was the daughter of the engraver John Raphael Smith (for the Aders collection see Waagen, 1838, Vol. 2, 231–6).

[232] A copy of the Ghent altarpiece, from which John Linnell had engraved *The Just Judges* panel, (see plate 33). This copy, which is now in the Koninglijk Museum voor Schone Kunsten in Antwerp, came from the Chapel of the Schepenhuis, Ghent, and was bought by Aders from the widow of M. Charles Hisette in 1819.

[233] Michiel van Coxie (1499–1592), painter. Schinkel was presumably interested in the Aders copy of the Ghent altarpiece because of its relative completeness. He would have been familar with the original wing panels of the Ghent altarpiece in Berlin, and with the Coxie copy of the *Adoration of the Lamb*, which had been bought by Berlin in 1823. He would, therefore, have been in a good position to comment on the qualities of the Aders copy. Other parts of the Coxie copy had been acquired in 1820 by the King of Bavaria. (I am indebted to Dr Catherine Reynolds for information on this and other paintings in the Aders collection.)

[234] This is almost certainly the painting in the National Gallery, no. 1083, described as 'style of Aelbrecht Bouts'. It was noted in Henry Crabb Robinson's Diary for 10 November 1817 (Dr Williams Library, London) as already in Aders Collection.

[235] This might be the Netherlandish School painting of the *Virgin and Child in a Garden*, with a prominent church façade in the background, in the National Gallery, London, no. 1085, which was attributed to Margaret van Eyck, and which belonged to Aders. However, the description does not quite fit and the painting is described as being in Aders's villa in Godesberg in 1828.

[236] St Pancras Parish Church was built 1819–22 by the Inwood brothers. It is the earliest and most important example of Greek revival church building in London. The close imitation of Athenian models – the Erechtheum and the Tower of Winds – can be seen in the portico, the galleries with caryatids on the north and east sides, and the tower. Wegner (114, e 33) argues that the plan of the church was influential on Schinkel's later work.

34. T.H. Shepherd, *St Pancras Church, West Front*, from *London in the Nineteenth Century*, pub. 1827

35. A.C. Pugin and T. Rowlandson, *Westminster Hall*, from *The Microcosm of London*, pub. by Ackermann, 1809

36. G. Cooke, *Blackfriars Bridge from the West*, 1827, engraving (see also plate 177)

37. George Scharf, *View of the building of the British Museum*, 1828, pen, pencil and watercolour. On the left is Montagu House, middle left the Townley Gallery of Antiquities, and at the right the North division of the West Wing of the new British Museum. British Museum

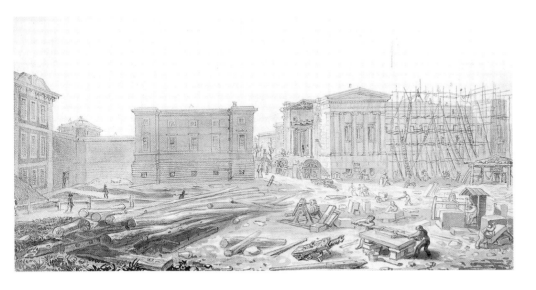

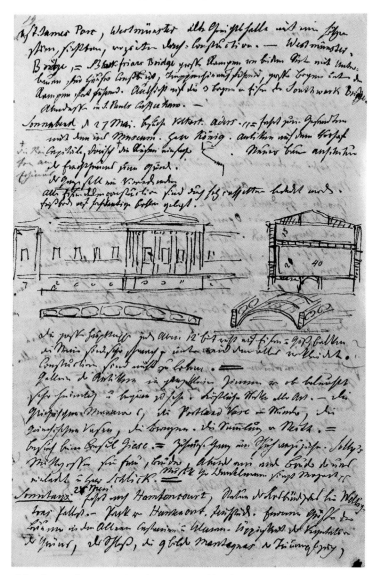

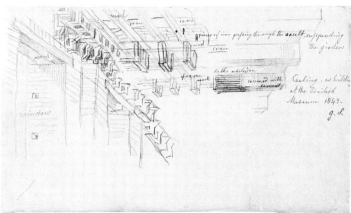

39. Henry Shaw, FSA, *Interior of the King's Library*, *British Museum*, 1834, engraving

40. George Scharf, *Sketch of the construction of the ceiling in the British Museum*, showing structural use of iron, 1843, pencil. British Museum

38. *Journal*, p. 19, (on line 9) profile drawing of capital, British Museum, (middle left) view of façade of new British Museum, east interior side of King's Library, (middle right) section of building with measurements: upper story 15; lower 20′ high, 40′ wide, (beneath) sketches of iron construction of roof, on the right a vault held up by iron supports

41. George Scharf, *The Townley Gallery of antique sculpture, British Museum*, 1827, pen and watercolour. British Museum

42. *Journal*, p. 20b, (top) sketch of a reproductive device in the workshop of the engraver Turrel, (upper middle left) section of a street drainage pipe, (bottom) stamping devices at the Mint

237 Schinkel saw the park before the landscaping by John Nash in 1828.
238 Westminster Hall is a late eleventh-century building remodelled under Richard II. The timber roof was constructed between 1394 and 1401. It and the façade had been restored in 1820.
239 Built 1738–50 from a design by Charles Labelye.
240 Built 1760–69 from a design by Robert Mylne.
241 Built 1814–19 from a design by John Rennie (1761–1821). The iron construction of this bridge, and Waterloo Bridge (1811–17), is the major work of this important engineer and bridge builder.
242 When the original premises of the British Museum in Montague House, which it had occupied since 1759, could no longer accommodate the collections, the Townley Gallery was built in 1804–8, to which was added a further building to house the Parthenon sculptures acquired in 1816. Work had begun on a new building to house the whole museum, designed by Robert Smirke, in 1823. In 1826 it was still at an early stage; only the east wing, intended for the King's Library and the paintings from the Angerstein collection acquired in 1824 (which were, however, to become the core of the National Gallery collection, see note 323) was finished. The building was not finally completed until 1847. (See J. Mordaunt Crook, *The British Museum*, Harmondsworth, 1972)
  Schinkel was mainly interested in the iron roof construction of the library and the stairway. The gallery of antiquities was only partially and provisionally stocked. Back in Berlin, Schinkel wrote (letter of 11 December 1826 to Franz Catel; National Library, Munich): '. . . The beautiful Greek marbles in the British Museum will perhaps be accommodated in a suitable building much later than our small collection of antiquities in Berlin. At the moment they are still stored in sheds, although their beauty makes one forget their surroundings . . .'. (For additional bibliography see Wegner, 115, note 34.)
243 Karl König (1774–1852), originally from Germany, from 1807 director of the natural history section of the British Museum.
244 Discovered in Rome in the seventeenth century, it belonged to the great collector William Hamilton, then to the Duchess of Portland. An amphora of blue glass with a white veneer, with depictions of Peleus and Thetis, it found its way into the British Museum in 1810. It dates from the Augustan period.

Erechtheum Temple, Tower of the Winds. Quite good except the tower. Stark interior, especially the flat-coffered ceilings, low galleries, two pulpits.

St James's Park,[237] – Westminster, old lawcourt with a beautiful timber roof[238] (plate 35), its contruction exposed and decorated. – Westminster Bridge.[239] Blackfriars Bridge[240] (plate 36), large ramps on both sides with substructures constructed for houses, steps leading up to it, great arches continuing underneath the ramps. View of the 3 iron arches of Southwark Bridge.[241] Supper in St Paul's Coffeehouse.

Saturday, 27 May

Visited Volkert, Aders etc. – Drive to the Ambassador, with him to the Museum,[242] Herr König.[243] Antiquities in the forecourt, Doric capitals, simple fluting (plate 38) New building, based on the architecture of the Erechtheum (plate 37). It is intended to be square when finished. All the iron ceiling construction has been enclosed in wooden coffering (plates 39 and 40). Floor laid upon up-ended boards. The great main staircase, each flight 12 ft wide, rests on cast iron beams, the bricks are very weak, everything below is wainscoted. None of the construction particularly praiseworthy. Gallery of antiquities (plate 41) in very small rooms, lit from above, very restful and satisfying. Precious objects of all kinds. The Greek marbles, the Portland vase[244] a wonder, the Greek vases, bronzes. Knight's[245] collection.

Visited Consul Giese. – Home to change shoes. Solly's[246] dinner, his wife, brother, in the evening another brother, who invited us for a meal, and Herr Schlick. – Music, Count Danckelmann sang Mozart etc.

245 Richard Payne Knight (1750–1824), scholar and aesthete, theorist of the Picturesque movement. He published *The Landscape – a Didactic Poem*, and *Analytical Enquiry into the Principles of Taste*. His important collection, consisting mainly of drawings, was left to the British Museum in 1824.
246 Edward Solly (see note 226). His brother Isaac Solly was Governor of the Royal Exchange Assurance Office and Chairman of the London Docks.

Sunday, 28 May

Drive to Hampton Court, statue of the horse-tamer outside Wellington's house.[247] – Hampton Court park. Breakfast. Enormous height of the trees, chestnuts and elms in all the avenues. Lushness of green vegetation. – The palace, the 9 pictures by Mantegna, the Triumph of Caesar,[248] the 7 cartoons by Raphael,[249] splendidly hung as frescoes in their own special room. The interior of the room, brown wood, Corinthian pilasters, is rather eerie and gloomy, and it is not wide enough. I have not had so much pleasure from painting since the Vatican in Rome.[250] – Ferry crossing in a small boat, and walk through fields and part of Richmond park to the terrace. Wonderful view of the leafy valley and the river. Walks. – Dinner in a handsome room of the inn with Herr and Madame Aders and drive home in their carriage with them.

Monday, 29 May

Presentation of the prizes of the Society of Arts, Manufactures and Commerce, under the presidency of the Duke of Sussex,[251] brother to the King, in the Opera House.[252] (Boring.) The interior is large and tasteless. Gas lighting, glass chandelier which is of little use, not very bright, poor music. Long speech by the secretary. Answering speeches by the prize-winners after the Duke's address. Ladies. – Exhibition of works of art near the Opera.[253] Exhibition of watercolours: much skill, landscapes predominate, everything daubed [*geschmiert*], inaccurate, sometimes successful in effect, more often bland and overdone. All the portraits insipid. Many of the miniatures clever and harmonious. – Holtzapfel and Deierlein's mechanical workshop.[254] Lathes. – Academy exhibition in Carlton House,[255] similar in character to all the others. Small picture in which the projected silhouette of a sleeping father had been drawn on the wall by a boy, the family is watching, and the mother sleeps

[247] In 1822 the statue of Achilles, cast by the sculptor Sir Richard Westmacott from the metal of French cannon captured at Waterloo, had been set up in honour of Wellington outside the latter's residence, Apsley House. The sculpture was strongly influenced by one of the antique *Horsetamers* of the Quirinal in Rome. Apsley House was built 1771–8 by Robert Adam at the entrance to Hyde Park; it was presented by the state to the Duke of Wellington in 1820. It was enlarged in 1828, and later became the Wellington Museum.

[248] The great series of a Roman triumphal procession by Andrea Mantegna (1431–1506), of nine tempera paintings. They were acquired by Charles I in 1628, and with the Raphael Cartoons are the most important paintings from Charles I's collection to remain in the Royal Collection (see following note).

[249] In 1623 the seven Raphael cartoons were acquired for Charles I. They remained for a long time in the Cartoon Gallery of Hampton Court, which dates from 1695. They are now on loan to the Victoria and Albert Museum.

[250] Schinkel is referring to his visit to Rome in 1824, when he saw the Raphael Rooms in the Vatican on 28, 29 and 30 August. He reiterated his high opinion in a letter to Franz Catel (Berlin, 11 December 1826; Staatsbibliothek, Munich): '. . . as to pictures, Raphael's magnificent cartoons at Hampton Court particularly delighted me, recalling as they did my impressions of the Vatican, with their size and fresh colour. . .'.

[251] Augustus Frederick (1773–1843), son of George III, from 1801 Duke of Sussex. Brother of George IV (1762–1830, Regent from 1811, King from 1820).

[252] The Royal Opera House in the Haymarket, originally built at the beginning of the eighteenth century, rebuilt 1816–8 by John Nash in collaboration with George Stanley Repton.

[253] The Royal Society of British Artists, founded in 1823, which put on annual exhibitions, had its exhibition rooms in Suffolk Street, Pall Mall, near the Opera.

[254] See note 284.

[255] The Royal Academy of Arts, founded in 1768, had been in Somerset House in the Strand, since 1780 and remained there until 1837. Schinkel is probably confusing it with Carlton House – begun in 1783 by Henry Holland, completed in 1816 and pulled down 1827–9 – the residence of the Prince Regent, later George IV.

[256] This must be William Mulready's *The Origin of a Painter*, now lost, but the composition is known from a drawing in the Victoria and Albert Museum, reproduced in K.M. Heleniak, *William Mulready*, New Haven and London, 1980, pl. 110.

[257] In 1808–9 the original eighteenth-century building had been replaced by a new theatre designed by Robert Smirke.

[258] This is probably the *Operatic Drama* by F. Fortescue, written in 1822, which attempted to adapt the epic material as a musical piece.

[259] Richard Westmacott (1775–1856), from 1811 member of the Royal Academy. He produced many monuments throughout Great Britain and the colonies (see also notes 287 and 482).

[260] Edmund Turrel (dates not known) engraver, especially of architecture. Also contributed to Beuth's *Vorbildern für Fabricanten und Handwerker*, published in Berlin from 1821 by the Prussian Royal Commission for Trade. His 'parallel machine' was presumably a device for creating parallel shading lines on a copper plate.

[261] It is not clear in what form or where Schinkel saw Cockerell's 'Aeginetan temple'. Schinkel appears to refer to a model or drawing of it or possibly casts of the sculptures, but he only called on Cockerell the following day (without finding him in). Casts of the Aegina marbles were installed in the Literary and Philosophical Institution in Bristol in 1825 (D. Watkin, *The Life and Work of C.R. Cockerell*, Cambridge, 1974, 96).

Charles Robert Cockerell (1788–1863), architect and archaeologist, pupil of his father, Samuel Pepys Cockerell, and collaborator with Robert Smirke (see note 242). He was in Greece from 1810 to 1817, and also visited Asia Minor and Italy. He took part in excavations, including the Temple of Aphaia in Aegina in 1811 with John Foster (see note 489) and a group of German amateurs. The Aegina figures were acquired to Cockerell's regret at that time by Ludwig I for the Munich Glyptothek. In 1812 Cockerell took part in the excavation of the Temple of Apollo in Bassae, and in 1815 he acquired the reliefs for the British Museum. After devoting his early years to archaeology he then turned to architecture more fully in the 1820s. In 1826 he became a member of the Royal Academy. He published works on ancient architecture and its reconstruction.

[262] There were two arcades in London in 1826, and it not clear which one Schinkel is referring to here – the Royal Opera Arcade (built 1816–8 by J. Nash and G.S. Repton) or the Burlington Arcade (built 1815–9 by Samuel Ware).

in another corner.[256] – In the evening Covent Garden Theatre,[257] pleasant interior, good actors, superb subject, Robinson Crusoe,[258] unbearable vapour and stink from the gas light.

Tuesday, 30 May

To Consul Giese, with him to see the sculptor Westmacott[259] and his work. – To the engraver Turrel,[260] saw his inventions of the parallel machine, die compasses, an ellipse machine. (plate 42) Cockerell's Aeginetan temple.[261] – Market for carriages, horses and other things (large ox 1 shilling). – Arcade.[262] – Interior of Westminster Abbey. Henry VII's Chapel,[263] monuments. – Sadler's Wells Theatre.[264] Grotesque dancers.

Wednesday, 31 May

Voigt,[265] die-sinker. London pavements with iron gutters set in them. 4 ins in diameter. – Museum.[266] Rooms 15 to 18 ft, 13–14 ft high, lit from above, rotundas 21 ft in diameter. Remarks and drawings in the catalogue until half past 2. – Visited the architect Cockerell, who was not at home. – St Stephen's church in Walbrook,[267] by the architect Christian [*sic*] Wren. [This sentence crossed out.] St Martin's church[268] by James Gibbs. – Old wing of the palace begun by Jones.[269] – Shops, chairs, furniture. – Ackermann.[270] – Ambassador, supper, fast walk home, took 1½ hours.

[263] This was built 1503–12, and represents London's main example of late-Gothic Perpendicular style. During the years 1807 to 1822 it had been carefully restored under the direction of Thomas Gayfere.

[264] This was opened in 1777 as a theatre.

[265] Carl Friedrich Voigt (1800–1874), die-sinker and engraver, pupil and colleague of Vollgold and Posch in Berlin. In 1825/6 he was working in London under Pistrucci (see note 280) at the Royal Mint. He moved to Munich in 1830.

[266] Presumably a return visit to the British Museum.

[267] Built 1672–9 by Christopher Wren.

[268] St Martin-in-the-Fields, built by James Gibbs between 1721 and 1726.

[269] This is the Banqueting House, an annexe to the old Whitehall Palace (demolished in 1695) and intended as part of a palace for Charles I which was never completed. It was designed by Inigo Jones and built from 1619 to 1622. The Banqueting House was one of the few buildings in London which Schinkel sketched on his return to London shortly before he left England on 2 August (see plate 179). Inigo Jones (1573–1651), architect, from 1615 Surveyor General of Works under Charles I.

[270] Rudolph Ackermann (1764–1834), publisher originally from Germany who had been in London since 1794. His publications include *Repository of Art* and *Microcosm of London* (see J. Ford, *Ackermann, 1783–1983*, London, 1983).

43. T.H. Shepherd, *Bank of England*, from *London in the Nineteenth Century*, pub. 1827

44. After Thomas Malton the younger, *Lothbury Court, Bank of England*, aquatint

45. A.C. Pugin and T. Rowlandson, *Royal Exchange*, from *Microcosm of London*, 1809, coloured aquatint

46. A.C. Pugin and T. Rowlandson, *The Mint*, from *Microcosm of London*, 1809, coloured aquatint

Thursday, 1 June

Visited Mr Bischoff, wool trader, tables of price rises in export, and of bankruptcies, arranged like a map for quick reference. – Town Hall [Guildhall],[271] medieval style. Monuments to Nelson,[272] Pitt and his father, badly made, too big, the plinth new and in the wrong style. – Bank[273] (plate 43), many rounded corners, Corinthian, handsome courtyard, much that is useless, a simple set of pillars divides two courtyards, one of the triumphal arches is the best thing about the building[274] (plate 44). – Stock Exchange[275] (plate 45), inner courtyard, wide arcades all the way round, flat vaulting, 25 ft wide, rotundas inside the building, barrel vaulting, incomplete domes etc., strangely simple in ornamentation. – Lord Mayor's house. – Mansion House,[276] fine portico, Corinthian, simple upper construction. – Monument,[277] narrow streets, dreadful noise of carriages and people. – London Bridge,[278] view of the ships. – Tower Hill, old cobbled-up buildings with nothing really ancient about them. – Royal Mint[279] (plate 46). Cutter two sides. Coins stamped through vacuum chamber, 12 coin-cutting machines in a circle all round. The medallist Pistrucci,[280] producing the most delicate work with the coarsest of hands. Large medal of the Battle of Waterloo (plates 47 and 48), on one side 4 monarchs' heads above each other, around them Hercules, Themis, Castor and Pollux, Plenty etc. On the other side Blücher, Wellington on horseback, Victory in the middle, Jupiter above, with the fallen giants round about. Executed in the best style and taste, carved red stone with an archangel, many heads which are on sale as antiquities, and other compositions. – Inside the Tower, guides in red uniforms and caps, archaic. The weapon collection, all the kings on horseback armed, not worth seeing. The new weapons are splendidly arrayed upright in repositories standing directly behind these (plate 50). – Tower where the two princes were murdered,[281] William the Conqueror's tower.[282] – Breakfast in St Paul's Coffeehouse. Drive to Westmacott, who was not at home. – Walk to Solly's, who was also out. – Bramah's warehouse[283] and walk to his factory. That pleasant gentleman had an overseer show us all round. Hydraulic presses, fine iron smelting, careful, not too hot,

[271] The Guildhall was built 1411–38 as the seat of local government for the City of London. In 1788–9 George Dance the Younger added a façade in a mixture of classical and Gothic styles.

[272] Monuments to: Horatio Nelson (1758–1805) by James Smith (1775–1815), 1810; William Pitt the Elder (1708–78) by John Bacon, 1782; and William Pitt the Younger (1759–1806) by George Bubb, 1813.

[273] The interior of the Bank of England, an eighteenth-century building (central section 1732–4 by George Sampson and wings 1766–83 by Robert Taylor), was rebuilt in a completely new style by John Soane (see note 360) between 1788 and 1808. In 1927 the interior and much of the exterior was destroyed (see D. Stroud, *The Architecture of John Soane*, London, 1961, 65f.).

[274] Schinkel is presumably referring to Lothbury Court.

[275] The Royal Exchange, built 1667–71 by Edward Jerman (destroyed by fire in 1838).

[276] The official residence of the Lord Mayor of London, built by George Dance the Elder, in 1739–42, with alterations by George Dance the Younger, in 1795/6.

[277] A Doric column designed by Christopher Wren and erected in 1671–77 at the spot where the Great Fire of London started in 1666.

[278] See note 299.

[279] A large workshop had been built 1807–12 for the Royal Mint by James Johnson and Robert Smirke.

[280] Benedetto Pistrucci (1784–1855), gem and coin cutter, medallist, model-builder and sculptor, was of Italian extraction and had been in London since 1815. From 1817 he was Chief Engraver of the Royal Mint. His main work was the medal commemorating the Battle of Waterloo: begun in 1817 it was not finished until 1850, and was never officially issued (see L.P. Biroli Stefanelli, *Benedetto Pistrucci* in *Bolletino Numismatico*, monograph series, Rome, 1989).

[281] The 'Bloody Tower'.

[282] The White Tower, built *c.*1080 by William the Conqueror, is the oldest building in the group.

[283] Joseph Bramah (1749–1814), machine manufacturer and entrepreneur, invented the combination lock in 1784, the modern water-closet in 1793, and the hydraulic press in 1795. His workshops, continued and extended by his sons, were the first in England to produce tools by machine. The 'pleasant gentleman' was probably Timothy Bramah, one of Joseph's sons. Henry Maudslay (see note 285) collaborated initially with him (see I. McNeil, *Joseph Bramah: a Century of Invention*, London, 1968).

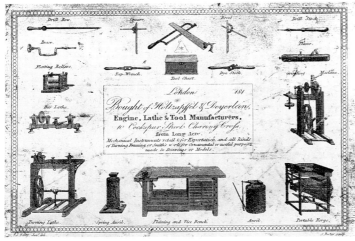

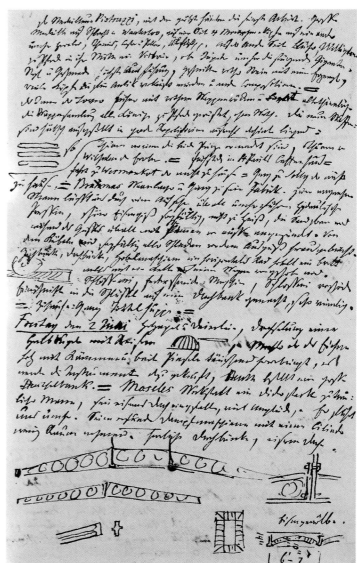

47 and 48. Benedetto Pistrucci, *The Waterloo Medal* (recto and verso) 14 cm. diameter. British Museum

49. Holtzapffel and Deyerlein, label on tool box, engraving, 1820s. Museum of London

50. *Journal*, p. 21, (upper left) stands for the display of armour in Tower of London. (middle left) planing machine in the Bramah workshop, (below centre) ornamental lathe, making wooden fluting in the workshop of Holtzapffel and Deyerlein, (bottom) details of the iron roof construction of the Maudslay workshop, including (bottom right) an iron vault 6–7 foot wide

the sand box is heated with flames from outside during the casting. All the slag is carefully removed from the buckets before moulding. Draw benches, lathes, planing machines, a horizontal wheel planes a board moved on a carriage with a chain. Machine for producing springs, locksmith's workshop, different notches made in the keys on a lathe, very cleanly done. – Walk home, turtle soup.

Friday, 2 June

Holtzapffel and Deierlein[284] (plates 49 and 50), turning of a fluted wooden hemisphere. Painter who brings up the grain of the oak with combs and wide brushes; the instruments for this can be bought; Beuth ordered a large lathe (plate 51).

Maudsley's workshop[285] (plate 53), [Maudslay] a stout, friendly man, his iron roof had collapsed, much damage. He took us round. A steam-engine (plate 52), his own invention, with one cylinder takes up little room. Magnificent lathes, iron roofs. Iron vaulting (plates 50 and 55). Iron staircases. The slender iron columns supporting the roof of one of the rooms also function as outlets for waste water. The foundry is installed on an iron-and-brick vault; roller which makes holes, slits and incisions, for nail holes in the steam boiler (plate 54). A hammer simultaneously punching profiles, with a clamped head. A cut-off worm acts as a brake on the fall of the hammer.

From Maudsley's to the Office of Gaslight[286] (plates 54 and 56). Enormous plant, 17 sheet-iron gasometers, 40 ft in diameter, 18 ft high, set up in great sheds. The gas passes through all the retorts into a common horizontal pipe and is then redistributed.

Westmacott's huge statue of King George III[287] on horseback, 24½ ft high, the horse 16 English ft[288] to the beginning of the neck. The horse has many good points, rather heavy-looking, flowing mane not a success. He has cast it in individual sections, 4 legs, body, head, tail and chest separately, similarly with the human figure; he intends to join the parts by casting, he casts from a cupola furnace, not a flame furnace,[289] the latter seems to be unreliable.

[284] The firm of Holtzapffel and Deyerlein (1804–27) of 64 Charing Cross Road, was famous for its precision lathes for the production of ornamental turned wares, a subject of particular interest to Beuth and Schinkel. From the tiny drawing on this page

(see plate 50) Schinkel must have watched a lathe in action, turning a piece of wood and applying fluting to it. As it happens Beuth's purchase of a lathe is recorded: on 26 October 1826, after his return to Germany, he paid £160 for a 5″ screw lathe (W. Greene Ogden, Jr., *Notes on the History and Provenance of Holtzapffel lathes*, 1987, 32).

The reproduction and duplication of works of art of all periods by the latest technical means was one of the main aims of Beuth and the Berlin Institute of Trade. This was reflected in his *Vorbilder für Fabricanten und Handwerker* published in instalments since 1821. In a summary of these publications in 1837 he remarked: 'If it becomes possible to disseminate a work of art among all classes by faithful reproduction and duplication, so that it is no longer necessary to visit museums or inaccessible private collections in order to see it, we may hope that one of these scattered seeds will grow and bear fruit.'

[285] Henry Maudslay (1771–1831) was the greatest figure in the development of precision machine tools of the early nineteenth century. He was particularly admired in Prussia and set up a workshop in Berlin in 1830. Apart from the fame of his lathes he was known for his invention of a small-scale table steam engine, which Schinkel notes with approval. A few days before Schinkel's visit, on 24 May, a new roof being erected over the workshop collapsed with some loss of life, to which Schinkel refers. Despite this Schinkel was still extremely interested in what remained of the roof (K.R. Gilbert, *Henry Maudslay*, Science Museum, London, 1971).

[286] In his Itinerary (see page 211) Schinkel wrote 'Gasworks in Petersstreet' which makes it certain that he visited the Westminster Gas Light and Coke Company. It was the first operational public gas works, opening in 1813, and by 1822 it had 18 gasholders (not 17 as Schinkel states), with four of them enclosed in brick buildings (see E.G. Stewart, *Historical Index of Gasworks, 1806–1957*, London, n.d., 109). Gas street lighting had been installed in London in 1814, Paris in 1815 and Berlin in 1826.

[287] The equestrian statue of the king, who died in 1820, had been commissioned by Liverpool in 1822 and was later erected in the London Road.

[288] One English foot was equal to 30.4 cm. The Rhenish foot used in Prussia was equal to 31.3 cm.

[289] Vertical cylindrical furnace used in the smelting of iron and other metals, as opposed to the flat flame furnace.

51. Holtzapffel and Deyerlein, lathe for ornamental cutting of the kind bought by Beuth in 1826. Science Museum, London

52. Model of Maudslay's table steam engine, of the kind Schinkel would have seen in the workshop. Science Museum, London

53. Anon., *The Maudslay workshop in Westminster Road*, watercolour. Guildhall Library, London

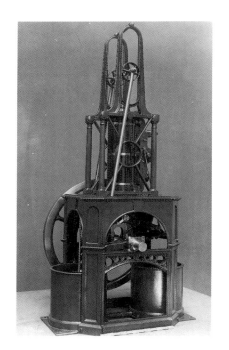

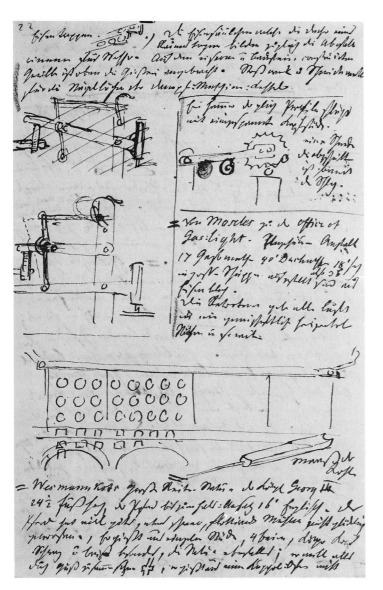

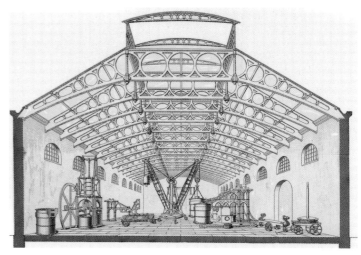

54. *Journal*, p. 22, (top left) iron staircase in the Maudslay workshop, (left below) two views of a trip hammer in the Maudslay workshop, (right above) metal cutting machine in the Maudslay workshop, (bottom) system of gas retorts at the Westminster Gas Company. The instrument below to the right is captioned by Schinkel: 'measure for coal'

55. Anon, *The Main Erecting Shop of Maudslay's workshop in 1830*, engraving from a report on Maudslay in the *Verhandlungen des Vereins zur Beförderung des Gewerbefleisses in Preussen*, 1833, a society of which Maudslay was an honorary member. Science Museum, London

56. Anon., *Gas Works*, 1819, engraving. Probably an ideal view of a gasworks to demonstrate their workings

57. T.H. Shepherd, *Egyptian Hall, Piccadilly*, from *London in the Nineteenth Century*, 1827

58. G. Jones, eng. Wise, *Astley's Amphitheatre, Surrey Road*, 1815, engraving

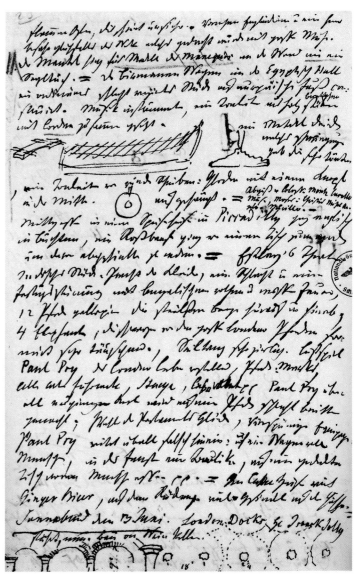

59. *Journal*, p. 23, (above) Four sketches of musical instruments on exhibition at the Egyptian Hall, (bottom) Wine vaults at London Docks in section and plan with measurements

Distinguished-looking English lady and a gentleman were also looking at the work, which was being turned with a great deal of effort. The coat for the dummy model hung on the wall like a piece of sailcloth. – The Burmese coach in the Egyptian Hall[290] (plate 57), a crude, badly decorated piece set up on a European base. Musical instruments, a scale made of sticks, little wooden bars tied together with cord (plate 59). A metal triangle which vibrated loudly. A scale made of round discs: bells hung up by a knob in the middle. Casts of statues [from] Monte Cavallo. Museum, Moses and Christ [by] Michelangelo.[291] Murillo.

Dinner in an eating house in Piccadilly, in booths in the English style, a joint of roast beef was taken from one table to another to be sliced. – Astley's Theatre[292] (plate 58). Indian play. Magnificent costumes, a battle and storming of a castle with red and white Bengal flares, 12 horses galloped up and down the steepest mountains, 4 elephants, the black ones made up from big London horses, very convincing. Graceful tightrope-walking. Comedy Paul Pry,[293] presenting London life, horse market, all kinds of coach transport, stage, cabriolet etc. Paul Pry everywhere, curious fellow, is made to ride his horse badly. Election of Members of Parliament, coach and four. Paul Pry careers into everything on his horse: a coach full of people, a shop-window, a fully laid table where people are eating etc. – A fair amount of ginger beer in a coffee house, on the way home a whole lot of rabble in the streets.

Saturday, 3 June

London Docks[294] (plates 60 and 61), Mr Isaak Solly as guide, new construction of wine cellars. Dock basin for 250 ships, storerooms, stone steps and double iron doors, iron rails, iron cranes; wine cellar with 22,000 barrels, above these storerooms for tobacco, around 400 ft wide, 800 ft long. New basin (plate 62), construction of locks, erection of a weir beam. Swing bridge. Surrounding walls. Boat trip on the river between the Thames ships, across the stretch where the tunnel is being built.[295] To the West India Docks[296] (plate 63). New construction, good planning: sheds of iron and wood right round the basins, well-constructed roof, covered with corrugated

[290] The Egyptian Hall had been built in Piccadilly in 1810–12, with an Egyptian façade (builder W. Bullock, architect P.F. Robinson). It contained natural, ethnological and historical objects, often augmented by panorama displays. It was open to the public. For the Egyptian Hall see R. Altick, *The Shows of London*, Cambridge, MA, 1978, *c*.18, 235–252. The Burmese State Carriage, captured in 1824, was also noted by the German traveller Pückler-Muscau. It is reproduced in Altick, p. 250, ill. 75.
[291] Presumably casts of Michelangelo's *Moses* (1513–42, S. Pietro in Vincoli, Rome) and *Christ* (1519/20, Sta Maria sopra Minerva, Rome).
[292] An amphitheatrical building, erected in 1774 as a riding school; it had been a theatre since 1780.
[293] A well-known contemporary actor and acrobat.
[294] Begun in 1796 by Daniel Asher Alexander for the wine and tobacco trade. In 1811 an entrance with terraced buildings was added, and in 1820 the Docks were completed.
[295] See note 317.
[296] These warehouses, built 1799–1802 by George Gwilt, were seen as architecturally the most successful in London and greatly influenced subsequent warehouse construction.

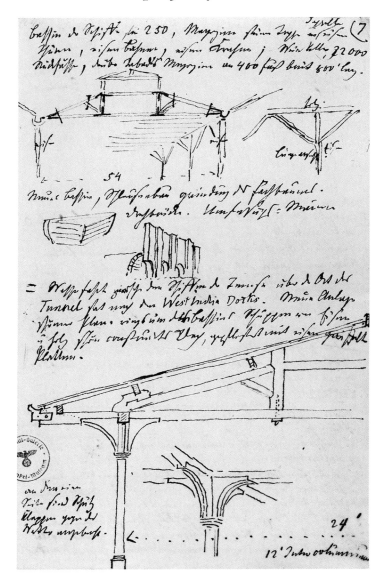

61. H. Moses, *London Docks*, 1825, engraving

62. T.H. Shepherd, *London Docks, looking West*, from *London in the Nineteenth Century*, 1827

60. *Journal*, p. 24, (top) warehouse at Tobacco Dock with detail sketch. Left view with width of 54ft.: right view inscribed: 'wood, iron, long view'. The joists are of wood with iron fastenings, which Schinkel indicates in thicker pen. They can still be seen. (below) London Docks, lock in course of construction, (bottom) Section of roof construction at West India Docks, with iron columns. Measurements of 24ft and inscr.: '12ft intercolumniation'

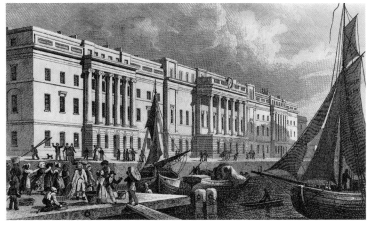

63. T.H. Shepherd, *West India Import Dock, Poplar*, from *London in the Nineteenth Century*, 1827

64. T.H. Shepherd, *The New Custom House, from Billingsgate*, from *London in the Nineteenth Century*, 1827

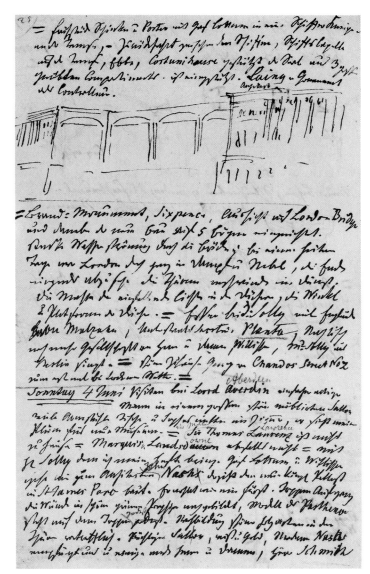

65. *Journal*, p. 25, Custom House, exterior before Smirke's alterations to Laing's façade were completed

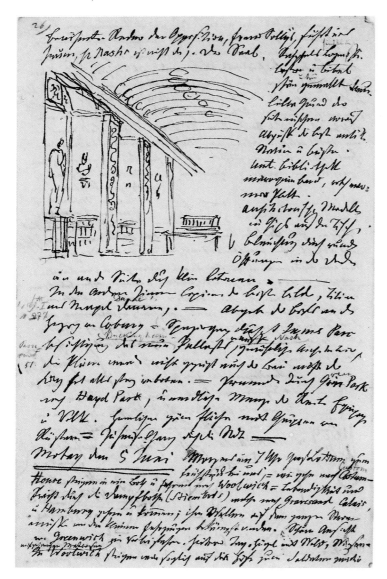

67: A.C. Pugin, *Gallery in the House of John Nash Esqr. Regent Street*, 1836, engraving

66. *Journal*, p. 26, the Gallery of John Nash's apartment in Lower Regent Street, showing elaborate decorations and display of architectural models

iron sheets. On one side there are flaps for protection against the weather. Intercolumniation 12 ft.

Breakfast, ham and porter, with Count Lottum in a sailors' tavern on the Thames. – Boat trip back between the ships, ship's band on the Thames, tide out, Custom House[297] (plates 64 and 65), column supports, the Long Room, consisting of 3 large vaulted sections, has iron supports. Laing, architect, and Garment as overseer.

Great Fire Monument,[298] sixpence. View of London Bridge[299] with the new bridge next to it constructed on 5 arches. Strong current flowing under the bridge. Although the weather was fine London was wrapped in fog and smoke; you could not see to the edge of the city, the towers were invisible in the haze. The mass of roof-lights, the angles and platforms of the roofs. – Ate at I. Solly's, many Englishmen, Baron Maltzahn, Undersecretary of State Planta, after the meal more company of gentlemen and ladies, Willisen, Madame Solly from Berlin sang. – Pleasant walk home from 2 Chandos Street, for the first time in dry weather.

Sunday, 4 June

Visited Lord Aberdeen,[300] a simple noble person, in a large beautifully furnished drawing room, many armchairs, tables and sofas in the middle of the room; he looked at my plans for the new museum. – Sir Thomas Lawrence[301] was not at home. Neither was the Marquis of Lansdowne.[302]

With Mr Solly, to whom I brought my portfolio, Count Lottum and Willisen, went to see the architect Nash,[303] who at present is building the new royal palace in St James's Park.[304] He lives like a prince. Stairway upwards, the walls covered in beautiful imitation green porphyry, model of the Parthenon on the landing, excellent imitation wood in the doors. Magnificent drawing room, white and gold, Mrs Nash received us and other gentlemen and ladies, Mr Smith,[305] famous Opposition orator, also the Sollys, and took us round, Mr Nash was not there. The hall (plates 66 and 67). Raphael's Loggie[306] pilasters and pediments finely painted, faithful, purple background of the side niches, where casts have been

[297] Built 1812–7 by David Laing, this building had been enlarged around the central section, which contains the room mentioned by Schinkel, and on the Thames side 1825–7 by Robert Smirke. Laing's work had proved structurally unsound, and the central section had to be demolished: it was reerected rather differently by Smirke (see Colvin, under Smirke).

[298] See note 277.

[299] This medieval bridge had been enlarged 1758–62. Schinkel saw a new iron bridge, designed by Rennie in 1820, which was being built (1823–31) alongside the old bridge.

[300] George Hamilton Gordon, Earl of Aberdeen (1784–1860), known as 'Athenian Aberdeen'. He visited Greece in 1804, after which he founded the Athenian Society in London and interested himself in archaeology. During the Coalition against Napoleon he played a diplomatic role, and after 1826 he was variously Foreign, War, and Colonial Minister.

[301] Sir Thomas Lawrence (1769–1830), portrait painter. Member of the Royal Academy in 1814, in 1820 its president. His portraits were notable for their freedom of handling and elegance.

[302] See note 364.

[303] John Nash (1752–1835), architect and town-planner. (See p. 15).

[304] In 1825 Nash had designed Clarence House as an annexe to the sixteenth-century St James's Palace. It was completed in 1828, and was the residence of the Duke of Clarence until he became King William IV in 1830. Schinkel may be referring to this building or possibly to Buckingham Palace, designed by Nash in 1825 and under construction in 1826.

[305] It has been suggested that this is Sydney Smith (1771–1845), author and theologian and wit. He was a member of the Whig party then in opposition, but it is more likely, however, to have been his brother Robert Percy Smith (1770–1845).

[306] Presumably in imitation of the paintings on the walls and ceilings of Raphael's Loggie in the Vatican (1513–18).

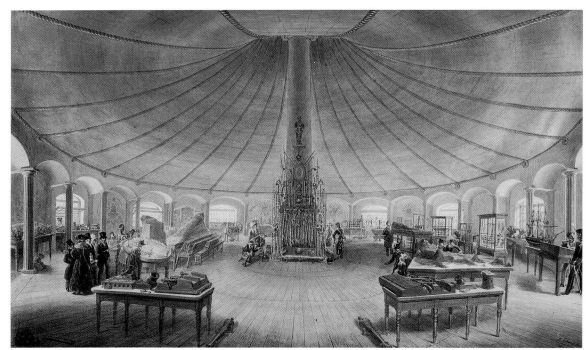

68. George Scharf, *Woolwich*, watercolour. British Museum. Nash's Rotunda for the Royal Artillery Museum is middle left, and Woolwich Barracks can be seen to the far left in the distance

69. George Scharf, *The Rotunda, Woolwich*, watercolour. British Museum. The ceiling is of canvas held up by ropes, and supported on a massive central column

mounted of the best statues and busts of antiquity. Below, books bound in morocco, slabs of red marble. Plaster architectural models on the tables,[307] lighting by means of round openings in the ceiling and small lamps at the side. In the other rooms, copies of the best paintings, Titian's Naples Danae.

Handed in the letter to the Duke of Coburg. – Walk through St James's Park, looked at the new palace by Nash,[308] very ordinary architecture, the plans may not be seen, nor the building site, the King has expressly forbidden it.

Promenade through Green Park to Hyde Park, endless stream of riders, carriages and people out walking. Wonderful stretch of green with clumps of elms. – Walk home through the town.

Monday, 5 June

Count Lottum breakfasted with us at 7 o'clock in the morning, we went to the Custom House, got in a boat and set off for Woolwich. – Splendidly lively scene provided by the steamboats coming and going from London to Gravesend, Calais and Hamburg, the small boats have to struggle against the wash they make across the whole river. Fine view of Greenwich as we sailed past. Good weather. Wooded hills, fields with sailor-prisoners.

In Woolwich (plate 68) we immediately climbed the hill to the barracks,[309] and asked the Commandant, to whom we had letters of introduction, for permission to look round. Superb elevated position, with hills, large clumps of trees. A very green, flat parade-ground on an enormous scale is surrounded by trees and shrubs like a park, and there happened to be a parade of guards on it with music; the main façade of the barracks runs the length of the parade-ground, in front is a wide gravel area. Behind the barracks are the stables; from everywhere one has a view over the Thames valley and London, which is however never visible owing to the smoke from the chimneys. On the other side of the parade-ground is the cadets' house in a castellated style,[310] and behind these a wooded hill on which stands the Commandant's house.

We inspected first the model collection in the pavilion[311] (plates 69 and 70) constructed specially for it. Ropes tied fast to a central

[307] Some of these architectural models, apparently made in France for Nash, still survive and are in the Victoria and Albert Museum, Furniture Department. (I am indebted to Dr Tessa Murdoch for this information.)
[308] See note 304.
[309] The Royal Artillery Barracks in Woolwich, built 1802–8 from designs by James Wyatt (1746–1813) or Jeffry Wyatt. Wegner seems to have confused this enormous building with the Royal Military Academy (see Wegner, 121–2, note 50 and note 310 below).
[310] The Royal Military Academy in Woolwich, built 1796–1805 from designs by James Wyatt; a neo-Gothic brick building in the castellated style (see *Buildings of England: London 2*, 454 and plate 40a).
[311] This was in fact a temporary ballroom built by John Nash (1814) in St James's Park. It was removed to Woolwich and turned into a military museum in 1819. It is now the Royal Artillery Museum. The ropes still remain and hold up the canvas tenting in the interior.

312 The Royal Arsenal, a complex of brick buildings built 1716–19, probably from a design by John Vanbrugh. It had undergone several extensions. (See *Buildings of England: London 2*, 453 and plate 30).
313 The Old Royal Observatory in Greenwich Park, built in 1675/6 by Christopher Wren.
314 First built 1664–9 from a design by John Webb. In 1696 Christopher Wren began on the great baroque ensemble, centred on Inigo Jones's Queen's House (1616–35). Hawksmoor and his successors continued the building into the middle of the eighteenth century.
315 Presumably the 'Painted Hall' (1698–1705) within a building by Christopher Wren, with ceiling and wall paintings (1708–12) by James Thornhill, celebrating in an allegorical mode the Protestant Succession (see *Buildings of England: London 2*, 149 and plate 25b).
316 Rebuilt 1780–9 in a classical style by Athenian Stuart and William Newton.

post, with metal sheets in between. Among the models Gibraltar, Rio de Janeiro and Quebec were of interest. A copperplate engraving machine which automatically does the printing and removal [of the print]. A rain machine from Drury Lane Theatre. In one of the rooms Napoleon's field-kitchen wagon and hearse can be seen. The soldiers' quarters, 8 men were eating mutton chops and potatoes, food looked well prepared. – Stables, riding arena. – Stores. – The Royal Arsenal,[312] thousands of cannon in neat rows on the floor. – The prison ship, tack stores, here we heard complaints about moths. – Iron rails. – Very fine sawmill with steam-engine. There are extra gadgets for cutting cross-section by circular saw; a cog-wheel is attached for decoration. Old drill. Breakfast of ale and ham in an open lodge by the water, fine view. – The dockyards. Huge sheds, usually 2 standing next to each other. Awesome anchoring equipment. Excellent smiths' workshop, big iron construction, steam-engine, bellows, enormous great hammers. Smiths' workshop in Woolwich dockyards (plate 71).

Drive to Greenwich (plate 72). Through the beautiful park to the Observatory,[313] magnificent green and over the wood the view across the palatial buildings of London itself. Deer, roedeer. An old sailor from Saxony spoke German. He and his companion let us look through telescopes for a small sum. One can hardly make out Westminster even in good weather. The Hospital building[314] (plate 73), good in many aspects but so made up of different forms rather than decorative elements, that the unity is lost; it is built of fine material. A long colonnade on each side of the open central space. A large state-room for the sailors to walk in contains pictures of maritime heroes and sea battles.[315] Opposite is the chapel[316] with a completely flat roof, quite pleasing, some decoration, very big. – In the streets there are many women inviting one to tea.

Return to London, disembarked at Custom House. Looked at Southwark Bridge (see plate 177) from above and below, enormous span, effect of the iron arches from below, the iron 3 ins thick including the edge, the individual sections up to 14 ft long, cast 7–8 ft high. – Supper with Count Lottum.

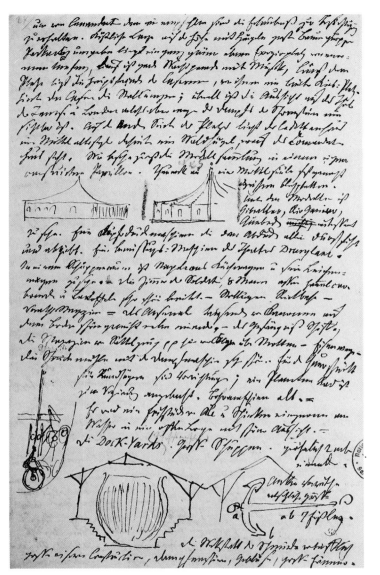

70. *Journal*, p. 27, (above) Two views of Nash's Royal Artillery Museum, exterior and interior, (below left) possibly a circular saw in Woolwich dockyards, (below right) Woolwich dockyards, section of a dry dock with iron roof, (far right) anchor, inscr.: '7′ long'

71. *Journal*, p. 28, (top) workshop buildings in Woolwich dockyards, seen from the front and side, with measurements, (below) view of Greenwich Hospital from park, with London in distance, (bottom) Thames Tunnel, steam engine for water pumping mechanism

72. William Westall, *London from Greenwich Park*, 1826, aquatint

73. S. Read, *Greenwich Hospital*, steel engraving

74. *Sketches of London Bridge*, 1826, pencil

75. *Sketch of St Paul's from the river*, 1826, pencil

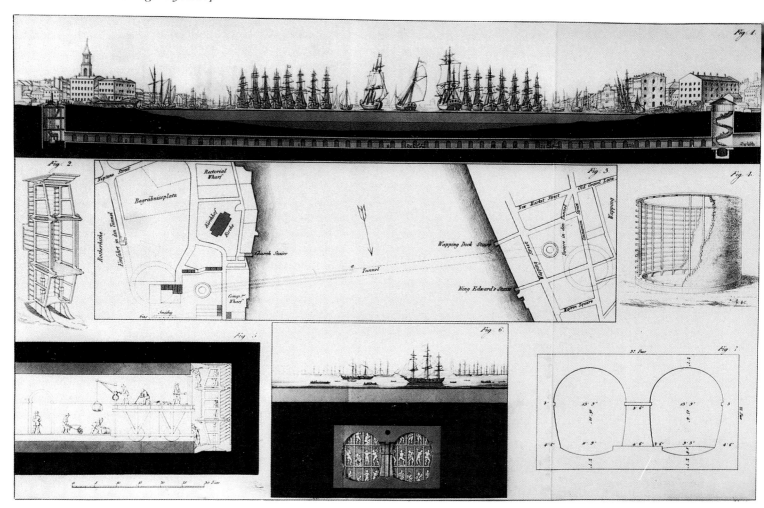

76. F.W. Schwechten, Plan and details of the Thames
Tunnel, from *Verhandlungen des Vereins zur Beförderung des
Gewerbefleisses in Preussen*, 1827, engraving

Tuesday, 6 June

Walk to Mr Brunel's office;[317] from there across Blackfriars Bridge, fine weather, superb view of the city from the streets along the water opposite St Paul's (plate 74). St Paul's (plate 75) particularly striking, also Southwark Bridge.

We walked through a poor part of the city, and took a boat to the tunnel[318] (plates 77 and 78). A steam-engine with 2 horizontal cylinders pumps the water out in the 20 ft wide bricked well. The boiler is outside it, the steam is channelled into the building. Work has progressed as far as the edge of the river. More moisture seeps through at the entrance than at the further end; the earth seems more compact nearer the river; the connections between the two tunnels will be dug later, they were in the process of digging the first of these; the vault is three bricks thick. The sections or rings are bricked together without any bonding, with Roman cement ¾ in. thick. They progress 2 ft per day; 10 ins are always left clear of the roof for the bricking of the vault. Light for the work is provided by transportable gas (plate 76).

Mr Brunel told us that there was a problem because a slight curve in the tunnel would have to be made at this point. He is confident of the success of the project. The Commission finds everything satisfactory. He has already built several tunnels in Chatham,[319] to rechannel sea water. When the work was finished everything would be as dry as a living-room. Giant screws move forward the ramming machine, which is made entirely of iron.

To the East India Docks: a Chinese clipper was brought in, large ships of all kinds, all armed. Drive back in the city coach to the boat.

To Captain Browne's chain factory.[320] Testing machine, a chain was burst under a pressure of 8,000 hundredweight, 3 men operated the machinery.

Return journey, half by water (expensive), then by coach.

Drive to Islington, to Mr Bischoff, there had been a misunderstanding, however; the invitation had been for 2 days later, but we were nevertheless kindly received. We had quite a pleasant evening in the family circle, there was indifferent music,

[317] Marc Isambard Brunel (1769–1849), engineer, bridge and ship builder, originally from France; in England from 1799. The Thames Tunnel was his most famous achievement (see note 318).

[318] In 1825 work was begun on what was to be the first successful tunnel under the Thames, from the London Docks to Rotherhithe. It was designed by M.I. Brunel (see note 317), who had invented a new tunnelling system. It was the greatest engineering achievement of its time (directed by Brunel's son, Isambard Kingdom Brunel). It was over 400 metres long and consisted of two parallel tubes. It ran into serious problems in 1827, when the river broke in, and it was not completed until 1843 (*OHT*, 463–4).

[319] Since the sixteenth century the Royal Dockyard had been sited at Chatham, at the mouth of the Medway.

[320] Sir Samuel Brown (1776–1852), a naval officer, took out a patent for flat wrought iron links in 1817. They were adopted for Telford's Menai Bridge (see p. 188), and for many other suspension bridges (*OHT*, 459–60). Beuth had visited the factory already in 1823 (Wegner, 125, note 54).

77. B. Dixie and T.T. Bury, *The Thames Tunnel*, coloured aquaint

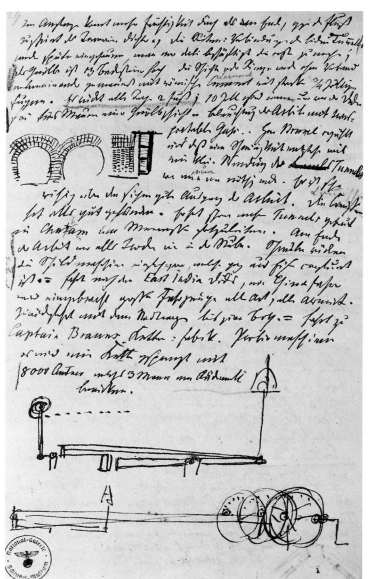

78. *Journal*, p. 29, (upper left) The Thames Tunnel, section showing the brick casing, and view of the boring apparatus (see fig. 5 on plate 76), (bottom) Brown chain factory, sketches of a machine for testing chains

80. David Wilkie, *The Blind Fiddler*, oil painting. Tate Gallery, London

79. Anonymous, *The National Gallery, 100 Pall Mall*, lithograph; part of a print contrasting the meagreness of the British National Gallery with the splendour of the Louvre

81. *Journal*, p. 31, Londonderry House, plan of the entrance hall and stairwell, and section of the staircase showing the gallery and vaulted ceiling with overhead lighting

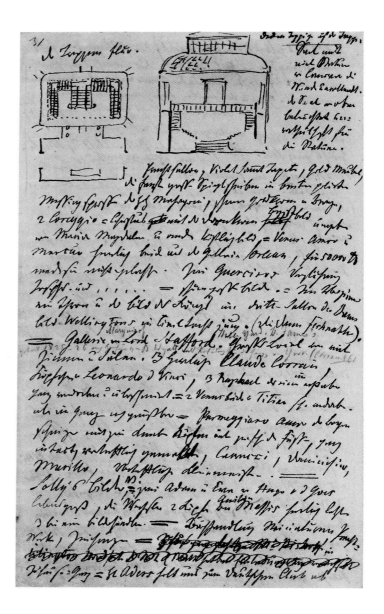

we looked at books etc. (spoke French, they replied in English). House pleasantly situated, with space all round. Walk back through the city, about ¾ mile.

Wednesday, 7 June

We learned of Weber's death,[321] Herr Dannenberger[322] from Berlin visited us. At 10 o'clock I went to the National Gallery[323] (plate 79) (the others went to Deptford) – Hogarth's paintings full of genius and intellect.[324] Solly found me there and showed me the pictures. Claude Lorrain wonderful, they seemed to me absolutely authentic. Poussin's landscape magnificent. Sebastiano del Piombo, Awakening of Lazarus from the Dead, large sumptuous painting, the figure of Christ in robes with superbly styled folds, the whole in wonderful colours, beautiful heads, somewhat full in composition and occasionally reminiscent of Michelangelo. – Correggio: small picture, 1 ft high, 7 ins wide (pearl), Mother and Child, the child seen from the front, has his shirt pulled up over his stomach and his little legs wide apart, the mother is holding one of the child's hands loosely in hers, she is pressing the child's arms to her breast. – 3 Rembrandts. – Nicolas Poussin. – Copies of Titian by his pupils, good. – Copies of Correggio, Christ on the Mount of Olives, black.[325] – A Rubens landscape,[326] excellent like those in the Pitti Palace in Florence. – Minor painters Teniers, Van de Velde, Potter, also landscapes of the English school[327] and genre pieces. The painter Wilkie[328] (plate 80) is extremely graceful in his domestic scenes, has a genius for colour, character and effect, his tone is mild and harmonious, both the light and dark colours are toned down.

Solly took me to Lord Londonderry's house[329] (plate 81) sumptuous, 80,000 pounds income. – The hallway and stairs. Thick carpets on the staircase. Room with many statues by Canova,[330] the walls unfinished. The room lit from above, unfavourable for the statues. Magnificent drawing-room, purple velvet wall-coverings, golden furniture, the windows large panes of glass in the best polished brass mullions, the wood mahogany, heavy gold-coloured bronze chandelier, 2 Correggios: Christ with Crown of Thorns,

[321] Carl Maria von Weber (born 1786) had died of tuberculosis in London two days earlier, on 5 June. He had come to London in March, and on 12 April had conducted the first performance of his opera *Oberon*, which had been commissioned by Covent Garden Opera.

[322] Johann Friedrich Dannenberger (born 1786), textile manufacturer, from 1812 owner of a textile-printing works in Berlin. Co-founder of Beuth's *Verein zur Beförderung des Gewerbefleisses* [Association for the Promotion of Trade and Industry] in 1821. During his frequent visits to England he acquired technological ideas which he put into practice in Berlin.

[323] The basis for the National Gallery, founded in 1824, was the banker John Julius Angerstein's collection of 38 paintings, which were kept at his house at 100 Pall Mall until 1834. A special gallery was built for them in 1832–8. Paintings from other collections were also displayed.

[324] The following paintings mentioned by Schinkel in the National Gallery can be identified:
1. Hogarth's *Marriage-à-la-Mode* and *Self-portrait*
2. Claude Lorrain, *Landscape with Death of Procris*, *Landscape with Narcissus*, *Landscape with Isaac and Rebecca*, *Seaport*, *Embarkation of the Queen of Sheba*
3. N. Poussin, *Landscape with figures*
4. Sebastiano del Piombo, *Raising of Lazarus*
5. Correggio, *Holy Family*
6. *Woman taken in Adultery*, *Adoration of the Shepherds* and *Christ taken from the Cross*.

[325] Apart from *Christ on the Mount of Olives*, there were 'two groups of heads' in the collection, according to contemporary sources.

[326] Schinkel is probably referring to the *Landscape with the Château de Steen*.

[327] Schinkel is possibly referring to Richard Wilson's *Maecenas's Villa* and *Landscape with Apollo and Diana*, already in the collection by 1826.

[328] David Wilkie's (1785–1841) *The Blind Fiddler* (1806) and *The Village Fête* (1809–11) already belonged to the National Gallery by 1826 (both now in the Tate Gallery).

[329] Londonderry House in Park Lane, built 1760–5 by James Stuart and rebuilt 1825–8 by Benjamin Wyatt for Charles William Vane, Marquis of Londonderry (1778–1854, general and statesman). The interior, which included a magnificent art collection, particularly classical sculptures, was one of the most sumptuous in London along with those of Lancaster House (see note 333) and Apsley House (see note 247).

[330] The most important of these was the early work *Theseus and the Minotaur* (1782), now in the Victoria and Albert Museum.

[331] This great collection of paintings formerly owned by duc Philippe d'Orléans, originally in Paris, had been sold in England in 1793 and 1798. The two Correggios are now in the National Gallery.

[332] According to Francis Russell, the two Guercinos are clearly *Joseph and Potiphar's Wife* and *Amnon and Tamar*, now in the National Gallery of Art, Washington, D.C. (see *Burlington Magazine*, July 1991, *Guercino in Britain* supplement, 10, figs. 11 and 12).

[333] Stafford House, later known as Sutherland House and York House and now Lancaster House, was built 1820–7 for the Duke of York, by Robert Smirke and continued by Benjamin Wyatt, and later enlarged. At the centre of the rich interior was a gallery containing an important collection of paintings, although it is not mentioned by Schinkel.

[334] Here and later, Schinkel confuses these with paintings in the nearby Bridgewater House. K.F. Waagen mentions four paintings by Claude Lorrain in the Bridgewater Gallery in *Art and Artists in England*, 1838: *Morning Landscape*, *Morning Landscape with Shepherds*, *Landscape with Moses and the Burning Bush*, and *Landscape with an Old Man*.

[335] The head of a girl by Bernardino Luini (*c*.1475–1532) in the Bridgewater collection was once attributed to Leonardo da Vinci.

[336] These are the Bridgewater Madonna (*c*.1508), now on loan to the National Gallery of Scotland, Edinburgh, and the *Holy Family under the Palm-tree* (*c*.1508). There is no record of a third painting by Raphael.

[337] These are *Diana and Calisto* and *Diana and Actaeon* (both 1559), now on loan to the National Gallery of Scotland, Edinburgh.

[338] In his description of the Bridgewater Gallery (see note 334) Waagen mentions one painting by Parmigianino, eight by Lodovico and Annibale Carracci, and six by Domenichino. There is no mention of Murillo.

[339] Edward Solly, who had sold most of his collection of paintings to the Prussian government in 1821 (see note 226), also owned other, mainly Italian, pictures.

[340] Johann Karl Ludwig Schorn (1793–1842), art historian, worked in Munich and Dresden, then published *Schorns Kunstblatt* in Stuttgart. From 1826 Professor at the University and Academy in Munich. In 1826 he travelled to Holland and England. There he called on John Flaxman, among others. In 1833 he was invited to reorganize the Art School in Weimar, and in 1835 the Grand Duchess asked him to commission Schinkel to design a Goethe gallery in the Palace of Weimar.

half-length, enfolded by Mary Magdalene, and a round, superb picture, Venus, Cupid and Mercury, magnificent, both from the Galerie Orléans,[331] they could not have been bought for less than 50,000 pounds. Two Guercinos: the Kidnapping of Joseph and [illegible]- large, beautiful pictures.[332] – In the anteroom a throne and a picture of the King in the third drawing-room and of a lady, a picture of Wellington in civilian clothing, young. (The lady fashionable.)

Lord Stafford's gallery.[333] Large, with many rooms and halls. 3 wonderful Claude Lorrains,[334] small head by Leonardo da Vinci,[335] 3 Raphaels, only one genuine, but quite ruined and smudged.[336] – 2 Venus pictures by Titian,[337] in bad repair, but on the whole still worth seeing. – Parmeggiano [*sic*]:[338] Cupid the archer, with two boys' heads below between his feet, quite intact, excellently executed; Carracci, Domenichino, excellent minor painters. – Solly's pictures:[339] two of Adam and Eve by Hugo van der Goes, lifesize, the money-changers, 2 heads by Quentin Massys, superb, the last 3 with a dealer. – Bookshop: miniatures, wonderful examples, drawings. – Went home.

Herr Aders called for us to take us to the German Club, Professor Schorn[340] from Munich, poor music, English formality, song books (*Freut euch des Lebens*) – Haymarket Theatre[341] (Paul Pry), terrible auditorium, rectangular, lit without gas, dark. A pleasant aria. Packed house, at the beginning we had to stand on the stairs to the stalls.

Thursday, 8 June

Mr Bischoff fetched us to go to a special festival in St Paul's[342] (plate 82), he had managed to get tickets in the front row. Many thousands of children were standing in 16 rows on a high semi-circular podium under the dome.[343] Every parish had dressed its

[341] The Haymarket Theatre, dating from 1720, had been rebuilt by John Nash in 1820/1.

[342] Schinkel revisited St Paul's on 3 August, taking special note of the impressive dome construction which was to influence his plans for centrally-planned churches (Nicolaikirche in Potsdam and suburban churches in Berlin).

[343] This was the occasion of the Anniversary Meeting of the Charity Children.

82. R. Havell, *Anniversary Meeting of the Charity Children in St Paul's Cathedral*, 1826, watercolour. Museum of London. This is the actual ceremony that Schinkel attended

children differently, in simple and attractive clothes; each one had a banner with an inscription on it, the children of each parish were led into the church by stout old beadles with silver staffs, and were put in their allotted places. The Duke of Gloucester[344] was present, also the Lord Mayor with 2 Sheriffs. A clergyman read the psalms etc. from a low pulpit, the Bishop of London gave the sermon from the higher pulpit. Chorales on the organ and sung by the children. Many thousands of people in the church. Later we looked down from the organ loft and had a good view of the packed building, we could see right down onto the podium. The magnificent Lord Mayor's and Sheriffs' equipages at the entrance below me, in front of the former a great sword was carried and prominently affixed to the splendid coach, everything was stiff with gold. The Lord Mayor's costume is a scarlet coat with fur and a gold chain. Everything very ceremonial. – Many thousands of people round the church, which we could see quite well from our hotel. – Herr Schiffert from Berlin and his father-in-law were also in the church. – Drive to Herr Aders's party, very good supper, in the evening excellent music, the little Schulz brothers from Vienna, virtuosi on the piano, guitar and harmonium, with their father. – A French lady sang Rossini wonderfully [4 illegible words]. – Other ladies and a gentleman sang Scottish songs and other things in harmony, Madame Aders's Goethe songs.

Friday, 9 June

Good weather at 9 o'clock on the journey to Brighton, 12 German miles covered in 5 hours. I sat inside, the others outside. – The countryside is a garden, magnificent trees and luxuriant green. Lord Conyngham[345] had refused the Ambassador's request for permission for us to view the Pavilion in Brighton, as the King does not allow anyone in; but later he wrote again, and apparently when the King heard that it was me he then gave his permission. (The journey costs 1 pound 1 shilling, and 2½ shillings tip for the coachman from everybody.)

Arrived in Brighton at 5 o'clock, had a meal, then walked along the sea to the Chain Pier[346] (plates 83 and 84), which is only a

[344] William Frederick, Duke of Gloucester (1776–1834), son-in-law of George III, from 1816 invested with the title Royal Highness.
[345] Lord Steward of the Royal household, his wife was reputedly George IV's mistress.
[346] In 1822/3 the Chain Pier had been built in Brighton, a three-span landing stage 345 metres long. On each side four lengths of chain hung down between the cast iron posts, bearing the bridge itself. It was built by Captain Samuel Brown and others. Schinkel had visited 'Browne's chain factory' in London on 6 June (see note 320).

84. John Constable, *The Chain Pier, Brighton*, 1827 oil painting. Tate Gallery, London

83. *Journal*, p. 33, (top) Brighton, beach and Chain Pier, (below) detailed studies of the Chain Pier: section with measurements, and a chain link from two views, (middle right) St Mary's Chapel, detail of Doric capitals, which Schinkel found to be 'badly constructed', (bottom) Brighton Pavilion, kitchen. The sketch on the far left shows the steam outlet system, and those on the right the roasting apparatus, inscr.: 'spit, vertical roast, 7″ & 8″, where the coal is placed underneath', (Middle left) is a section of the kitchen, inscr.: 'the kitchen supported by 4 palm trees'

85. C. Fielding and A. Pugin, *Brighton Pavilion, West Front,*
1824, from J. Nash, *Views of the Royal Pavilion at Brighton,*
1826, aquatint

86. *Brighton Pavilion, the Kitchen*, from J. Nash, *Views of the Royal Pavilion at Brighton*, 1826

87. *Brighton Pavilion, the Corridor with Staircase*, from J. Nash, *Views of the Royal Pavilion at Brighton*, 1826

88. *Journal*, p. 34, (top) Brighton Pavilion, details of staircase: 1. steps from the top, inscr.: 'a. Grey, granite-like cloth b. red cloth striped c. screwed-down bronze plate'. 2. sketch beneath, step from front, inscr.: 'front view broken through' 3. far right, side view of steps, inscr.: 'side view broken through' 4. middle, detail of bannister on staircase, (upper right) perspective view of the ceiling of the Banqueting Room, (below right) wall hangings in the Music Room

landing stage for ships and steamers. At the sea end the chains are fixed to the posts which have been rammed in, and held fast in bolted blocks. 4 chains each side. The town spreads out along the coast, a fine sight from the seashore. The deck over the sea is planked with wood. Pleasant promenade along the sea. The entrance and exit are controlled by a turnstile which takes a toll of 2 pence. New church in medieval style.[347] – New church, Doric, brick columns, the arched lintels in the architraves very inaccurately constructed.[348] The Royal Pavilion[349] (plate 85) from outside in the Moorish style of royal tombs in India. Huge glass dome. The citizens of Brighton have started to spoil the King's view of the sea from the Pavilion by building in front of it, so the King wants to pull down the Pavilion; he does not come to Brighton any more. Went back to the Old Ship Inn on the seafront.

Saturday, 10 June

We learned that Count Lottum and Count York had come to Brighton on the night-coach, to join us in seeing the Pavilion. We all walked again to the Chain Pier in the hot sun, the three counts went in the sea, then we went to find the man who had been recommended to show us the Pavilion.

The interior of the building is magnificent. First the kitchen[350] (plate 86), all the apparatus for cooking with steam, very fine; table with an iron plate into which the steam can be fed, on which everything can be kept warm. Iron pots, into which the steam is fed inside double walls, with stopcocks to siphon off the condensed water. Cooking apparatus with coal (see plate 83) The kitchen is held up by 4 palm trees. Sheet-metal dome.

After a long corridor (plates 87 and 88) one enters a pleasant, long, low gallery, where at each end light steps lead upwards and allow light through. The banisters are of cast iron, in a delicate imitation of bamboo tracery.

1) State Banqueting Room[351] (plate 89). Wall-covering of shimmering silver material (painted), various groups of Chinese figures. Dome culminating in a banana-tree, the chandelier also

[347] St Peter's, built 1824–8 in neo-Gothic style by Charles Barry.
[348] Either St Mary's Chapel, a building with Doric columns, completed in 1827 by the architects Clarke and Wilds, or, as suggested by Wegner, (128, note 64 and fig. 48) Christ Church, New Road, Brighton by A.H. Wilds.
[349] Since 1784 the Prince of Wales, had shown increasing interest in visiting Brighton, and commissioned Henry Holland to design a country house there. It contained Chinese elements and was enlarged around 1800. Plans by Humphrey Repton for further alterations, which were not carried out, introduced Indian themes. Nash worked on the building 1815–21.
[350] The Great Kitchen, built in 1816, before most of Nash's alterations, was considered to be a technological marvel, with all the latest cooking devices (J. Dinkel, *The Royal Pavilion*, Brighton, 1983, 89).
[351] The most spectacular tour-de-force in the Pavilion, a domed room in the Chinese style, with an extraordinary chandelier stemming from a gigantic cluster of plantain leaves.

89. *Brighton Pavilion, The Banqueting Room*, from J. Nash, *Views of the Royal Pavilion at Brighton*, 1826

90. *Brighton Pavilion, The Music Room*, from J. Nash, *Views of the Royal Pavilion at Brighton*, 1826

of the same tree. Candelabra of Indian porcelain, vases and banana forms. – Various stained glass in the lunette. Long banqueting tables.

2) Gallery,[352] white and gold, palm trees.

3) Domed hall.[353] In the ceiling a painted gold-leaf dragon. Crimson and yellow wall-covering (French taste), but embossed with an elegant silver frieze. – Tables with inlaid work, sumptuous chairs in gold.

4) Gallery,[354] white and gold, palm trees.

5) Great state room[355] (plate 90). Organ. The walls laquered in crimson, with Chinese landscapes painted in gold, the dome imitation mother-of-pearl. The four corners of the ceiling in laquered wood and scaled like a gallery. Magnificent fireplace of white marble. Dragons everywhere. 8 Chinese towers forming a candelabra of porcelain, genuine.

The small rooms upstairs, almost all for ladies, Chinese, the upper gallery and corridors have stained-glass ceilings to provide light. Upstairs there are fine ivory models of ships etc. (genuine), very delicately worked.

The stables[356] (plates 91 and 92) built around a large glass-domed building 85 ft in diameter. Each individual stable with 3–5 horses has its own ventilation. Too hot inside, really crazy: it was designed to be a greenhouse.

The riding arena. Covered walk in the garden from the Pavilion to the stables, lit by glass globes on the lawn. The whole very pleasant.

Return journey to London in glorious weather from 3 to 9, I sat outside, in the coach a bride, bridegroom and sister; I spent the first half of the journey looking at them, which task I then left to Count Lottum.

[352] Presumably the South Drawing Room, decorated, though unemphatically, in the Chinese style.
[353] The Saloon, designed by Robert Jones in 1823.
[354] The North Drawing Room, also in the Chinese style.
[355] The Music Room, with the Banqueting Room, the most dramatic space in the Pavilion. It is dominated by a large organ at one end, and has large Chinese landscapes on the walls. It was designed and executed by the Crace family workshop.
[356] The round stable building in Brighton (later the 'Dome', used for balls and concerts) was built 1804–8 by William Porden. With its great dome 24 metres in diameter it was one of the most important early glass-and-iron buildings in England.

91. *Brighton Pavilion, the Stables,* from J. Nash, *Views of the Royal Pavilion at Brighton,* 1826

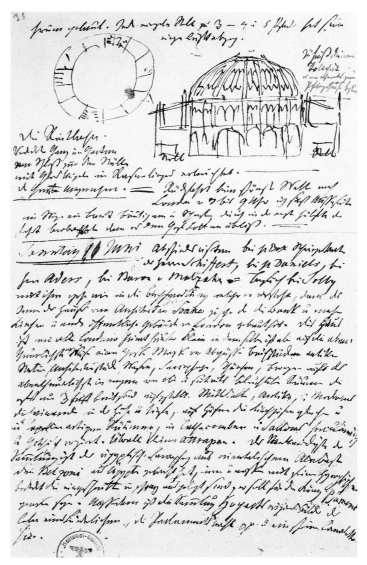

92. *Journal,* p. 35, Brighton Pavilion, Stables, plan and section

London, 10 June 1826

Dearest Susanne. You will by now I hope have got my letter from London in which I acknowledged receipt of your letter in London and told you of my pleasant crossing from France. Now I must again give you news of my stay here, as I shall be leaving London in a few days to go into the country. You can imagine how full every day has been; I now know London quite well, there are only a few things left to see, some of which I shall save for when I come back from my journey into the country.

Everything here is enormous. The city is, it seems, never-ending; if you want to visit three places you need a whole day; even within the town distances are reckoned in miles when you go by carriage. 10,000 houses are built every year, all speculative, and they are made to look attractive by all sorts of peculiar forms. You often see long rows of grand houses, which in fact are nothing but groups of private houses 3 or 4 windows wide, all joined together by a common architectural style.[357]

I have seen the museums, many private galleries, exhibitions, churches, the Raphael cartoons in Hampton Court, the famous Richmond, Greenwich, Woolwich, the work on the tunnel underneath the Thames, Maudsley's big mechanical workshop, the great gas installations for the city, the London Docks, West and East India Docks, many architectural interiors in private houses and in the homes of the wealthiest lords, and yesterday I returned from Brighton, where we had gone the day before to see the Chain Pier and the Royal Palace. Permission to see the latter was at first refused to our Ambassador by Lord Conyngham, because the King has given strict orders that people should no longer be allowed to visit this remarkable oriental building, as he wishes to pull it down in his anger at the citizens of Brighton, who have spoiled his view of the sea by building private houses. But when the King learnt that *I* had come on purpose to see the building, he made an exception and instructed Lord Conyngham to allow us in, and also to visit Windsor, where we go tomorrow. We covered the distance to Brighton, 12 German miles, in 5 hours, 4 horses at full gallop all the way; I tried to spend part of the journey outside, as you see so

357 In effect the new buildings around Regent's Park were narrow terraced houses behind common façades (see p. 14).

much more that way. In summer almost everyone rides on the outside.

We have enjoyed much pleasant and interesting company, at Solly's house and his brother's, at a Mr Bischoff's house, where we appeared for dinner on the wrong day owing to a misunderstanding on Beuth's part, but were nevertheless very well received and could appreciate all the more the private family life of an Englishman. On 7 June we attended a grand festival of orphan children from all the London parishes in St Paul's Cathedral; Mr Bischoff kindly obtained seats for us among the peers right next to the dome and very near to the Duke of Gloucester. Beneath the dome a large podium had been erected with about 16 rows on top of one another for the children. Thousands of well-dressed children were lined up, each parish with a different costume and marching in with a banner. The Lord Mayor of London and two Sheriffs were also present on this festive occasion, arriving in splendid state equipages stiff with gold; the former had a great sword carried in front of him, there was a sermon by the Bishop of London, and choir and organ music, and all the children joined in very well in unison. Thousands of people filled the church and the streets outside. At the end of the service we were taken up to the organ loft to have a view of the church and podium from above, which was really very impressive.

As always I long for letters from you, but I doubt whether I shall receive further news of you before we leave London. I often think of you all very fondly, and hope and pray that you are all well. The time is also approaching when you will be on your way back to Berlin, where you will perhaps have a quieter life. I am not sure what the situation is regarding letters sent from other parts of England, but I shall be sending brief news from various places, please do not be anxious if letters do not arrive punctually, this does happen on occasion.

I am in excellent health. I find the way of life here most congenial: we get up at half past 6, write our journals, then breakfast on tea, rolls, butter and eggs, go out at 9 to look at buildings etc., come back tired out at 6 for something to eat or go on to somebody's house, where we have a great deal of rich food, and if we are not going to the theatre we go to bed at about 11.

Unfortunately I cannot seem to do anything about my spoken English; I find people's accents particularly difficult and never understand what they are saying. I've given up hope, as Count Danckelmann knows far more than I do and he is not faring much better. Sometimes when in company we have been able to get by quite well with French. I don't know whether I told you that I had a letter from Rauch in Paris to say that he arrived there on the day we left. He had not sent word that he would be there, and in Berlin we were given to understand that he probably would not be going to Paris.

Monday, 12 June 1826 – Farewell, dearest Susanne, I'll seal this letter today so that it can be posted in good time. My best love to the children, Wilhelm, Karoline and Mother. Your Schinkel.[358]

Sunday, 11 June

Farewell visits to Mr Box, Herr Schiffert's father-in-law, Mr Daniels,[359] Herr Aders, Baron von Maltzahn. – To Solly's, went with him to the bookshop which he runs. – Then we went to see inside the house of Soane[360] the architect (plate 93) who built the Bank of England and several churches and other public buildings in London. Like all private houses in London this house is small, but it contains a great number of casts, fragments of antique statues and buildings, vases, sarcophagi, little panels and bronzes, all exhibited in the most ingenious way, in the smallest of spaces lit from above and the side, often only 3 ft wide. Medieval, antique and modern works are intermingled at every level; in courtyards resembling cemeteries, and in chapel-like rooms, in catacombs and drawing-rooms, ornamented in Herculanean and Gothic styles. Everywhere little deceptions.

The most remarkable object of the collection is the Egyptian sarcophagus[361] made of eastern alabaster, which Belzoni brought back from Egypt, covered inside and out with delicate hieroglyphics carved and inlaid in black: it is said to have been made for King Psamenite. The collection of Hogarth paintings[362] is also here: the Rake's Progress, Election etc, also a fine Canaletto.

[358] The letter is no longer extant.

[359] This is perhaps William Daniell (1769–1837) or Thomas Daniell (1749–1841). Both, nephew and uncle, were well-known landscape painters and printmakers.

[360] John Soane (1753–1837), perhaps the most gifted architect in England at the time, had built himself a house in 1812–14, in Lincoln's Inn Fields. The interior was and remains extraordinary. The rooms were brilliantly designed to use natural light, and to display his varied collections, including paintings, sculptures antique and modern, architectural and ornamental fragments, and models and drawings of his own buildings: a private museum even during Soane's lifetime, it has been preserved in its original state (Sir John Soane's Museum). Soane became a member of the Royal Academy in 1806 and was responsible for, among others, the 1788–1808 rebuilding of the Bank of England (see note 273), 1811—14 Dulwich Art Gallery, and 1809–17 Chelsea Hospital stables.

[361] The alabaster sarcophagus of King Seti I (1313–1292 BC; not Psametich, as Schinkel suggests), discovered by Belzoni in 1815 near Thebes and acquired by Soane in 1824, was displayed in a specially constructed sepulchral chamber.

[362] The series of paintings Rake's Progress (1734–5) and The Election (1754–5) by William Hogarth (1697–1764). Soane's collection also included paintings by Canaletto and Turner.

93. J.M. Gandy, *Views of different rooms in Sir John Soane's house and museum*, 1822, pen and watercolour. Sir John Soane's Museum, London

94. J.P. Neale, *Lansdowne House, Mayfair*, 1815, from J.P. Neale, *Views of the Seats of Noblemen and Gentlemen*, 1818–29

363 Since 1824 Schinkel had been involved in plans for the rebuilding of Prince Karl of Prussia's summer residence at Glienicke on the Havel, near Potsdam. At the same time he was planning an extension of the palace of the Knights of St John in the Wilhelmplatz, which was to provide a town residence for Karl (built 1827/8). While in England, and especially in London, Schinkel acquired furnishings and new ideas for these buildings.

364 This had been built 1762–8 in Berkeley Square by Robert Adam. George Dance the Younger had built a sculpture gallery c.1792 which had been completed 1816–19 by Robert Smirke. Wegner illustrates the Salon (131, fig. 53). The collection of antiquities was particularly outstanding: some pieces came from Hadrian's Villa near Tivoli. Of the sculptures noted by Schinkel the following can be identified:

    a. Mercury. probably Michaelis 85, a version of a famous statue in the Louvre restored as Cincinnatus. The Lansdowne version notable for having the original head though not of the best quality. Found by Gavin Hamilton in Hadrian's Villa.

    b. Amazon. probably Michaelis 83, a work of high quality found by Hamilton in Tor Colombaro.

    c. seated Juno. Michaelis 87, a female figure seated, not thought to be Juno.

    d. restored Diomedes, Myron's Discobolos. Michaelis 89, a copy of the Discobolos restored by Cavaceppi as Diomedes. Found by Gavin Hamilton.

    e. Minerva head. Michaelis 93, colossal fragment of statue of type from Velletri to be found in the Louvre. Found in Roma Vecchia by Hamilton.

    f. Statue of a Roman emperor. Michaelis 63, probably Marcus Aurelius, of unusual size but of low quality. Found by Hamilton at Tor Colomabaro.

See A.H. Smith ed., A. Michaelis, *A Catalogue of the Ancient Marbles at Lansdowne House*, privately printed, London, 1889. Waagen (Vol. II, 150) notes that the reclining figure by Canova is a version of the classical *Hermaphrodite*, and that the Canova *Venus* is a copy of the *Venus Italica* in Florence.

365 Henry Petty Fitzmaurice, Marquis of Lansdowne (1780–1863), politician, was variously Home Secretary and Foreign Secretary after 1826. His father William Petty had bought the house in 1768 from the Earl of Bute, and begun the collection. Lord Darnley's collection was kept at Cobham Hall near Rochester and in London (see note 369).

Monday, 12 June

Changed money at Rothschild's for Edinburgh, Liverpool and Bristol. – Saw the Bank and Royal Exchange again. – Had a look around a beautiful glassware shop with Herr Dannenberger, vases, knife-handles, doorknobs, etc. of cut glass. – Small carpets for Prince Karl[363] Fireplaces also. – The collection and great house of the Marquis of Lansdowne[364] (plate 94), among the antique objects: Mercury, Amazons, a heroic female figure, Minerva, a seated Juno, restored Diomedes, Myron's discobolus, fine heads in the ancient style, a Minerva head like that from Velletri, statue of a Roman emperor, Canova's Venus Pitti, a reclining Venus, his last work, a cast of Hebe. These last are exhibited in two extremely tasteful rooms. Golden-yellow wall-covering and curtains, the walls hung with pictures, a yellow carpet with simple brown pattern, white pilasters painted with colourful arabesques, purple frieze, ceiling white, decorated with bright arabesques and pictures, old paintings in gold frames on the golden-yellow wall-coverings. Sumptuous mirror behind the sofa niche, furniture arranged all around in the room, mahogany doors, pleasing arrangement (plate 95). The Marquis[365] received us in his room, he had gout, very pleasant, a Lord Darnley was with him, offered to show us his gallery in town and in his country seat near Rochester.

    I went to Solly's, saw his pictures and discussed their value, then went to Regent's Park (plate 96) with him in glorious weather to see the new buildings there. Immense plan, all private houses built in palace-like terraces which have a view of the whole park with beautiful hills behind. There are artificial lakes and ponds in the park. Marylebone Church[366] (plate 98) is not without effect. – Walk home of over one German mile. – After a meal we went to see *Der Freischütz* at Drury Lane Theatre[367] (plate 97), dreadful depiction of the Wolfs' Glen, poor musical performance, also the oratorio *War*

366 St Marylebone New Church, built 1813–17 by Thomas Hardwick with a large Corinthian portico by Nash, looks across to Regent's Park through York Gate.

367 The Theatre Royal Drury Lane, the fourth on this site, was built 1810–12 by Benjamin Wyatt.

95. *Journal*, p. 36, Lansdowne House, panelled door, and corner of door frame

96. T.H. Shepherd, *Plan of the Regent's Park*, from *London in the Nineteenth Century*, 1827

97. T. Kearnan & G.B. Moore, *Interior of Drury Lane Theatre*, 1808, engraving

98. J. Coney eng. W. Wise, *St Marylebone Church*, 1817, engraving

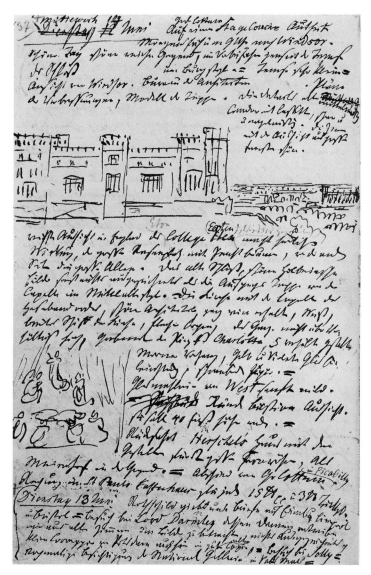

99. *Journal*, p. 37, (above) View of Windsor Castle from the Terrace, with Eton College at far right, (below) Rapid sketch of M.C. Wyatt's monument to Princess Charlotte in St George's Chapel, Windsor

and Victory,[368] where a Handel march from *Samson* was badly played. – It is a fine theatre, the boxes flush, gold pillars, crimson background with pilasters, white and gold balustrades, round ceiling, double proscenium, the first one a very narrow arch, the second with Corinthian columns which are however too high.

Tuesday, 13 June

Rothschild gave us letters to present in Edinburgh, Liverpool and Bristol. – Visited Lord Darnley, whose ladies we drove out of all the rooms so that we could view his pictures, nothing of excellence, small Caravaggio like the one in Potsdam,[369] also very good, a fine old copy. – Visited Solly. – Went to the National Gallery in Pall Mall again. – Walk to a plaster-castmaker, who had nothing of note. – Supper in St Paul's Coffeehouse. – Had a walk alone across Blackfriars Bridge to Westminster, the views, the light architectural style of the private houses, the roof-joists of the great Law Courts. – Back via Charing Cross.

From London to the North

(Oxford, Birmingham, Dudley, Derby, Sheffield, Leeds)

Wednesday, 14 June

To Windsor at 9 o'clock in the morning with Count Lottum, sitting outside on a stagecoach. Beautiful day, fine rich countryside, passed . . . Country house on the other side of the Thames, castellated style.[370] Thames very narrow. View of Windsor (plate 99). Office of the architect [Wyattville][371] Improvement plans, model of the staircase. Details all indifferent, passage with coffering, heavy and irregular. The rooms with a view from large windows handsome.

Finest view in England. Eton College,[372] creates a magnificent effect, the great playing-fields with splendid trees, the wide avenue

[368] Probably the *Dettingen Te Deum* by George Frederick Handel, written in 1743.
[369] Schinkel is possibly referring to the *Portrait of a Young Woman* or the *Portrait of a Man with a Dark Beard*, both of the Caravaggio school and acquired for the Prussian collections as part of the Giustiniani collection in 1815. It is not possible to identify the paintings from Waagen's account of his visit to the Darnley collection (Vol. III, 17–20).
[370] This is probably Claremont House, built 1771–4 by Henry Holland and Capability Brown, but could also be one of the neo-Gothic buildings in Claremont Park.
[371] Jeffry Wyattville (1776–1840), who began the radical alterations of Windsor Castle for King George IV in the castellated style (see note 373).
[372] The buildings of Eton College, founded in 1440 by Henry IV, lie opposite Windsor Castle on the other side of the Thames.

on the other side. The old castle,[373] fine Holbeins,[374] nothing else of note apart from the chapel stairway in medieval style. The church with the chapel of the Order of the Garter,[375] beautiful architecture, kept in perfect condition, white, wide nave in the church, flat arch, the whole not disproportionately large. Monument for Princess Charlotte,[376] 5 veiled figures, marble curtain, yellow and violet glass lighting, hovering figure. – Stained glass by West,[377] subtle, restrained. Round bastion, view, it is to be made 40 ft higher. On the way back Herschel's[378] house with the stands for the great telescopes, a small estate.

Took our leave of Count Lottum in Piccadilly. Bill in St Paul's Coffeehouse: 15 pounds each and 3 pounds tip.

Thursday, 15 June

Drove to Oxford, the road to Windsor again. Windsor looked very well in the distance. The countryside the same character all the way. We rode outside (plate 100). Fine view of Oxford, wonderful drive in over a bridge, on the right a college with a fine tower,[379] the old buildings, a garden with huge trees within. On the left the trees round the Botanical Gardens. – Parliamentary elections, voters with banners and a great crowd of folk were coming towards us in the streets. We drove up to the Mitre Inn, where our waiter from St Paul's Coffeehouse had booked rooms for us; the innkeeper, a respectable old lady, received us very amiably. Candidates and their committees were at the inn, and the voters soon appeared with banners, cheering outside the house, and the candidates for the election made long speeches from the window upstairs, which were applauded and cheered; the women too, everybody was excited. A crowd from the other party tried to march past with their banners, but were not allowed through. There was some scuffling but after a while everyone calmed down. – Walk through and round the various colleges, then in the park next to one of these colleges, and saw boxing matches in a field. Four seconds were busy with the half-naked boxers, looking after them at the end of each round, washing the blood off them with vinegar and water, also brandy, and letting them rest on the knee of one of them. One was so

[373] Windsor Castle, begun by William the Conqueror and Henry I, had been enlarged under Edward III, and also in the following centuries.
[374] The paintings in the Picture Gallery included Holbein's portraits of Henry Guildford and Dierick Born.
[375] The late Gothic St George's Chapel (begun 1475) is one of the finest buildings in the Perpendicular style. It is also the chapel of the Knights of the Garter, an order founded by Edward III in 1350.
[376] In the chapel next to St George's Chapel stands the monument to the princess, showing her lying in state. It was designed by Matthew Cotes Wyatt and erected in 1825.
[377] A stained glass window showing the Adoration of the Shepherds, designed by Benjamin West (1738–1820), had been placed in St George's Chapel 1792–6.
[378] Friedrich Wilhelm (Sir William) Herschel (1738–1822), an astronomer originally from Germany, had been in England since 1757 and lived in Slough since 1786. He invented the reflecting telescope, and having discovered Uranus in 1781 went on to make numerous other astronomical discoveries.
[379] On entering Oxford from the direction of London across Magdalen Bridge, one sees Magdalen College (1474–81) on the right, with Magdalen Tower (1492–1505).

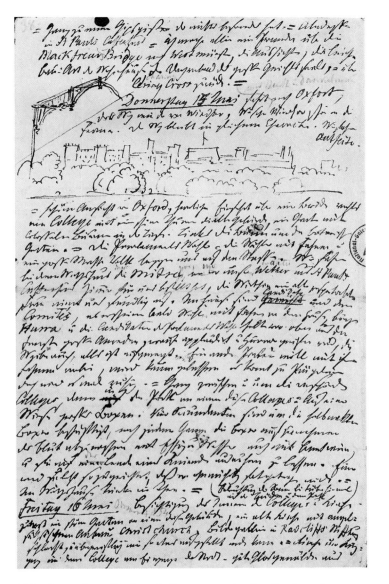

100. *Journal*, p. 38, (top left) apparently detail of roof construction of one of 'the great Temple Courts' seen on the way back from Windsor, (just beneath) a distant view of Windsor Castle

101. *Journal*, p. 39, (9th line down) tiny plan of Radcliffe Camera, Oxford, (near bottom left) sketch of part of the façade of an Oxford College

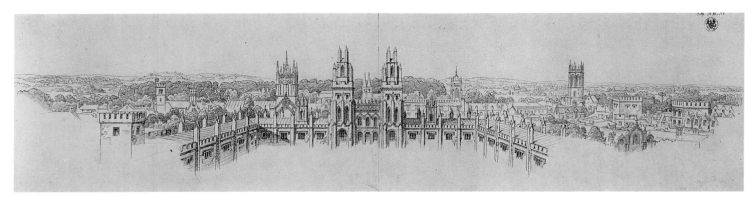

102. *Panorama of Oxford, looking into All Souls,* 1826,
pen and pencil

103. *Views of Magdalen, Merton and New Colleges,
Oxford,* 1826, pen and pencil (recto)

104. *Details of St Mary's Church, Oxford,* 1826, pen and
pencil (verso of plate 103)

beaten up that he was carried away unconscious. – Drank tea in the inn. – (Sunlight on the bridge and the park, grey sky.)

Friday, 16 June

Looked at interiors of colleges and churches. First a beautiful garden outside one of these buildings, an old church,[380] part of which is Anglo-Saxon, Christ Church. Picture gallery in Radcliffe's foundation, bad, incomprehensible how such things can be exhibited. – Chapel and cloister in the college at the entrance to the town [Magdalen] (plates 103 and 104). Good stained glass from Rubens's time, new glass opposite, vestibule of the church with an iron stove in the middle, where the smoke is drawn away under the floor. – Another courtyard and church at the entrance to the park, vestibule, 4 pinnacles on the tower. – Church in the main street,[381] the wooden roof construction without beams and with flat pointed arches, as small iron roofs are now made. – Library [Radcliffe Camera],[382] circular building with arches all round; 2 fine candelabra, especially the one with the 3 ibis figures. One can see clearly how the circular shape is retained in a triangle (plate 101). View from the gallery of the Library (plate 102) into the various colleges,[383] quite distinctive and opulent but very repetitive architecture. – Collection of natural history specimens and antiquities in another ponderous building[384] (next to it execrable herms), Druid rings in glass mosaic, perhaps Phonoecian. Models of Stonehenge near Salisbury. – The church of another college[385] with stained glass windows by the old Dutch school and that of West.

Tumult in the streets, election platforms, everyone carrying the flags and banners of his party, dark blue and light blue; the royal party seems to dominate in the county here,[386] where for the most part landowners live. The opposition is red and orange. – Two elected members of parliament on chairs garlanded with wild laurel, carried around the town by the people amidst dreadful music, all the windows, roofs etc were packed with onlookers. – Afternoon walk in the park, wonderful weather, walk round the town. – Trouble with a drunk at teatime in the sitting-room at the inn: he

[380] This could be either St Peter in the East or St Ebbe's.
[381] The university church of St Mary the Virgin, dating from the fifteenth century. The tower was begun *c*.1300.
[382] The centrally-planned Radcliffe Camera or Library, built 1737–48 by James Gibbs.
[383] The nearest are All Souls College (*c*.1440, 1720) and Brasenose College (seventeenth century).
[384] The Old Ashmolean Museum, next to the Sheldonian buildings, built 1679–83 for the collection of curiosities donated to the university by Elias Ashmole. The 'herms' must be the notorious stone heads outside the Sheldonian Theatre.
[385] The late Gothic chapel of New College, which has stained glass windows of Flemish origin and by Joshua Reynolds not Benjamin West.
[386] Schinkel presumably means Tories.

was smashing crockery. The landlady apologized to us and ticked-off the troublemaker, saying that her house was not going to be brought to shame: three of the most eminent gentlemen from Prussia were honouring her house and what were they to think.

Saturday, 17 June

Drive to Birmingham. Outside at 4 o'clock in Warwick, having passed a small spa[387] where a good deal of building was going on because some members of the royal family had made the town fashionable following a visit last year. – We had 3 hours in Warwick and saw the castle.[388] Magnificent vegetation. At the entrance through the gate there is a path hewn in the rock leading to the park, the walls are covered in ivy and wonderful plants, above is a most beautiful south-facing wood. You emerge in front of the castle, a splendid courtyard, the old towers and walls half concealed by tall trees wound about with climbing plants. Across a bridge and through a gate one arrives at a courtyard with a lawn; all around stands the whole ancient castle building, in perfect preservation, everything is covered in ivy and ancient trees grow high above the castle walls.

The whole of the interior is old and sumptuous, but not furnished until the seventeenth century. Fine pictures, portraits by Van Dyck and Rubens,[389] landscape by Poussin, Queen of Aragon by Raphael,[390] very fine picture. – Great hall of weapons: furniture with inlaid brass. – Etruscan vases, cinquecento bronze, wood panelling. Superb view from the windows, the whole resting on an 80 ft high foundation. Down by the castle an old-style mill, a ruined bridge with supports completely covered in green. – In the conservatory the great and famous Warwick vase[391] (see plate 107) found in Hadrian's villa in Tivoli and brought to England by Hamilton. About 6 ft in diameter. Beautiful park. At the exit in the gateway a huge punch-bowl is displayed, 3 ft in diameter, very deep, also the armour of the great Earl of Warwick etc. – Had an excellent meal at our inn and left at 7 o'clock in another stagecoach; on the way we were entertained by our co-passengers, factory workers and a farmer, who argued and joked with each other,

[387] Leamington, where mineral springs had been dicovered in 1797.

[388] Warwick Castle, the oldest part of which dates from the eleventh century (Caesar's Tower), was built mainly in the fourteenth and fifteenth centuries. In the sixteenth and seventeenth centuries it was extended as a castle, and is one of the most picturesque in England (see Wegner, 135, fig. 57).

[389] Waagen (Vol. III, 212–4) lists a number of portraits by both artists.

[390] This is a copy of the portrait of Johanna of Aragon, 1518/19 (Louvre, Paris). Waagen mentions it favourably but doubts its authorship (Vol. III, 213).

[391] This immense fourth-century BC marble vase was discovered in 1771 in Hadrian's Villa near Tivoli. It became one of the most frequently copied works of antiquity (now in the Glasgow Museum). Beuth and Schinkel included an engraving of it in Section II of their *Vorbilder für Fabrikanten und Handwerker* (see R. Marks and B.J.R. Blench, *The Warwick Vase*, Glasgow Museums, 1979, and note 393 for Thomason's full-size copy).

105. Anon., *View of Birmingham*, steel engraving

106. David Cox, eng. W. Radcliffe, *High Street Market in Birmingham*, 1827, engraving

another farmer galloped behind us all the way on a little grey.

At 10 in Birmingham (plate 105), we found a cramped space at the inn, the rooms are high up and have a view of the town which looks Egyptian with the pyramids and obelisks of the factory furnaces. The road goes uphill to the market, it was the Saturday-evening or night market, and driving in there felt like entering an amphitheatre full of people (plate 106).

Sunday, 18 June

The sight of an English industrial town like this is most depressing: nothing pleases the eye, and there is also the Sunday silence. Breakfasted with our Consul Mr Thomason, a pleasant elderly man with a good-hearted wife and a son. After walking around the cheerless town, with much poverty to be seen, I was persuaded that there was nothing here of any value to me. Some ugly churches – an awful bronze statue of Nelson[392] in the market-place notable only for a large ship's bow and [the admiral's] missing arm. Quite unremarkable redbrick houses for 120,000 inhabitants create a very melancholy impression. After our meal we spent the evening at Mr Thomason's, where I showed him my portfolio.

Monday, 19 June

Went to Mr Thomason's at 10 o'clock and saw his stock of silver-plated goods, bronzes, glass etc, and his factory. He has had the great Warwick vase cast in bronze[393] (plate 107): 4 workers produced the moulds over a period of 6 months, then it was worked on in the factory for 6 years, only to end up as a most wretched piece of manufacture on a huge scale; it must have cost him at least 12,000 thalers. All the sculptured parts look as if they are stuck on, which is why the thing is so deplorable; not one section of it is even moderately well modelled, it is all beneath criticism. Even worse is a bronze statue of the King of England, 6 ft high: any baker could do it better in dough. The factory is an antiquated affair; the man is rich and does not have to do much, being Consul for all the European powers. Visited a papier-mâché

[392] Westmacott's statue of Nelson, unveiled 1809.
[393] In fact the copy was made in iron, not bronze, but had a bronze finish to retard the corrosion which set in early. It is now in the grounds of Aston Hall, Birmingham (see Marks and Blench, op.cit. in note 391, 21). In their text in *Vorbilder für Fabricanten und Handwerker*, Schinkel and Beuth mentioned Thomason's method of reproduction: 'For manufacturers whom this concerns, it may be of interest to note that the manufacturer Thomason in Manchester [*sic*] has recently produced this vessel in the original dimensions in patinated bronze, with the handles and ornamentation in gilded bronze.' In 1826 a specimen found its way to Berlin, and in 1827 the vase was modelled for casting on a smaller scale in the Berlin iron foundry. Later, probably after Schinkel's death an enlarged version of the vase was set up on the top landing of the stairway of the Museum am Lustgarten (Altes Museum).

107. Medal commemorating the
casting of Thomason's life-size replica
of the Warwick Vase. Collection of
Mrs Ruth Rubinstein, London

factory and a wire mesh manufacturer. Anything of artistic merit is eclipsed by horrific surroundings.

Dinner at Thomason's, good English repast. First course: soup, salmon, roast beef, roast lamb, chicken pie, potatoes; second course: roast duck, pudding, peas, cream, fruitcake; third course: dessert and wine; the ladies had only one glass and then withdrew. Then the bottles circulated round the table. – Home at 10 and packed our luggage.

Tuesday, 20 June

Drive to Dudley. – Passed Boulton and Watt's[394] Park (inventor of the steam-engine). – Canal in Birmingham, 12 ft wide, 12 locks which the boatmen can open themselves, iron reinforcements on the lock walls. The locks are not filled through movable barriers in the gates, but through channels from the upper to the lower level. New canals are being built. Pleasant location, in the distance you can see the smoke of the ironworks, which stretch for miles.

Arrived in Dudley by post-chaise at 9, and drove to the ironworks straight after breakfast and tea. Overwhelming sight of thousands of smoking obelisks (plates 108 and 109). Coal, iron and lime are mostly brought up from the mines by winding engines. Then a big tholus for the glassworks etc. Only the cylinders of the steam-engines are under cover, the arm with the winder and the flywheel, also the boilers (2 boilers on each machine) are in the open.

Had a look at Gospel Oaks Ironworks[395] (plate 110), which is of horrific proportions. 15 steam-engines, canals, puddling furnaces, blast furnaces, rolling mills, tin-plating machinery, drills. The 3–4 inch thick iron from the annealing furnace is processed into fine sheet iron by 2 hammering machines, planing apparatus in front of the roller, operated each time by a boy pushing a lever with his hand and foot. A pair of cutters easily slices right through each 4-inch piece of iron. – Roof construction of iron. Very wide, shallow arch of brick, which bears a heavy load and shudders a good deal. Roof construction of iron and tiles. The columns also function as gutters for the water. Cylinder for a blower 9 ft in diameter very precisely angled.

[394] Matthew Boulton (1728–1809), engineer and machine-builder, and James Watt (1736–1819), engineer and inventor of the steam engine. In 1769 they joined forces and in 1784 started a foundry in Soho, Birmingham, which was continued by their sons after 1800.
[395] The Gospel Oak Iron Works was south-west of Wednesbury on the road out of Dudley (see W.K.V. Gale, *The Black Country Iron Industry*, 1979, 1812 map on front endpaper).

108. *View of the industrial scene around Dudley*: 'thousands of smoking obelisks', 1826, pencil

109. J.M.W. Turner, *View of Dudley*, 1832, watercolour. Lady Lever Art Gallery, Port Sunlight

By chance saw Wednesbury Oaks Iron Works,[396] a fine new well laid-out plant, on the way back to Dudley.

Return via Dudley castle;[397] in a park on a wooded hill lie the ruins of the castle, still moderately preserved, surrounding a courtyard, on one side an old half-ruined castle, on the other the rest of the buildings. Walls and stretch of grass, double moat and outer constructions; magnificent view, the hill in the park honeycombed with drains, caves, tunnels etc underground. In the afternoon we visited a glassworks in the town. Tholus 40 ft in diameter, 1½ bricks thick, the furnaces inside, apparently a Bohemian invention or at least introduced here 100 years ago by Bohemians. In Germany these thick shells for furnaces have generally been abandoned. Glasses, especially fired rims and wine-glass stems, are beautifully made here. – Drive back to Birmingham, view of the smoking ironworks (plate 111). Constant fine weather. Bought a padlock. Going to bed soon. In England every factory has a customs official allotted for the enormous duty payments. He keeps the raw materials under lock and key. The glass factories pay 8–10 pounds sterling on every hundredweight of cohering material. If it is exported, about 8 pounds sterling is refunded on the goods. Breakage and waste are not counted.

Wednesday, 21 June

Drive to Newcastle in a new stage at 7 o'clock, on the outside a young Catholic priest who spoke French, my neighbour. Conversation about languages, metre, poets etc., a very pleasant man. He got off in Stafford; my other neighbour, a good-natured young Englishman who made an effort to make himself understood and to teach me some English; he told me the names of everything we saw. He gave out oranges and let us taste from his bottle of cider. Breakfasted in Newcastle at 1, then drove by post-chaise half a German mile out of the town to Hetruria [*sic*][398] to see the Potteries;[399] a wide valley which contains as many potteries as Dudley has ironworks. Wonderfully Egyptian-oriental forms of the towns because of their factory buildings. Under the Wedgwood son Hetruria is no longer what it was under the father; since his time many larger works have sprung in the region.

[396] The Wednesbury Oak Iron Works was a short distance from the Gospel Oak works in the direction of Bilston. It does not appear in the 1812 map cited in note 395 above, but it is in the 1831 Ordnance Survey (see Wegner, 137, note 81 for bibliography).

[397] The ruins of Dudley Castle date from the eleventh to the sixteenth century.

[398] Josiah Wedgwood had built a factory in 1769 named Etruria for the industrial production of high-quality earthenware. He developed an unprecedented number of colours and shapes, and his influence was decisive throughout Europe in the adaptation of current ideas of taste for the Antique to relatively inexpensive pottery.

[399] From the 1760s onwards Wedgwood was able to distribute his wares throughout Europe, but he had to face competition from imitators. After his son took over in 1795 this competition increased greatly, and many of the imitators also set up their factories in the same area of Staffordshire, which became known as the Potteries.

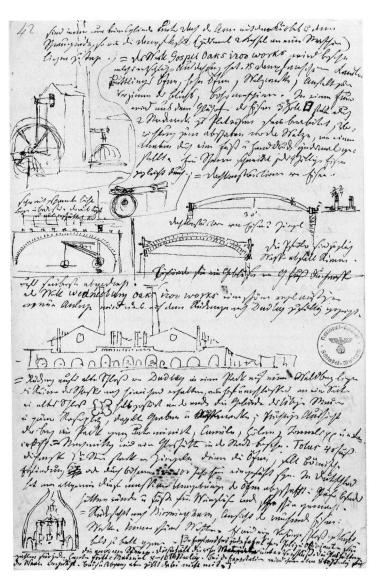

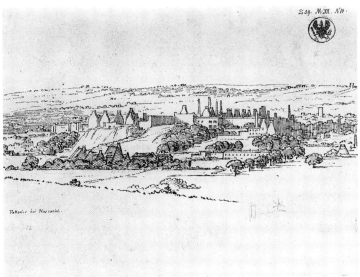

110. *Journal*, p. 42, (top left) Gospel Oak Iron Works, steam engine, (below left) detail of a sawing machine? (to the right) girder, with measurement 30′, with details of fastenings; (on the far left) brick arch with crane; (to the right) brick vault with iron fastenings; (below) view of Wednesbury Oaks Iron Works; (beneath left middle) groundplan of Dudley Castle; (bottom) Dudley, glassworks, section of furnace

111. Anon., *Bilston near Dudley*, ca. 1830, engraving

112. *Potteries near Newcastle*, 1826, pen and pencil

On the way back we saw many more potteries from the outside, most impressive plants in beautiful surroundings; from a church quite high up on a hillside we had a magnificent view of the region and all of the Potteries: I drew a part of it (plate 112). Got back to the inn in Newcastle at 5, wrote my diary while Beuth and Danckelmann visited a silk mill. Very good supper.

Thursday, 22 June

To Leek early in the morning by post-chaise. Many things of interest on the journey; you often see separate steps outside the houses for the women to mount their horses, for they could not swing over a high saddle without such steps when a groom rides in front of them. – Beautifully situated church, an ancient cross of little note, completely weathered. – Stone houses with gable windows decorated with balls and acroteria, thatched roof above. – Brick buildings with attractive mouldings and brick gables. Apertures for barns, storerooms and for the beam-heads (plate 113).

Fine factory building at the end of the town, quite new, most splendid position in the whole place. – Letter and appointment with Mr Badnal; we spent the time waiting for his return talking to his 3 sisters, pleasant ladies who even in the morning were well but simply dressed; the eldest takes precedence in England, she gave orders and was waited on by the others, but in a refined manner without any unpleasantness. Mr Badnal had us shown round a silk mill; a young man, the owner's son, was very willing to show us everything. Much impressive machinery (plate 114).

Nearby a tannery, the lye is brought up by pumps and spread through the whole building in pipes, the skins are hung up like sacks between iron frames and filled up with lye. In 3 weeks everything is tanned. The leather is grey, an artificially produced colour.

Continued on to Matlock, via Ashbourne, the scenery becoming increasingly mountainous, stone walls around green alpine meadows. – Beside the churches, which are all in the same style, ancient great yew trees, some of them thought to date back to Saxon and Roman times. Magnificent maple trees – splendid view

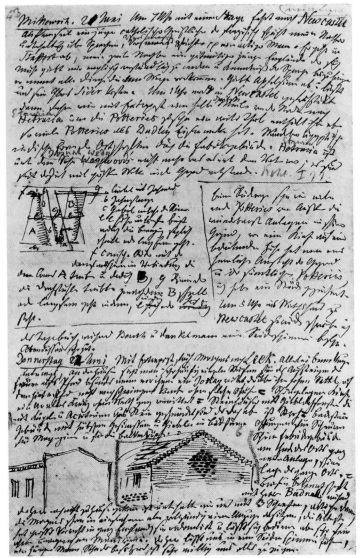

113. *Journal*, p. 43, (middle) diagram of rotating cones for regulating the speed of a potter's wheel, inscr.: 'a. crank with cog-wheel b. rack c. bracket, which moves the strap either higher or lower, so that the movement becomes slower or faster f. conical wheels connected to the steam engine, which drive cone A and through Bg drives the turntable, so that B goes fast or slow, according to how low or high it is fixed'; (bottom left) Leek, Staffs. house and barn

114. *Journal*, p. 44, Badnal's cotton mill, sketches of spinning apparatus, inscr.: 'a. wood with loops, through which the threads go, which by means of the hooks b and of the crank c, go in and out, so that the threads in the manner of d become wound around the bobbin. gg straps, which go snake-like through the iron rollers fff, through the ones behind and opposite, as the further ones become twisted, then through the attached bobbins, then wound on and around, to thread the cotton. Glass comb, over a glass tube, upon which the threads go with a device that keeps them still the moment the threads start to tear'

400 Richard Arkwright (1732–92) had constructed the first spinning frame in 1768, and in 1771 he built a textile factory in Cromford. His nearby country seat, Willersley Castle, was built 1789–90 by William Thomas.

401 William Strutt, FRS (1756–1830) owned one of the largest cotton mills of the time. It was a 200 ft long, six-storey building in which even before 1797 iron pillars and supports had been used, and a great number of spinning and knitting machines accommodated. Other buildings had been added by the time of Schinkel's visit. The reason for the refusal to allow Schinkel and Beuth to visit them may have been a not wholly unjustified fear of industrial espionage, for which Prussians were well-known (see Introduction, p. 12).

402 Dominique-Vivant Denon (1747–1825), General Director of Imperial Museums under Napoleon I. His own collection had been auctioned after his death.

403 This is one of the two Victory figures (Roman copies of Greek originals of the fifth century BC) which had stood outside the New Palace in Potsdam until 1806. They were taken to Paris by Denon (see note 402) and copied there.

404 The Derbyshire General Infirmary in London Road, Derby, had been not only funded but also apparently designed by William Strutt (see note 401), with the help of a local architect, and built 1806–10. It was a functional building well ahead of its time, with comfortable furnishings and modern equipment, and many of its more ingenious features would have derived from Strutt's experience with the great iron-frame mills at Belper. As Jeremy Taylor explains (see below), the doors of the water-closet operated within a kind of drum so that fresh air was brought in by the person entering and exiting, as well as from the ventilator noted by Schinkel. The construction of the baths in the basement also avoided any use of wood. A view of the Infirmary and a plan showing the water-closets are reproduced in J. Taylor, *Hospital and Asylum Architecture in England 1840–1914*, London, 1991, plates 1 and 2, and the system is discussed on pp. 1–3.

of Matlock valley. The entrance to the town is between high cliffs covered in wonderful vegetation (plate 116), which had been blasted to make a road through. In Cromford, seat of the famous Arkwright[400] (plate 115) who built the first cotton mill, beautiful country house in a park on top of the hill. Matlock is surrounded by cliffs covered in magnificent vegetation, at the foot of them is a river. Factory buildings below in the valley. The inn is on a plateau halfway up a hill outside the town, with a beautiful flower garden containing a huge maple tree, the branches 80 ft in circumference. The bathing huts of Matlock extremely picturesque on the slope opposite the cliff. We climbed the hill to the cave, which goes deep into the mountain, it is lit with many lights and they raise torches high up to show the rock fissures above. The path winds round as it goes up, and daylight filters through into the mountain down a narrow crack high up at the back. When we came out of the cave we bought a few small things made of the fluorspar which glitters inside the cave. Fine evening, Italian weather, beautiful sunset, supper. My bedroom has a magnificent view of the cliffs.

Friday, 23 June

A request sent by Beuth the previous evening by special courier, asking the cotton manufacturer Mr Strutt[401] in Belper for permission to see his factory (plate 117), the best in England, was turned down, so we drove straight through Belper and on to Derby. A request to Mr Strutt's brother, also a factory-owner, was, however, kindly received. He showed us his house and his pictures, for which he has built a special room; the furnishings are splendid, he has marble and bronzes, but all mediocre, bought at great cost. He has just acquired objects from Denon's[402] auction in Paris, among them the Potsdam Victoria[403] in bronze. Late cast or original?

Visited the famous Infirmary[404] with Mr Strutt, fine, pleasant building in every way. Magnificent staircase. The steps faced with lead plates. The famous hot-air heating (plate 118), water-closet with shutters, movement of air in and out of the rooms, the stale air is drawn off by a rotating ventilator on the roof. Very practical

115. W. Thomas, architect, eng. J. Cartwright, *Willersley Castle, Richard Arkwright's house*, 1805, engraving

116. Sketch of woody cliffs at Matlock, 1826, pencil

117. Anon., *Strutt's Mill at Belper*, mid-19th century, wood engraving

118. *Journal*, p. 45a, Derby, Infirmary, diagram, groundplan and section of a sanitary facility, inscr.: 'On the wall a b the tablets commemorating the donors are hung. in cc opening for light into the cellars. d place for the water closets. e a bar, which when pushed firmly, makes the door f open. and the bad air in k is drawn out through a hole in the ceiling, e comes to rest against the fixed wall g, one is then inside and the room is closed, then f rests in h. When going out one pushes the door h forward: the flap, after d has first opened the door, in the same way pushes the air back through the hole. In i is the entrance'

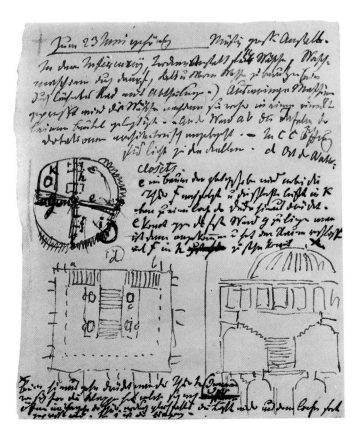

cooking equipment. Magnificent baths, a whole room, the anteroom through a canvas curtain, warmed by air wafted in from the bath. The doors made of slate, so that the steam does no damage, everything thought out to the last detail. – White lead factory, tall shot tower, wonderful view, pits, rollers, while the white lead is being separated from the lead it is sprayed with water so that contact with the harmful dust is avoided. Red lead (patent) boilers fed by steam. – Lancaster school,[405] circulation heating, the floors on an inclined plane, lavatories visible from the teacher's chair through a glass door. Heating with warm air to save wood, only moderately heated, but continuously. The flow of cold air always originates a long distance away, underground from clean, healthy locations, gas light. On our departure Mr Strutt was given a large bronze medal of Blücher. – Visited Mr Fox's workshop,[406] fine lathes, the famous planing machines, drills etc. Beuth placed a large number of orders. – After our meal we went to Mr Fox's workshop again, Count Danckelmann ordered a lathe, we were treated to soda water when we took our leave; this burly, pleasant man started his present large and successful enterprise as an ordinary workman. Visited another factory-owner, who makes kitchen ovens. – Then shop selling ornaments made of fluorspar,[407] where we bought a few small things. The owner showed us his workshop, very good sawing and cutting equipment. In the evening wrote my diary in the inn.

Fairly large area in the Infirmary for drying clothes, steam washing-machines, hot and cold water is used (a continuously turning wheel with compartments). Mangles, the washing is pressed after being placed in a square linen bag.

Saturday, 24 June

Drive to Leicester, short stay there, saw a new church in medieval style.[408] Buildings of this kind are much favoured in this area, but they are all the same, though this one has a vaulted ceiling. To Mr Simpson's house in Rearsby, he was not at home, we stayed for a while with his imposing-looking wife, who though a farmer's wife we found already very presentably dressed at 11 in the morning.

[405] A school designed on 'Lancasterian' principles of organisation, which involved older pupils teaching the younger under the direction of the teacher. It was pioneered in England by Joseph Lancaster, and was taken up especially by religious dissenters (P. Horn, *Education in Rural England 1800–1914*, New York, 1978, 34).

[406] James Fox of Derby, manufacturer of lathes and textile machinery, appears to have built a planing machine for metal as early as 1814 (*OHT*, 433).

[407] The particularly fine fluorspar formations in Derbyshire had been used for the production of bowls, vases, lamps, mantelpieces and other ornamental objects.

[408] Probably St George's Church, built 1823–6 by William Parsons.

The door was also opened by a servant in corduroy trousers [*Manchesterhosen*], so that everything was in the English-gentleman style. While we were there there was also a visit from a doctor and his wife, a pleasant man with whom we had some conversation. We did not wait until Mr Simpson's return, as he was probably staying in Leicester because of the election, and drove instead to the little town of Melton Mowbray, where Beuth expects to hear from him when we may see the local flocks of sheep, in order to purchase thirty cross-breeds from Leicestershire and Lincolnshire flocks for our government. Picturesque old church[409] (plates 119 and 120) in the town with an imposing tower and cruciform construction, very light. In 1556 the whole upper section was rebuilt, almost without a roof, with battlements all round, coffered ceiling the same shape as the roof in two oblique slopes. Terrible bells.

Sunday, 25 June

Wrote in the morning, in the evening I had another look at the church, walked around, sketched the church (plate 120). Mr Simpson has invited us for a drive to Knighton on Monday, to look at the best sheep in the district at his father-in-law's, Farmer Stone, then for a meal with him, and on Tuesday to see his farm, then to another meal with him, this time in company.

Monday, 26 June

Took the post-chaise to Rearsby, found the doctor still there, about to go, the post-horses were harnessed to Mr Simpson's carriage and we drove through Leicester to Farmer Stone in Knighton. We found Mr Stone to be a stout old Englishman, a family of one son and several daughters, not good-looking but quite stylish even this far out in the country. Saw the fat rams and ewes in the various paddocks, all very carefully shorn; rams 2 ft wide, very fine boned, all meat, no fat. The wool is long but not fine, meat seems to be more important here. – Breakfast in a cool conservatory. – Drive back to Leicester. Visited the gaol.[410] The prisoners on a treadmill. In the middle a chapel, above in the houses vaulted dormitories,

[409] The church in Melton Mowbray is a Gothic building dating from the late thirteenth and early fourteenth centuries. The tower is sixteenth-century Perpendicular. (Ill. Wegner, 140, fig. 63. Wegner also notes the importance of this church for Schinkel's later churches).

[410] The New County Gaol designed by William Parsons (d. *c.* 1860) was one of the two gaols under construction in Leicester during Schinkel's visit. It appears to have been built on rational principles defined by Jeremy Bentham, but was also castellated (*Buildings of England, Leicestershire*, 224).

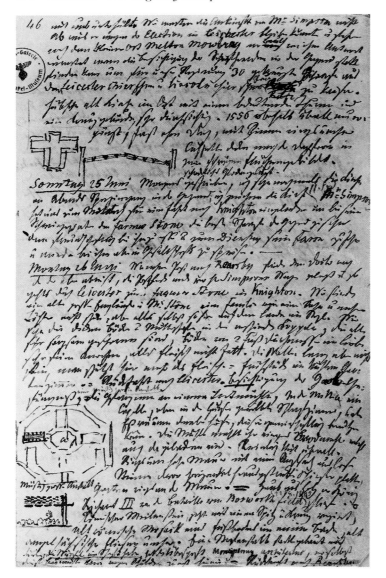

119. *Journal*, p. 46, (upper left) Melton Mowbray Church, groundplan; section of sloping coffered ceiling; (lower left) Leicester New County Gaol, groundplan; (below) part of a wall

120. Sketch of Melton Mowbray Church, 1826, pencil

121. C. Reis, eng. W. Wallis, *Sheffield*, steel engraving

below the dining-room, with yards next to them which they can use all together. The mill grinds their own flour, and the bread is baked there as well. Everywhere very clean. High walls all round topped with loose stones, horizontal slates sticking out in front of them, garden all round the wall. Fairly large institution.

House constructed of wood, where Richard III slept before the battle of Bosworth Field. – Roman milestone, now decorated with a point and a cross, ancient Roman mosaic in the floor of one of the bathrooms, old Anglo-Saxon tiles all round it. A prison,[411] sturdily built, columns with cubes in the shafts, has inscribed: Moneypenny architectus, who was himself the first to be imprisoned here for debt. – Return to Rearsby. Dinner. Mr Simpson, a simple, jolly country fellow, was quite entertaining. Drove back to Melton Mowbray at 10 o'clock.

Tuesday, 27 June

Beuth went back to Leicester on his own, to talk to Mr Robinson about sheep. Count Danckelmann and I drove to Rearsby at 11. Found old Mr Stone with his son and two clergymen already there, all in morning clothes having lunch (second breakfast). Mr Simpson went with us in the intense heat into the paddocks to show us his sheep and fine cows, the grass was scorched as there had been no rain for 4 weeks. Plough with double share, which does excellent work. Mr Simpson showed himself to be an able farmer, ploughed for us and rounded up the oxen and sheep, everything done with skill and method, in his picturesque garb of white hat, light grey smock, leggings and bootees of the same material. At dinner, very elegantly served in proper English fashion, with fine table linen, everyone was dressed in their best clothes and shoes. I talked to the clergymen in French about church affairs. After tea served in big silver vessels we returned to Melton Mowbray, having been warmly received in Rearsby and repeatedly assured by our host that we should always be welcome at Farmer Simpson's in Rearsby, Leicestershire.

[411] The County Gaol in Leicester had been built 1790–92 by George Moneypenny (born 1768 – date of death unknown), an architect who specialized in prisons. (Illustrated in Wegner, 141, fig. 64; see also notes 86–7 on p.142).

412 Nottingham Castle was built 1674–9 by Samuel Marsh.

413 All Saints' Church in Rotherham, a Perpendicular building.

414 Despite Schinkel's confusing reference to a 'Schloss' the house he visited was not Wentworth Castle but the nearby Wentworth Woodhouse with its magnificent east front and portico designed by Henry Flitcroft and begun 1734 (*Buildings of England, Yorkshire: West Riding*, 539 and ill. 596). The 'main hall' is presumably the Marble Saloon. The antique statue Schinkel mentions cannot be clearly identified as Michaelis did not visit the house, but there are occasional mentions of such a work, for which see the article by Nicholas Penny, to whom I am indebted, in the *Getty Museum Journal*, 1991. The tortoiseshell furniture was also one of the attractions of the house: a description of the house in the *Universal Magazine*, October 1770, 169f. singles out the Foggini *Sampson* group (now Victoria and Albert Museum) and 'a curious cabinet of tortoiseshell, ebony and ivory' (reference also due to Nicholas Penny). Waagen (Vol. III, 338–41) mentions several pictures by Van Dyck, and notes that the very expensive Raphael is a copy of one in the Pitti (house illustrated in Wegner, 142, fig. 65).

415 Friedrich Leopold Bürde (1792–1849), painter of horses and battles, resident in Berlin. Brother of Heinrich Bürde (see note 560).

416 Joseph Rodgers and Sons, founded 1724, were well-known for razors and penknives, and had a famous showroom which was set up in the 1820s. It became the largest cutlery factory in the world (see G. Tweedale, *Sheffield Steel and America*, Manchester, 1987, 129–30).

Wednesday, 28 June

Drive to Sheffield in a post-chaise, reached Nottingham at midday; castle[412] splendidly situated on a cliff, the rest of the town similarly hilly, walked to the end of the town where there was a pleasant flower garden on a terrace alongside pretty, isolated houses. (Lovely chapel.) Large, interesting market-place. – Continued on to Mansfield and Chesterfield, a twisted church spire, reached Sheffield at 8 o'clock. Smoke from hundreds of tall obelisks (plate 121). Grey, smoke-filled town built on hills and in valleys, the fires of many furnaces visible in the distance. – A one-horse carriage shaped like a nutshell has been hired to take us to Wentworth House [i.e. Wentworth Woodhouse] tomorrow, home of Earl Lord Fitzwilliam.

Thursday, 29 June

Drive to Wentworth, pleasant countryside with wooded hills, a new church outside the town, canals running along a river, on a higher level. – We passed Rotherham, a beautiful old church[413] high up with a tall, sturdy tower. Further on a magnificent park in Wentworth, with much woodland and hundreds of deer and roedeer. The housekeeper kept us waiting a long time until she was suitably dressed to show us round the house[414] (plate 122). The house with its fine portico, wonderful draped statue, antique, restored as Ariadne or Bacchus. Large and beautiful main hall, 60 ft (square) with a gallery. Other large rooms, paintings by Van Dyck. Gallery: Salvator Rosa, seascape, Raphael, Virgin and Child, [illegible word], which cost 18,000 pounds. Some of the new rooms good, costly tortoiseshell furniture. Drove back through the park, Indian cattle with humps, Beuth found his friend, the old master of a stud-farm, now demoted to ordinary labourer, but still gave him the promised Bürde[415] horse drawings in the street outside our inn.

Arrived back in Sheffield at 12 o'clock, visited Rodgers's[416] iron and steel works, Count Danckelmann made many purchases, I bought sewing needles for 15 shillings. Dinner, coach to Leeds later at 5. The vehicle was overfull, we had three other people inside.

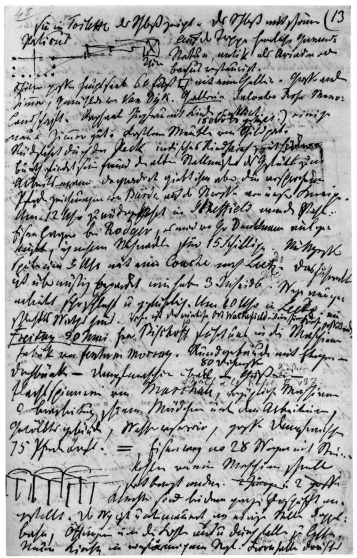

123. Anon., structural drawing of Fenton and Murray steam engine, designed 1802, pen and wash. Science Museum, London

122. *Journal*, p. 48, (top left) Wentworth Woodhouse, ground plan of portico, and right hand of building, inscr.: 'tower', (bottom left) Marshall's cotton mill, view of vault with iron columns

124. Anon., *Middleton Colliery Railway, with Christ Church in the background,* 1829, engraving

125. N. Whittock, eng. J. Rogers, *Corn Exchange, Leeds*, engraving

The roads are new, very bad and dangerous. 10 in Leeds, a bad inn. On the way we passed through the well-kept town of Wakefield with its fine church.

Friday, 30 June

Mr Bischoff took us into Fenton Murray's machine factory.[417] Circular building, 80 ft in diameter, with different storeys. Lathes, steam-engines (plate 123) everywhere. – Foundry. – Marshall's flax mill,[418] excellent machines and processing, pretty girls among the female workers. Vaulted building, water reservoir, huge steam-engines, 75 horsepower. – Iron rails,[419] where 28 carts of coal can be speedily transported by a machine (plate 124). 2 workers are employed on this. The rails are underpinned, in some places double rails, openings for the coal to fall through. – New church in monotonous style.[420] Corn Exchange[421] (plate 125), circular Doric building, not particularly well designed. The columns inside are too close together, those outside too far apart.

We had a meal, having first put on our best clothes, and drove in a comfortable open hired coach through a mass of factory buildings to the beautiful ruin of Kirkstall Abbey[422] (plate 126). Norman-Saxon style, wonderfully overgrown with ivy and full of very old lime trees (plate 127). The main parts of the church have survived, massive proportions. The nave had no vault, in contrast to the transepts. A pleasantly laid out path alongside a canal, which surrounds splendid factory buildings among which is a 120 ft high chimney; the path leads through flowering shrubs and through a watchman's house across a huge lock gate with movable sections to the meadow where the ruin stands.

We saw Mr Stansfield's factory for spinning and weaving worsted.[423] Steam-engine and a large water-wheel supplement each other. Girls demonstrated weaving for us. Setting-up the shuttles and the weft. Spinning there. They were not really working on this particular day. Beautiful children doing the work. In a new small building on top of a hill, next to the foundations of a new house, a collection of remarkable fossils from the area can be seen, imprints of antediluvian plants. Drive to Armley House (plate 128), Mr

[417] Fenton Murray machine factory, known as 'The Round Foundry'. Matthew Murray (1765–1826) was Boulton and Watt's first serious competitor in the development of the beam engine after the expiry of the former's patent (*OHT*, 186; see also Wegner, 144, notes 90–1).
[418] Marshall's Flax mill, Leeds. John Marshall developed new methods of spinning flax, and was adept at publicising them (*OHT*, 292).
[419] The railway operated from Middleton Colliery. The 'machine' is presumably one of the locomotives built in 1812.
[420] Christ Church, Leeds, a neo-Gothic building (1823–6) by Robert Dennis Chantrell, a pupil of Soane, stood in the immediate vicinity of Coal Staith, the iron rails which Schinkel mentions.
[421] Designed by Samuel Chapman, and previously thought to have been built 1827–8.
[422] An industrial landscape was already forming in the eighteenth century around the ruin of this Cistercian abbey, founded in 1152. The abbey had been frequently depicted by eighteenth and nineteenth-century artists, most notably by Thomas Girtin. The wall construction of this Norman building inspired Schinkel to make one of the preparatory sketches for an Architectural Textbook which he was planning (see G. Peschken, *Schinkel-Lebenswerk, Das Architektonische Lehrbuch*, Munich-Berlin 1979, plate 191).
[423] Parsons's Leeds Directory for 1826 records the firm of Stanfeld, Briggs and Stanfeld, Stuff Merchants, at Park Lane and at Burley Mill, Kirkstall Rd. It is probable that Schinkel visited the latter address.

127. Thomas Girtin, *Kirkstall Abbey*, watercolour. Victoria and Albert Museum

128. J.P. Neale, eng. C. Askey, *Armley House*, 1821, engraving

126. *Journal*, p. 49, (upper left) Kirkstall Abbey, Norman arches, (bottom left) Armley House, chair

Gott's[424] magnificent country mansion, on a pleasant hill in a beautiful park. It is a splendid construction of ashlar, with Ionic columns, and is in the best style both inside and out. Low, semi-circular courtyards, magnificent stone steps and terrace, other terraces all round. Sumptuous interior: beautiful paintings, library, golden room, chairs with lilac velvet and gold braid, extremely tasteful. Everything adorned with inlaid wood. Large coloured drawing of Athens in a gold frame; one of their sons died in Athens. Flaxman has done a model for his monument.[425] Mr Gott, a dignified and refined old gentleman, who has made millions in cloth manufacture, received us kindly. We were served with the finest fruits, wine and cake, then had a walk through the park to the workshops and greenhouses, everything richly stocked and well cared for (plate 129).

In the house we found the family at the tea-table, several nice-looking daughters, one of whom spoke very good French to me; they are all very well educated and musically and artistically talented. We were given letters of recommendation or introduction for Edinburgh. – Drove back to town, where we spent the evening at Mr Bischoff's. A pleasant family, the father, mother, 2 daughters, 2 brothers; they talked a lot, in good French. We spoke of Italy and Germany, which the gentlemen had visited. Church[426] with many square windows like a greenhouse, very old, in Leeds.

Saturday, 1 July

Drive to York, Count Danckelmann and I outside, a little rain before we left Leeds, then fine weather, the region is uniformly flat, well cultivated. 1 hour in York, very pleasant inn, the Black Swan. Visited the cathedral [Minster], varied architecture, very little stained glass, also some rather coarse wood panels. The octagonal chapterhouse, the choir, glass screen in the latter's stonework,[427] Anglo-Saxon crypt. Everywhere interesting details and fine proportions, though the vault and many other parts of the building from different ages do not quite harmonize. – Walk round the town. – Old castle on a hill, covered in fine vegetation, built of white ashlars, now a prison.[428] Walk along the river under tall lime

[424] Benjamin Gott (1762–1840), merchant and industrialist, had been building wool factories since 1792. Among these were Armley Mills in 1804 (using the new iron construction method). He had bought Armley House, which was near his new factory, in 1804. He commissioned Robert Smirke to extend the mansion (1816/17 in classical style, with rich interiors and iron staircases), and landscape gardener Humphrey Repton to lay out a park (from 1810). The garden vistas opened on to the Armley Mills and Kirkstall Abbey. The house still survives in neglected condition (see p. 16).

[425] The monument was to Gott's second son, Benjamin, who had died in Greece. Flaxman proposed several ideas for the monument, some of which are preserved in the family papers. It was to be a figure of 'Hope', and it is presumably this model to which Schinkel refers, and on the pedestal there were to be views of the Theseum. The monument was to go in Armley chapel, but Flaxman died (in December 1826) before the marble was completed, and the project was abandoned. All this information is taken from Veronica E.M. Lovell, 'Benjamin Gott of Armley House, Leeds, 1762–1840: Patron of the Arts', *Publications of the Thoresby Society*, n.d., Vol. LIX, pt. 2, no. 130, 192.

[426] The Late Gothic St Peter's church.

[427] It is not clear what Schinkel means by this observation.

[428] York Castle had been extended and converted into a prison in 1802 by Peter Atkinson and in 1826 by Peter Robinson.

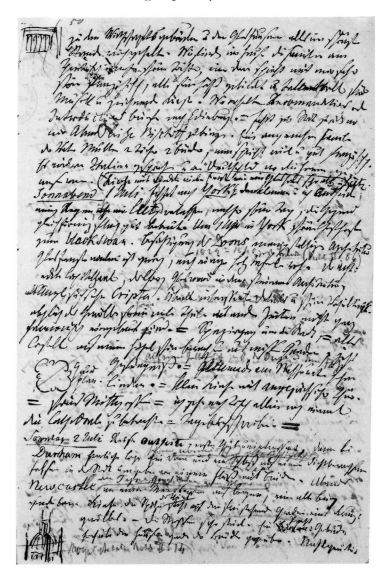

130. T. Allom, eng. E. Challis, *Durham, Castle and Cathedral*, 1832, engraving

131. T.H. Shepherd, *Edinburgh, Waterloo Place, Calton Hill with National and Nelson's Monuments behind*, from *Modern Athens*, 1829, engraving

129. *Journal*, p. 50, (top left) Armley House, greenhouse, (lower left) York Castle, groundplan. Inscr.: 'groundplan', (bottom left) St Nicholas's Cathedral, Newcastle-upon-Tyne, tower

S 59. M. XII. N 15.

132. *View of Edinburgh*, 1826, pen and pencil

trees. – Small church with an Anglo-Saxon door.[429] – Good dinner. – Afterwards I went on my own to have another look at the Minster. – Wrote my diary.

Sunday, 2 July

Travelled outside, first part uninteresting, then Durham (plate 130), magnificent setting. A cathedral and a castle[430] on a cliff thick with vegetation in the town, girdled by a river with a bridge across it. In the evening Newcastle, situated among hills on an inlet of the sea, an old castle,[431] strange. Church,[432] its spire resting on the exposed ribs of a vault. The streets very steep. A magnificent building high up above the houses, right opposite the bridge. Stopped for the night.

Scotland

(Edinburgh, Glasgow, the Highlands, the Hebrides)

Monday, 3 July

The countryside is uniform as far as the Tweed, then Scotland begins, wild and desolate slopes without trees, often covered in grass like velvet, occasionally with views of distant peaks and plateaux. At 8, from the slope of a wide mountain ridge, we could see the plain of Edinburgh, the sea coast with separate clusters of hills, Edinburgh itself like an isolated jewel, in the vicinity several hills, abundance of trees on the plain. The people are not handsome, the dwellings in the villages wretched. On the far side of Edinburgh you can see the shores of the bay with the hills beyond. We arrived in Edinburgh at 10. Splendid new wide streets, somewhat steep. To the side, glimpses of lower-lying streets leading off from under the one we were on. – The inn is opposite the Castle Rock and has an extensive view, at the end of the street stands Nelson's Monument,[433] also on a rock (plate 131).

[429] This could be the church of St Margaret's, with a portal in Romanesque style.
[430] Durham Cathedral was begun in 1093 and an Eastern transept and the main sections were completed by the mid-thirteenth century. The Castle was also begun in Romanesque times, and altered and enlarged in the seventeenth century.
[431] The Castle at Newcastle is Romanesque, dating from the eleventh and twelfth centuries.
[432] St Nicholas parish church (now Cathedral), dating from the fourteenth century, with an open tower.
[433] On Calton Hill, in the continuation of Prince's Street, stands a memorial column to Lord Nelson (1758–1805), designed 1807–16 by Robert Burn (completed by Thomas Bonnar).

133. T.H. Shepherd, *Edinburgh Castle, Interior Quadrangle*, from *Modern Athens*, 1829, engraving

134. T.H. Shepherd, *Edinburgh, Signet Library*, from *Modern Athens*, 1829, engraving

135. T.H. Shepherd, *Edinburgh, part of the Old Town*, from *Modern Athens*, 1829, engraving

136. *View of Edinburgh Old Town*, 1826, pencil

[434] James Gibson Thompson, Prussian Consul in Edinburgh.

[435] Apart from the earliest part, the twelfth-century St Margaret's Chapel, only recognised in 1845, and some fifteenth-century sections including Parliament Hall, most of the Edinburgh Castle complex is relatively modern.

[436] Mary Stuart (1542–87), Queen of Scotland, had given birth to her son by Lord Darnley, James VI of Scotland and James I of England, in 1566 in Edinburgh Castle. He had been lowered down in a basket from the Castle, to prevent his capture by her enemies.

[437] Formerly the Scottish parliament building, built 1633–40 by James Murray. The wooden roof was made 1637–9 by John Scott, Master Wright to the Town of Edinburgh. The sitting of the Lords Ordinary in the Parliament House ended 1844. There were several statues of judges in the hall, but Schinkel is probably referring to the most dramatic, Roubiliac's statue of Duncan Forbes of 1752.

[438] Later the Upper Signet Library, interior 1812–16 by William Stark (see A.J. Youngson, *The Making of Classical Edinburgh*, 1966, 134f).

[439] Schinkel could either have dropped south down into Cowgate, or down High Street and turned south on to the relatively recent South Bridge.

[440] The University was begun 1789–93 from a design by Robert Adam, and was one of his major works. It was completed 1817–26 by William Henry Playfair, who designed the interior. Schinkel is referring here to the Museum of Natural History or Upper Museum, which at the time was inside the University building (It is now the Talbot Rice Arts Centre). The sketch he mentions is no longer extant. The cross vaults, whose stonework Schinkel admired, are over the Anteroom between the staircase and Upper Museum (*Buildings of Scotland: Edinburgh*, 190).

[441] In Schinkel's preparatory work for an architectural textbook there are examples of wall constructions closely related to those of Edinburgh University (see G. Peschken, *Schinkel-Lebenswerk, Das Architektonische Lehrbuch*, Berlin-Munich 1979, Plates 41 and 106).

[442] The Observatory on Calton Hill was built 1818 by W.H. Playfair.

Tuesday, 4 July

Consul Thompson[434] came to fetch us, I wrote to Berlin and handed the letter in to be posted. We climbed up to the Castle[435] (plate 133), magnificent view of the town, hills and sea, the Castle has little in the way of old architecture. Everything is almost new. Mary Stuart's rooms,[436] window where the little prince was let down, everything very cramped. Highland soldiers with bare legs (Roman), skirt pleated like the leather strips in Roman armour. – From the Castle to the public Law Courts,[437] hall with a strange wooden ceiling, gilded in one niche, the Lord Chief Justice hearing a case amidst the noise of the public wandering round the room, secretaries etc. sitting around. The marble statue of a judge in the courtroom. – The Advocates Library[438] (plate 134) is in the same building. Good interior design, plain arches and book-niches in every window, Corinthian columns and behind them a small pilaster construction supporting a gallery for books above.

We walked down one of the old streets[439] to the Museum [of Natural History]: no greater contrast can be imagined than between the filthy cramped conditions of the coarse black dwellings and the poverty of their occupants, and the magnificence, elegance and airiness of the new streets (plates 132, 135 and 136). Several fine wide streets have also been built through the old town, so that a visitor is usually unaware of such pockets of squalor. – The Museum has been sumptuously set up in the University building[440] (plate 137). The design is similar to that of the Advocates' Library. – Like all the buildings in Edinburgh, it is constructed of magnificent stone which has allowed some very fine cutting. My system[441] is frequently in evidence here, but often with mistakes (plates 138 and 139).

There is much use of pilasters, and detail derived from Greek monuments, but lacking a feeling for proportion and its practical application. Everything seems more of an experiment than well-organized endeavour. – There is a splendidly constructed cross vault in the vestibule.

We climbed the rock to see Nelson's monument, where there is also an observatory[442] and where a faithful replica of the

137. T.H. Shepherd, eng. W.H. Lizars, *Edinburgh, The University, South Bridge Street*, copied from *Modern Athens*, 1829, engraving

138. W.H. Lizars, *Museum of Natural History, Edinburgh University*, engraving, used as letterhead by Prof. Robert Jameson, Keeper of the Museum

139. *Journal*, p. 52, (top left) Edinburgh University, (far left) inscr.: 'University', (to the right) 3 studies of window and wall openings, the last one, inscr.: 'private houses joined together, not characteristic', (last on the right) Signet Library façade, inscr.: 'Ionic façade on the side of the Advocates Library', (below left) Capital of pilaster, inscr.: 'This pilaster is often used', (below left) rapid sketch of Nelson's monument

140. *Panoramic view of Edinburgh from Calton Hill*, 1826, pen and pencil

141. T.H. Shepherd, *Edinburgh, View from the Calton Hill*, from *Modern Athens*, 1829, engraving

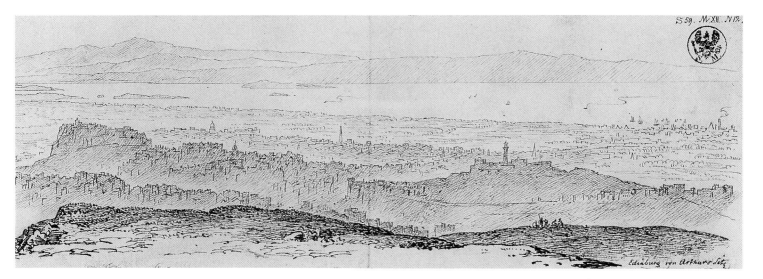

142. *Panoramic view of Edinburgh from Arthur's Seat*, 1826, pen and pencil

143. T.H. Shepherd, *St George's Parish Church and West Side of Charlotte Square*, from *Modern Athens*, 1829, engraving

[443] In 1824 work was begun on a Doric temple, which was intended to be a national monument in memory of the Battle of Waterloo. It was designed by W.H. Playfair under the direction of C.R. Cockerell, and modelled on the Parthenon. It was never finished, work stopping finally in 1829.
[444] Bridewell House, a Gothic revival building by Robert Adam.
[445] Holyrood House, periodic residence of the Scottish kings, was built at the beginning of the sixteenth century and enlarged 1670–79 by William Bruce and Robert Mylne.
[446] In 1566 David Rizzio, secretary and close friend of Mary Stuart, was murdered on the orders of her jealous husband, Darnley, in Holyrood House.
[447] By Jacob de Wit, 1684.
[448] Holyrood Chapel, surviving part of Holyrood Abbey, founded 1128, over which Holyrood House was built (see note 445). The church is early thirteenth century.
[449] Schinkel seems to have confused Louis XVIII with his brother Charles X, who, as the comte d'Artois, did have a period in exile in Edinburgh, living in Holyrood. (See M. Weiner, *The French Exiles, 1789–1815*, London, 1960, 131–2.)

Parthenon[443] is to be built as a national monument; the groundwork is already being dug, although not even a quarter of the necessary subscription of over 100,000 pounds has so far been raised. A general walk around [2 illegible words]. I sketched the town from Nelson's tower, another beautiful view of the surroundings and the sea (plates 140 and 141). We had delicious strawberries with sugar and cream, spirits may not be sold by the tower keeper.

Below the Monument rock lies a workhouse,[444] like a castle, with various battlements, turrets and gates etc. which offers from all sides a picturesque addition to the town. After dinner we walked down the old high street to Holyrood House.[445] Mary Stuart's room where her husband was murdered,[446] bloodstains on the floor, low doors where you hit your head, poor-quality tapestries, everything wretched and dark and small. – The wretched picture gallery of the kings of Scotland, all badly painted by a later hand.[447] – The old church, Norman architecture,[448] the kings' vault mediocre; even so some royal ancestors have recently been brought over from France and interred there. King Louis XVIII[449] of France stayed for a long period in Holyrood, only venturing out of the Castle on Sundays, because on working days he could have been arrested for debt, something which British law prevents on Sundays.

We climbed the rock to Arthur's Seat (plate 142), where one has Edinburgh below and a view of the whole estuary and surrounding countryside. A company of fine gentlemen and ladies on the summit; peasants with bagpipes, again not wearing trousers in Scottish costume. Spring at the bottom of the hill with drinking water. Up there one has the magnificent effect of the evening sunlight on the sea, a steamer was drawing its long smoke behind it like an island through the sea. – As we walked down towards our inn we saw the new road along the rock with Nelson's monument; a considerable section which slopes towards the town has now been built: a fine sight.

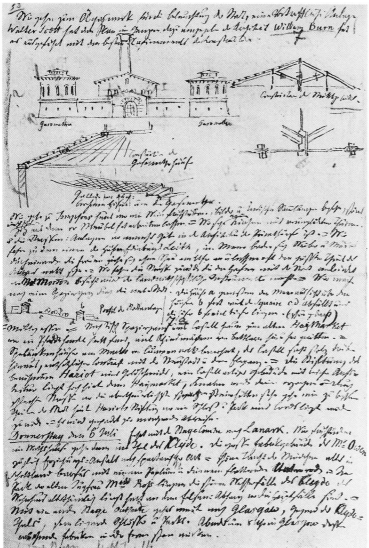

145. J.H. Clark, *New Lanark*, 1825, aquatint

144. *Journal*, p. 53, (top) Tanfield Gasworks. view of
gasworks with gasometers on either side, both inscr.:
'Gasometer', (right and below) roof construction with detail
of fastenings, inscr.: 'construction of the middle', (below left)
roof construction of the gasometers, inscr.: 'Construction of
the gasometer houses', (below) iron walkway around a
gasometer, inscr.: 'gallery of incised iron around the
gasometer) (middle left) Edinburgh, section of fall of ground,
inscr.: 'a–d. section of the position of the town. The houses a
enjoy a view of the lake right over the houses b, because the
square cd drops away and the houses bb which lie so much
further down, can be seen perfectly'

[450] The building of Edinburgh's New Town, begun in 1770 in classical, regular style, had been intensified after 1815.

[451] James Adam's St George's Episcopal Chapel, York Place, 1792–4.

[452] St George's Church in Charlotte Square, built 1811–14 by Robert Reid (see Wegner, 149, fig. 73). Schinkel is referring here to similar domed towers, designed by Karl Gontard, which were added in 1780–5 to the German Church (1701–8) and the French Church (1701–5) in the Gendarmenmarkt, Berlin (now Platz der Akademie).

[453] Tanfield Gasworks, Canonmills, built 1824 by William Burn. Sir Walter Scott was a partner in the Tanfield Gasworks Company, but is not otherwise recorded as having any part in the design. The plan was cruciform and an arm of it still survives. It became a Free Church assembly hall in 1843 (*Buildings of Scotland: Edinburgh*, 578; illustrated in its Free Church incarnation in Wegner, 149, fig. 74).

[454] George Heriot (1563–1624), goldsmith and banker to King James VI, founded this Gothic-style orphanage. It was built 1628–59 by William Wallace and William Aytoun, and continued 1671–93 by Robert Mylne.

[455] This is almost certainly Duddingston House, the seat of the Marquis of Abercorn.

[456] From 1800 onwards Robert Owen (1772–1858), social reformer and socialist, transformed the factory (built 1783, mainly spinning) and housing complex of New Lanark, running it on model lines. His aim was to solve the fundamental social problems of his employees. Among other things he introduced regular wages, a 10½ hour working day, non-employment of children under 10, security in sickness and old age, payment of wages during unemployment due to unforeseen circumstances, co-operative stores, and hygienic accommodation. From 1809 he worked towards systematizing a model of co-operative life at work and at home, and promoted his system elsewhere. New Lanark became well known and was visited frequently. In the years 1824/25 Owen sought to implement his ideas in the USA (New Harmony).

Wednesday, 5 July

Thompson collected us, after Beuth and I had been for a walk to the new streets of the town;[450] church in medieval style,[451] small, church with towers like our churches in the Gensd'armes-Markt [in Berlin][452] (plate 143).

We went to the gasworks[453] (plate 144) which provide the town's lighting; an excellent plant. Walter Scott designed the general lay-out, the architect William Burn carried it out using the most sophisticated construction.

We went to Thompson's house, where we refeshed ourselves with wine and looked at groups of pictures and Indian objects; beautiful Indian wood, which he had used for furniture. – We saw new churches with unfortunate towers, and the street lay-out which often reveals some good architecture in the private houses. – We drove to one of Edinburgh's ports, Leith; women and men bathe together in the sea, the women change on the beach without reserve, often exposing most of their bodies. – We drove back along the road linking the port and the town, visiting Mr Morton who makes agricultural implements. – We walked round the lower town again.

Dinner. – Then we walked round the Castle to the old Haymarket, where horse-dealing was going on; old nags being ridden up and down by beggars. – Wretched dwellings round the market-place, inhabited by riffraff, the Castle presiding over it all, appalling contrast with the new town and its elegance. The foundation of the noteworthy Heriot,[454] a goldsmith, a castellated building with rich architecture, stands high up behind the Haymarket; boys are educated there. – We walked along dreadful streets with strange black stone hovels, into the better parts of the town behind Heriot's foundation, where there was the house and park of a lord.[455] – Packed for our departure tomorrow.

Thursday, 6 July

Drove to Lanark in the stagecoach. We breakfasted at the inn, then walked down into the Clyde valley. Mr Owen's large factory buildings[456] (plate 145), also a school of a Spartan kind. – Girls in

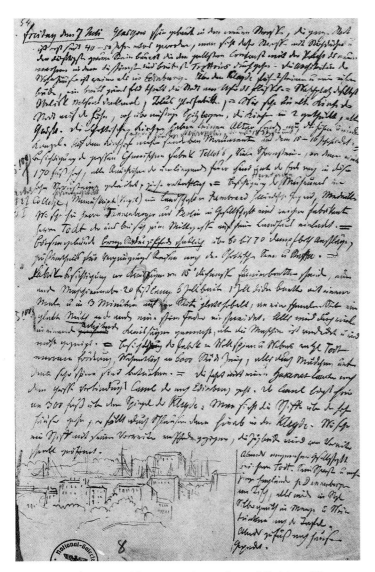

146. *Journal*, p. 54, Glasgow, view of canal linking Glasgow and Edinburgh

147. J. Knox, eng. J. Swan, *View of Glasgow from the farm of Shields*, from J. Swan, *Select Views of Glasgow*, 1828, engraving

148. J. Scott, *Glasgow Cathedral and Barony Church*, from *Glasgow Illustrated*, 1834, engraving

457 Erected on Glasgow Green 1806, from a design by David Hamilton. The tholus probably belonged to the Jamaica Street Bottle Works, 1730–c.1834.
458 Glasgow Cathedral (c.1197–c.1493). In the time of Schinkel's visit the Cathedral was divided into English and Gaelic-speaking congregations, divided by the Quire Screen or Pulpitum.
459 This must be Tennant's factory at St Rollox, as Wolzogen suggests. Charles Tennant (1768–1838) was famous as the developer of bleaching-powder for textiles, and the factory became one of the largest chemical manufacturers in Europe (*OHT*, 239–40, and N. Crathorne, *Tennant's Stalk*, Glasgow, 1983).
460 The Hunterian Museum, founded by William Hunter in 1781, was then in premises built 1804–5 by William Stark. There are four manuscripts of Virgil from Hunter's collection in the Glasgow University Library: it is not clear which one Schinkel was interested in, though one (Hunter 27; S.2.17) has some notes and commentary in German. The 'Rembrandt landscape' must be the *Panoramic Landscape* by Philips Koninck still in the Hunterian. Schinkel's name is recorded in the Hunterian Museum visitors' book (Glasgow University Library) and his companion is clearly recorded as Danckelmann and not 'Dannenberger' as Riemann has it, or 'Tannenberger' as recorded by Wegner! 'Mr Todt' is, according to the *Glasgow Post-Office Directory for 1828* 'Charles Todd, merchant, 79 Queen St works Commercial Road, Hutchesontown, house Plantation'. Plantation House, which Schinkel visited that same evening with Danckelmann, was situated one mile west of Tradeston, and was built c.1800 as a fine two-storey house with portico and wings. It is illustrated in anon., *The Old Country Houses of the Old Glasgow Gentry*, 1870, pl. LXXX.
461 In Trongate. According to Colvin, this was not built until 1827–9 (architect David Hamilton). The equestrian statue was of William III, dating from the 1780s, which stood near the Tobacco Exchange and was moved near the Cathedral in 1926. The timber factory is not identifiable at present. (I am greatly indebted to Paul Stirton for his help with the Glasgow entries.)

pretty costume, all girls in Scotland go barefoot wearing a pinafore dress and a thin, full underdress. – In the park of an elderly lady, Miss Ross, the finest waterfalls of the Clyde are to be seen, the house, antiquated, is right on the clifftop, where the main waterfalls are situated. – Drove on to Glasgow in another stagecoach, on the outside, Clyde valley region, grand houses and parks in the distance. In Glasgow at 8 in the evening; you can see its smoking factories from quite a distance (plates 146 and 147).

Friday, 7 July

The new streets of Glasgow are built spendidly, the whole town has only become something within the last 40–50 years, so one still sees streets full of houses with thatched roofs and in crude grey stone, which contrast strikingly with the splendour of the new streets with their fine wide pavements. The architecture of the ordinary houses is purer than in Edinburgh. 2 stone and one iron bridge span the Clyde, a broad green meadow divides the town along the bank of the river. – There is a washing area there, also an obelisk, Nelson monument,[457] the tholus of a glass factory. – We saw the old town church on the hill[458] (plate 148), crude unwieldy pointed arches, the churches divided into 2 [congregations], old crypt. The Scottish churches have no altar, just an upper and lower pulpit. Several strange monuments from the fifteenth-sixteenth centuries in the churchyard.

Visited Tellot's [Tennant's][459] large chemical factory, many chimneys, one of which is 170 ft high, all the steam pipes from the furnaces around go underground and discharge into these high chimneys, which draw very well.

Visit to the Museum in the College,[460] manuscript (Vergil), a Rembrandt landscape, Dutch scene, medals. Here we met Herr Danckelmann from Berlin in company with a wealthy factory-owner, Mr Todt [Todd], who invited us for dinner in his country house.

Stock Exchange,[461] equestrian statue, dreadful; over 60 to 70 steamboat notices, most of them offering pleasure trips to the Scottish lochs and Staffa. – Factory visit, where circular saws 15 ft in diameter splice veneer panels, another machine planes one side of planks 20 ft long, 6 ins wide and 1 in. thick in one operation in 3 minutes, cutting a smooth groove down one edge and a tongue down the other. Everything is done by circular saws working in conjunction with each other, but the machinery is covered over and could not be inspected. – Viewing of Mr Todt's wool-spinning and weaving mill[462] (plate 149), enormous production, about 6,000 bales of material a week, all done by young girls, some of them very pretty.

Drive in a hackney-coach to the great link canal which goes to Edinburgh. The canal is 300 ft above the Clyde here: you see the boats going along above the tall buildings, then it descends via locks down into the Clyde. We saw one boat with a rider in front, pulled by horses, the locks were quickly opened by the rider.

Pleasant evening in company at Mr Todt's. His sister and several young Englishmen, and Herr Danckelmann were at table, everything again stylish, silverware in abundance, and the drinking of wine after the meal. Walked home in the evening, packed.

Saturday, 8 July

At 6 in the morning we were on the steamboat together with a large company of English, French and Italians, ready to start our journey into the Highlands. The banks of the Clyde have been narrowed at intervals by stone barriers so that the river despite its width could be dredged to provide a very good route for shipping. Entrance and first lock of the link canal. Disembarked at the little town of Dumbarton. Castle on an isolated rock, Roman origin. Mountains all round. After breakfast a stagecoach stood ready, and most of the company got in to go to Loch Lomond. We covered the distance in an hour, and a steamboat was already waiting for the party, who were taken aboard by means of a large coal barge. The steamboat goes a way that passes the most scenic views of the lake and the mountains. There are wooded islands in the lake, the mountains are bare and rocky in the Scottish manner, but also green and marshy, right up to the summit (plate 150). We went ¾ of the way round the lake, and set down at a solitary cottage, Tarbet, an

462 For views of Todd's mill in Hutchesontown see the watercolours by William Simpson reproduced in *Glasgow in former times*, II, 147 & 183 (Mitchell Library, Glasgow).

149. W. Simpson, *Todd's Mill and Wingate's Works*, 1847, watercolour, Mitchell Library, Glasgow

150. *Scottish landscape*, inscr.: bei Sogodan, 1826, pen and pencil

inn and posthouse, agreeably situated among green trees and long grass in the pleasant sunshine. The waves were quite high on our way there in the little boat we hired. After a breakfast of cheese and ale we drove to Loch Fyne, in an uncomfortable two-wheeler with one horse, the local form of travel. Splendid view of this loch from above, a nice country house in a park as foreground. This scenery was all the more welcome as we had come through quite wild marshy and green rocky valleys between completely bare mountain peaks, with now and then a waterfall down a steep cliff in the middle of all the green. We had to wait a long time for a horse in another isolated posthouse, and had coffee there.

The road continues along Loch Fyne, with no habitation save cottages miles apart from each other, treeless, but the people inside looked quite gentlemenly in dress, now and then a peasant in archaic Scottish garb with no trousers, a checked skirt but with modern clothes over it. The women all barefoot, but wearing pretty bonnets on their heads, or hats; the common folk wear a cloak and hood, often of checked material, often in scarlet, brown, purple, yellow etc.

Late in the evening we reached Inverary (plates 151 and 152), an important place belonging to the Duke of Argyll, who owns practically all of the Ossianic islands [Hebrides].[463] Here he has built a modern Gothic castellated house[464] in a beautiful park. The mountain scenery round the large bay, which here looks exactly like an inland lake, is very beautiful, particularly with its magnificent woods. The vegetation is remarkably fine for Scotland, even chestnuts grow to a great height here. Maples, beeches, oaks, laurels, lime trees, elms etc. fill the woodlands. A tower stands on top of a high rock.

Elections had just taken place, we found everyone at the inn drunk, the landlady was just about holding things together, Beuth found himself drinking wine with an old Scotsman, bragging horribly, and a drunken young man, and could hardly get away from these two babblers. With great difficulty we managed to get supper and decent accommodation. – There is an awful church in the town, the inn is on the shore of the inlet and connected to other buildings by large arches and portals, which are intended to give the

[463] The islands off the west coast of Scotland. They derive their name from the mythical Celtic bard Ossian, made famous by the Scottish poet James Macpherson (1736–96) who purported to have collected and translated the third-century bard's songs (published 1760–65, definitive edition 1773). In fact the songs were for the most part written by Macpherson himself. Their melancholy, romantic tone was seized upon throughout Europe. They were translated into many languages and had an enormous effect on the literature and art of the late eighteenth and early nineteenth centuries.
[464] Inverary Castle was begun in 1745–60 by Roger Morris for the then Duke of Argyll.

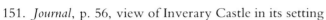

151. *Journal*, p. 56, view of Inverary Castle in its setting

152. J. Knox, *Inverary Castle*, lithograph

153. *View of Oban*, 1826, pen and pencil

situation a picturesque air and were probably built for that purpose by the Duke of Argyll.

Sunday, 9 July

We set off again in a carriage, magnificent route through the Inverary estate, fine trees, waterfall, outhouses, flower and fruit gardens, isolated cottages. – But soon the scenery becomes spare and Scottish-looking again. There was a steep climb, we had a view of a loch surrounded by high bens (mountain peaks). A country house with a terrace, on which stood a fine tree, lay down below us on the mountainside overlooking the vast desolate scene where only a cottage or group of black stone huts were occasionally to be seen. We had a second breakfast in an isolated posthouse and inn at the lochside, Port Sonachan,[465] and were then ferried over the loch together with a new horse and cart. On the other side the scenery was similarly wild and desolate, it began to rain, and uncomfortably huddled together on the cramped little open carriage we resigned ourselves to being soaked. It did not stop raining until quite late, we met some gentlemen on foot, which indicated habitation not far ahead, and to the side we saw the inland seawater overflowing, as more water comes in at high tide than the bay can hold. – Some of the inhabitants were busy clearing a landslide. – This far north the days last much longer than in Germany at the same time of year. We reached Oban (plate 153), a place by the sea of about 100 houses. From here you can see almost all the Ossianic islands and cliffs, picturesque, eerie and awesome in the confused way they are thrown together. We found a comfortable inn, had a meal and went to bed about 11, and it was still light enough to read.

Monday, 10 July

Long walks in the mountains above Oban and along the sea coast. The old castle[466] (plate 154) of one of the Douglas family (Dugle) has only recently fallen into ruin, and the owner (MacDugle), who was himself born in the old tower, has built himself an

[465] A ferry on Loch Awe, fourteen miles from Inverary, and next to the hamlet of Kilchrenan
[466] This is Dunollie Castle. The 'ordinary new house' must be Dunollie House, a plain two-storey house still surviving. The Castle is, in fact, largely fifteenth century with later additions. A castle on the site had originally belonged to the MacDougalls, but was confiscated by King Robert I in 1309. The MacDougalls were reinstated in Dunollie in 1451, from which the present castle probably dates. It was garrisoned against the MacLeans in 1675, and the latter did not succeed in taking it. The Castle was forfeited by the MacDougall owner in 1715 for taking part in the Jacobite rebellion, but it was restored to his son, who abandoned it to move to Dunollie House. See *Argyll: an inventory of the Ancient Monuments,* Vol. 2 *Lorn,* Royal Commission on the Ancient and Historical Monuments of Scotland, 1975, 194–98, 254. (Reference owed to Dr Ian Gow.)

unpretentious new house and farm behind the cliff, enhancing it with fine trees and a flower garden, a splendid oasis in those wild surroundings. The tower seems very old, round arches and horizontal roof construction indicate twelfth-century origins. The MacLeans are said to have taken the tower at one time, and Douglas, because he belonged to the revolutionaries, was driven out by the King, but was later pardoned and given back the castle. I sketched several views (plate 155). We went home, I wrote my diary while Danckelmann and Beuth went climbing again. – During the night a party of drunken Scots made a frightful racket beneath our bedroom windows. At first we thought someone had been murdered.

Tuesday, 11 July

At 9 the steamboat for Staffa arrived in the bay and we went on board. We sailed between the islands of Mull and Morvern (plate 156), their peaks are hidden by an almost endless mist, and their high coastlines, but there were magnificent flashes of sunlight which lit up the mountains, bare right up to their rocky and marshy summits; along the coast the bare rocks are blackish in colour, intermingled with brown. Many separate rocky islands and foothills project into the sea, with occasionally an old tower or castle on them. A few huts of black stone, badly thrown together, with thatched roofs over which a net of heather twine is laid, weighted down with stones, for protection from the wind (plate 157).

It is remarkable that the poor inhabitants of these huts manage to be almost fashionable in some things, especially their headgear. Wrapped in rags and going barefoot, the women still put on a pretty bonnet or a hat with a frill and ribbon over their unkempt hair. The boat often stopped on a wild bit of coast, where there was always a party of well-dressed people waiting on the edge, either to embark or see someone off; it is hard to imagine where they come from in this desolate region. The 60 steamboats which ply these coasts from Glasgow have brought closer connections, but how miserable and wretched everything here must have looked 20 years ago.

154. *The ruins of Dunollie Castle at Oban*, 1826, pen and pencil

155. *View taken from Dunollie Castle at Oban*, 1826, pen and pencil

156. *View of Morvern*, 1826, pencil

157. *Journal*, p. 57, stone house on an island between Mull and Staffa

At 5 in the afternoon we arrived in the coastal village of Tobermory[467] (plate 158), situated on a bay, where we found accommodation for the night; Danckelmann and I have a little room in a private house, clean and with good beds, Beuth is at the inn. Dannenberger and a brother-in-law, whom he met by chance on the steamboat in Oban, are staying in our house, also a gentleman-farmer and his wife and pretty daughters. We had a walk to a waterfall in an immense park, where a fine-looking house is being built.[468] This place is like an island in the wilderness. I made a few sketches from the waterfall of the picturesque lines of the bay and the sight of Ossian's Morvern in the distance, then we went back along marshy terrain and the terrible old Scottish military road, had a meal and we laid ourselves down to sleep.

Wednesday, 12 July

At 4 in the morning a boatman walked all round the whole village playing dreadful bagpipes, to rouse the party who were going to Staffa. At 4.30 we set off at speed, with a constant headwind and high waves. We took tea in the boat, as we usually did, but it will never again taste good to me. The coast became more and more desolate and eerie, and was matched by the frequent showers of rain. Whole walls of ancient weathered volcanic rock, containing traces of basalt, project out into the sea from the higher mountains, encircled by a thousand flapping seagulls, and forming deep black caves everywhere. Some of these are exceedingly picturesque. I was seasick, together with many others of the party, as we struck out into the open sea where Staffa and other groups of islands, of a highly characteristic form, could be seen in the distance.

We reached Staffa (plates 159 and 160) at about 12. As you arrive you see the whole of the architecture formed by the basalt, and sail into a very special first cave.[469] Here the party alighted on to the steps formed by the broken-off basalt columns which are all round the cave walls, while the sea foamed and pounded in the deeper columned recesses, through which one reaches the great Cave of Fingal (plate 161). Only one of the gentleman-farmer's daughters had come with us (mother and sister remained behind in

[467] The largest town on the island of Mull.
[468] In Ian Gow's view this is likely to be Aros House, about two miles from Tobermory. It was then known as Drumfin House, and was built in the early nineteenth century by the Macleans of Coll, who used it as a winter residence (see P. A. Macnab, *The Isle of Mull*, Glasgow, n.d., 151).
[469] This cave, famous for its rows of high basalt pillars and its colour and sound effects, was first entered by boat in 1772 and continued thereafter to be a tourist attraction. According to legend it was built by giants for Fingal, father of Ossian.

158. *Panoramic view of Tobermory Bay on the Isle of Mull,*
1826, pen and pencil

159. *The Isle of Staffa with entrance to Fingal's Cave,* 1826,
pen and pencil

160. *Staffa, entrance to Fingal's Cave, with rowing-boat entering*, 1826, pen and pencil

161. J.C. Schetky, eng. Manners, *Staffa, entrance to Fingal's Cave*, engraving

Tobermory because of seasickness), and she was notably fearless, climbing around the most dangerous parts which led into the innermost part of the cave. The sea is very deep inside the cave, which looks like a church, and with the incoming waves rising over 12 to 15 ft at the far end, a continuous thundering roar can be heard. Our Germans: Dannenberger, Danckelmann, the Swiss, sang in harmony at the back of the cave, which because of the waves sounded like an organ, and even looked like one because of the 50 ft high basalt columns standing in regular order. The roof, a rugged mass of rock, arches up to several points. The sea in the background appeared very green, but over the very black basalt created the optical sensation of the most beautiful crimson. When we had looked our fill, and negotiated the dangerous path back along the broken pillars lining the cave, where two boatmen at certain spots had to form a balustrade by holding up a wooden pole to protect us from the abyss; without this help we would not be able to get by, and passing a little boat with several boatmen rocking violently inside the cave, ready to come to the rescue in case of accident, we climbed up to the top of the island, along a narrow rock with a sheer drop on either side, and a ridge where you have to take special care. Some wild horses and a couple of cows, the only inhabitants of the island, darted off to the opposite cliff edge at high speed when they caught sight of the party emerging from below (I was reminded of Walter Scott's descriptions in *The Pirate*).[470] They have started building a little stone hut up there as a kind of resting-place, its walls looking very forlorn standing there in the bare landscape. From the top there are very fine views of the many clefts and outcrops of the island, which are all most remarkable due to the beautiful caves and basalt formations. I sketched one of the main views. Then we climbed down an easy path to another ravine and crossed a small, strangely formed outcrop of basalt to the steamboat.

We now went further out into the open sea, my seasickness got worse, at about 3 o'clock we reached the island of Iona,[471] Icolmkil Island, where a few wretched huts and the ruins of two churches mark the site of a former capital of the ancient Scottish kings. On the rock where we were set down by our rowing boat, and outside

[470] The novel *The Pirates* had appeared in 1822.
[471] Iona is the island whence Irish missionaries first set out to convert the Scots in the sixth century (foundation of a monastery in 563 by St Columba). The late twelfth-century cathedral is partly Transitional and partly late Gothic. The other church referred to, the Nunnery, is also Transitional. Tradition has it that Scottish, Irish and Norwegian kings are buried in St Oran's cemetery.

the door of every hut, there were children selling all sorts of strange rock specimens on little plates. Ugly folk in rags, half naked. The cathedral churches are about 600 to 800 paces apart, small, and appear to be twelfth-thirteenth century; very badly constructed, with some bizarre sculptures on the capitals and round and pointed arches, though one is almost entirely round-arched. The churchyards and the church floors, and the small renovated chapel nearby, contain a large number of very crudely carved tombs: knights and bishops and kings, dating from the fourteenth-fifteenth centuries. There are also stone crosses everywhere, some still in one piece, some broken, of the kind that are thought to be the oldest, with barbaric decoration of the old Caledonians, Picts etc., but this kind of decoration can also be found on fourteenth and fifteenth-century tombs. All round the churches and churchyards there are now arable fields and potato growing; only the old ruined stone road from one church to the other is used by the villagers, and nothing remains of the original dwellings. The present cottages are newer and nearer to the coast. Most of the knights on the tombstones are of the MacLean family; the verger who showed us these antiquities, an old man who compared with the rest of the village looked decent enough, but the rumour is does not do his job as a teacher well, is himself a MacLean.

Beuth had stayed behind on the steamboat, in his usual humour, and in our absence he had taken great delight in the fact that the poor people of the region had come out to the steamboat in rowing boats, and had stared like wild men at this incomprehensible being, and were enchanted to be offered some white bread; this bread is nothing but oatcakes, ¼ in. thick large slabs, quite tasteless. We went back on board, and passing Staffa again returned to the bay of Tobermory, where we took up our night quarters again.

Thursday, 13 July

Awakened by the bagpipes we went on our way back to Oban at 5, where Herr Dannenberger and the Swiss gentleman left us to visit those parts nearby which we had already seen. At 10 we continued on from Oban in the steamboat, we saw magnificent lofty cliffs in the sunshine, a country house with a park made a fine sight nestling in the mountains. New passengers were taken on board in the harbour of Scarba, others disembarked, the steamboat filled up with strange creatures, women of a fairly free-spirited manner (we discovered later that these were all bound for the fair in Glasgow). In the afternoon we reached the link canal[472] between the Knapdale islands formed by its construction and Argyll; the steamboats are built to fit within its width. This fine piece of engineering starts off immediately with two high locks, each about 15 ft, thus 30 ft in height, then continues along a water-logged mountain slope, close to inland marshland which at one time was probably sea, then on through pleasant scenery. The mountains are quite wooded again here. 7 locks during the ascent, 8 on the descent to the seacoast; on this side there are several fine country seats with parks near Loch Gilp[Head] Inn, where the canal flows into the sea. I stayed in the cabin as night fell, feeling extremely unwell, and did not go on deck until next morning when we reached the entrance to the Clyde.

Friday, 14 July

In Port Glasgow I saw a fine Doric customs house of impressive size,[473] then Dumbarton Castle again and the country houses along the Clyde, of which our fellow-traveller and his family own one of the finest. – At 9 we disembarked in Glasgow, I still felt ill and retired straight to bed, staying there all day to recover, as we are to set off for Manchester tomorrow morning at 6. Beuth and Danckelmann went out and enjoyed themselves at the fair in one of the town squares.

Liverpool, Wednesday 19 July

Dearest Susanne. I was overjoyed to receive your dear letter of 28 June on my arrival here yesterday, in which I find you happier back in your own home with the children, and that you and Mother and Karoline have been preparing everything for their future life in Berlin. Greetings to everybody, especially Wilhelm, whom I thank for his few lines, I would like to have heard more from him,

[472] The Crinan canal, built 1801, with a large number of locks. It cut through the long Argyll peninsular, making the journey from Glasgow to the Hebrides considerably shorter and safer.
[473] Schinkel probably means Greenock, in which case he would be referring to William Burn's Doric Custom House of 1818 (see *The South Clyde Estuary*, 1986, Royal Commission on the Ancient and Historical Monuments of Scotland).

especially on the subject of the Crown Prince's apartments.[474] Special greetings to Rauch and Tieck, tell them that this journey is so rushed that it is impossible for me to write letters to them, I must tell it all from my own mouth, but tell them that there was little to find in art that was really new in this otherwise very interesting country.

You will have received my letter of 4 July from Edinburgh. Since then I have been on a long journey by land and sea to the Scottish Highlands and round Ossian's islands, Mull and Morvern, as far as Staffa and Iona or Ikolmkil, where I did not escape severe seasickness, though I have arrived here in Liverpool in good health again.

The journey into this wonderfully wild, deserted country, between awesome cliffs around whose caves swarm thousands and thousands of seagulls; where the higher mountain peaks are almost always wrapped in mist, wonderful old, rough castles and churches are sparsely scattered on the plains and hills, uninhabited for centuries; where the homes of the people are like those of wild men, a poverty-stricken people, living in huts often several miles apart, nevertheless have some sort of modern air about them, they all go barefoot but wear bonnets and hats decorated with frills and ribbons; where one often, as far as the eye can reach, can see no trees, but unending mountain slopes of heather and bog mixed with rock, stretching right up to the highest point of the hills, on which live wild sheep that are like goats; where one is carried on roads by wretched two-wheeled carts, pulled by a single horse – all in striking contrast to the rich cultivation of England. Even so one sees in the roughest hamlet and on the country roads, and in the wild hill-slopes, and where boats pick up passengers, many people about who are just as finely dressed as one might see promenading about London; where they live, where they emerge from in the wilderness, one has no idea. Now and then one finds an oasis, a country house with a tree-lined park, whose owner must have been born in the region if he could feel at ease there.

In the last 10 years 60 steamboats have started up in Glasgow alone for these northern regions, and their regular journeys will so connect up these vast outlying areas that their character will soon

[474] In 1823, after the marriage of the Prussian Crown Prince Friedrich Wilhelm (IV) to Princess Elisabeth of Bavaria, Schinkel had been commissioned to redesign a suite of rooms for them in the Berlin Stadtschloss. This suite had formerly been occupied by Friedrich II, much revered by the Crown Prince. The alterations to the six rooms were carried out 1824–6 with the collaboration of Berlin artists including Friedrich Tieck and Carl Wilhelm Kolbe and formed one of Schinkel's finest interiors.

become something else, and get a more civilized aspect; indeed the process has already begun. These boats are always full of people, Scots going south to have a look at the new splendours of Glasgow and Edinburgh, or Southerners seeking the Highlands out of curiosity. 50 years ago the two aforementioned towns must have had a very primitive character, for there is a wondrous contrast in these towns between the stone huts covered with straw in the old parts, and the splendid streets full of palaces, 20 ft wide pavements of the finest stone, the iron railings and gaslight lamp-posts etc.[475]

Return to London

(Manchester, Liverpool, Wales, Bristol, Bath)

Saturday, 15 July

Feeling tolerably well I climbed inside a stagecoach, in which we travelled alternately through cultivated land and hill regions of a Scottish character. During the day we covered 22 German miles to Carlisle, back in England; the bare feet and the checked skirts cease, everything becomes more civilized. Here we rested in bed for a few hours from 10 to 4. Then the coach continued on.

Sunday, 16 July

I felt better. The scenery in Cumberland is very pleasant, still wild and hilly from time to time, here in particular there are lakes or lochs beloved by the English, which we saw with their surroundings as we drove past. Lunch tasted good again. We soon reached Lancastershire [*sic*], the most built up and hard-driving province of England, factories everywhere, especially bleaching works for cotton using chemical methods, rather than the open air. The country houses and parks of the factory owners always nearby [their factories] in pleasant valleys. Often a view of the sea. Passing through Lancaster, Preston and Bolton, we reached Manchester

[475] This letter is no longer extant.

(plate 162) at 9; we had covered 23 German miles, and 45 German miles since yesterday morning – 225 English miles, sleeping on the way. We found good accommodation at the Royal Hotel.

Monday, 17 July

I wanted to spare myself, I stayed in and wrote the diary, the others went to see factories. After the evening meal we went around: enormous factories, e.g. MacConnell, Kennedy[476] and another, Morris [Murray],[477] have buildings 7–8 storeys high, as long as the Palace in Berlin[478] and equally wide, with absolutely fire-proof vaulting, a canal at the side and inside (plate 163). The streets of the town go through these masses of buildings, and over the streets go connecting walkways. It is like this through the whole of Manchester, these are mills for cotton of the finest quality, from a pound of cotton 1,300 by 2,500 yards of material are made. – The cotton-bleacher Ainsworth[479] bleaches 500 to 1,000 rolls of cloth 60 yards long each week.

The great canal of the town goes above the streets[480] (plates 164 and 165). This canal then reaches a lock and goes this time under a street and under a tall building which rests on 2 unequal arches with small abutments. There lie above the streets great iron ways high up on supports. A big iron waterwheel, very lightly constructed.

6,000 Irish workers from the Manchester factories have recently been transported back to their homeland at the town's expense, because of the shortage of work. 12,000 workers are now coming together to rise up. Many workers work 16 hours a day, and then get a weekly wage of only 2 shillings. Establishments that cost 500,000 pounds sterling are now worth only 5,000. A dreadful state of affairs. Since the war 400 new factories have been built in Lancastershire; one sees buildings standing where three years ago there were still fields, but these buildings appear as blackened with smoke as if they had been in use for a hundred years. – It makes a dreadful and dismal impression: monstrous shapeless buildings put up only by foremen without architecture, only the least that was necessary and out of red brick.

There is a great English military presence in Manchester to ensure

[476] Schinkel is here referring to the celebrated cotton mill of McConnel and Kennedy (partnership 1795–1826) in Union St, Ancoats, Manchester. After 1826 it traded as McConnel and Co. Henry McConnel, the owner of the mill, was a collector of paintings by J. M. W. Turner. The mill still survives in a dilapidated condition. The records of the firm are held in the John Rylands Library, University of Manchester.
[477] The Murray cotton mill, like that of McConnel, continued to operate into the twentieth century.
[478] Schinkel is here referring to the Royal Palace or Stadtschloss, designed by Andreas Schlüter in the early eighteenth century, the palace of the Kings of Prussia.
[479] Probably Richard Ainsworth & Son, Brazenose Street, Manchester (Pigot and Dean's *Directory for Manchester, Salford, etc.*, 1824–5).
[480] Schinkel is here describing the part of the canal system which ran through the centre of the city of Manchester and over the Irwell on a viaduct, and which still partially survives. There appear to be no early views of it, but note Johanna Schopenhauer's description on p. 13 (see Wegner, 159, note 113, for a more precise identification of Schinkel's drawings). It is not to be confused with the Manchester Ship Canal which only opened in 1894.

162. G. Pickering, eng.
T. Higham, *Manchester*,
1834, steel engraving

163. S. Austin, eng.
McGahey, *Cotton Factories,
Union Street, Manchester*,
from *Lancashire Illustrated*,
1831, inscribed to Mr
Murray and Mr McConnel

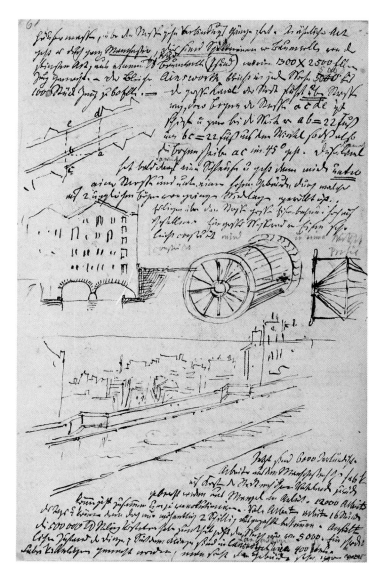

164. *Journal*, p. 61, Manchester canal system, (top left) groundplan of an aqueduct, inscr.: 'a–e the arch of the gangway a e is on a slant, and with the width from ab = 22 feet around bc = 22 feet from the corner, so that the round arch a c goes around 45 degrees', (below) View of the canal flowing under a house, (right) Iron water wheel in perspective and section, (below) perspective view of the canal crossing over streets beneath

165. *Journal*, p. 62, (above) View of Ancoats, with cotton mills. Union Street in foreground with the McConnel and Murray mills fronting the canal, (middle left) Manchester, doorway, (bottom) Liverpool, St John's Market, (above), section of the building, inscr.: 'abc. 140–150' deep, over 400' long', (below) details of roof construction: section & details of roof construction, (to the right) details of wooden joists and fastenings, inscr.: 'the long wooden rafter'

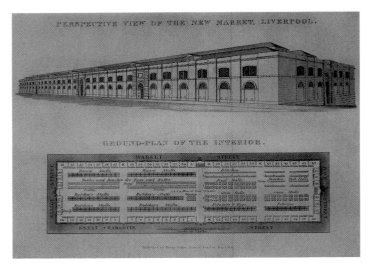

166. H. Fisher pub., *St John's Market, Liverpool*, 1822, engraving

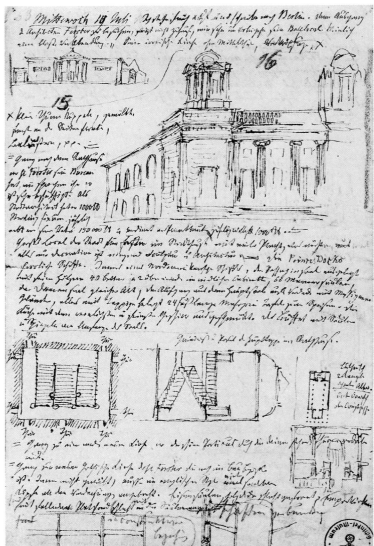

167. *Journal*, p. 63, (top left) Liverpool, Wellington Assembly Rooms, (right) St Andrew's Church, (below) Liverpool Town Hall, groundplan and section of central stairwell, inscr.: 'groundplan and section of central staircase in council house', (right) 2 sketches of St Andrew's Church: groundplan and section of interior, inscr.: 'Lutheran-2 chancels behind altar. Below Doric above Corinthian', (bottom) St Luke's Church, construction sketches

security:[481] fine-looking fellows, men and officers, splendid horses they ride on. – Tremendously wide pavements, 20–30 ft, of the finest stone, in undistinguished though wide streets. – The unfortunate door architecture of London is reproduced here as it is in the rest of England many thousand times over (see plate 165).

Tuesday, 18 July

We travelled through Warrington to Liverpool. Horse-market in Warrington, I was tired and stayed alone in the inn, watching the people in the street and in the dining room (similarity of manners of eating of all classes). Arrived in Liverpool by post-chaise at 5 in the evening. Westmacott's statue of George III on horseback,[482] the pedestal very high, but very poorly executed. Fine accommodation, Adelphi Hotel, good dinner. Beuth, Danckelmann, turtle soup their highest ideal. Magnificent bedroom for me. Walk round the town in the evening. – Doric church,[483] the beautiful covered market[484] (plate 166), a pity that the external architecture is not up to it. The columns iron, also water-pipes. Water (under pressure) everywhere for washing. Vaulted cellars. 140–150 ft wide, over 400 ft long.

Town Hall,[485] Nelson's monument[486] (plate 168), group with Nelson hanging crowns on a sword, which Victory hands to him between chaotic flags, while below on the round pedestal lamenting prisoners of the defeated nations. – The docks. Huge town, unattractive.

Wednesday, 19 July

I get up early and write to Berlin. Then go out to visit the architect Foster; he is not at home, we see in passing his Assembly Rooms,[487] smallish, a mere façade (plate 167). His Ionic church,[488] no central door, corner mouldings, small domed towers, vaulted windows along the sides, balustrade, etc. Go to the Town Hall, where Foster[489] has his office, we talk to him, he is very busy. As town architect he has a 1,000 pounds a year salary, he will inherit 150,000 pounds from his father, and earns about 1,000 pounds a year from private work. – Big town assembly room in the town

[481] In 1819, in St Peter's Fields ('Peterloo') Manchester, the workers of the industrial metropolis demonstrated for parliamentary reform and improved living conditions. The cavalry was ordered to charge, and there were many casualties. After that social tensions worsened, exacerbated by industrial overproduction and the impoverishment of a rapidly increasing proletariat.

[482] Richard Westmacott's statue of George III on horseback had been erected in 1822. It is in London Road in north-east Liverpool.

[483] Probably St Mary's Church for the Indigent Blind, Hotham Street, 1818–19, by John Foster the younger.

[484] St John's Market, a market hall built by John Foster, father and son, 1820–4, and demolished in recent years.

[485] This was formerly the Liverpool stock exchange, built 1749–54 from a design by John Wood, senior. Alterations were made 1789–92 by James Wyatt, and 1796–1820 by John Foster the Elder.

[486] Designed by M.C. Wyatt and executed by Richard Westmacott, erected 1813.

[487] Probably the Wellington Assembly Rooms. They were not designed by John Foster (1787–1846) but by Edmund Aikin (1780–1820) 1815–6 (*Buildings of England: South Lancashire*, pl. 36).

[488] St Andrew's Scottish Church, built 1823–4 by John Foster the Younger. Badly damaged by fire in recent years (Wegner, 162, fig. 93).

[489] This was John Foster the younger (1786–1846), whose father, also John Foster (d. 1824), was surveyor to the Corporation of Liverpool. Father and son were frequently involved in the same buildings and the latter succeeded to the former's office as architect and surveyor to the Corporation. The younger Foster had spent time in Greece with C.R. Cockerell and his German companions (see note 261).

hall of great splendour, somewhat empty, because everything is only decoration, nowhere any sculpture or architecture.[490]

The Prince's Docks (plate 169), magnificent ships. Interior of a north American ship, the passengers' quarters panelled in fine wood, 40 beds, one above the other in twos, in pleasant cubicles, 60 marble columns, the ladies' quarters similarly fitted out, the stairway from the main room to the deck has a brass rail, everything is carpeted, 24 ft long mahogany table for meals. The kitchen equipped with the finest, cleanest pottery. The sideboard with columns and mirrors at the entrance to the room. Go to another new church,[491] where the fine portico is spoilt by the doors standing inside.

Go to Mr Foster's new Gothic church,[492] which is still being built. Interior not vaulted, the outside in the English style with many grotesque heads fixed to the roofing. Wooden roof badly formed, choir with sloping ceiling, badly attached to the columns.

In the evening a walk outside the town on the bare hill where the streets run out. Then to the water below, observed the locks in the docks, where the water was let out to be filled up at high tide. Fine swing bridges over the lock gates, the latter without props.

[Continuation of the letter to Susanne of 19 July]

For the last 50 years, for as long as machines have been in operation, England has doubled, and in some places tripled and quadrupled, its population, and has become much improved. This is an extraordinary phenomenon which any discriminating traveller must note. But the peak has now been reached, and speculation has now surpassed itself. In Manchester, where we were yesterday, 400 new cotton mills have been erected since the war, among which several are as big as the royal palace in Berlin, thousands of smoking obelisks from steam-engines around them, whose height of 80 to 180 ft destroys all the impact of the church towers. All these structures have produced such an enormous mass of goods that the world is glutted with them, now 12,000 workers are gathering on the streets because they have no work, and after the town has, at its own expense, sent 6,000 Irishmen back home, other workers can only earn 2 shillings a week, about 15 groschen, for a

[490] In 1795 the Town Hall interior was destroyed by fire and rebuilt to the designs of the elder Foster under the supervision of James Wyatt.
[491] St Michael in Pitt Street, built by Foster, father and son, between 1816 and 1826. This church was destroyed in the Second World War. (For a fuller account of the original church see Wegner, 162, note 118).
[492] St Luke's Church, begun 1811 by the elder Foster and altered after 1827 by his son. Severely damaged in the Second World War.

168. G. & C. Pyne, eng.
T. Dixon, *Liverpool,
Exchange Buildings and
Nelson's Monument*, from
S. Austin, *Lancashire
Illustrated*, 1831, engraving

169. Harwood, eng.
F.R. May, *The Prince's Dock,
Liverpool*, from S. Austin,
Lancashire Illustrated, 1931,
engraving

170. Thomas Harrison, *The Propylaea viewed from inside the portico of Chester Castle*, pen and sepia wash. Grosvenor Museum, Chester

171. L. Haghe and T. Bailey, *West (Entrance) Front of Eaton Hall*, lithograph

172. W. Wallis, *St Winefrid's Well, Holywell*, engraving

16-hour day. – One is very much in doubt as to what might come of this frightful state of affairs. – More of this from my own mouth. You see that there is much of interest to observe here.

Unfortunately I cannot give you any firm times for my return journey to London via Wales and Bristol, as this hangs on Beuth's business. But we shall certainly be in London in 4 weeks and ready for the return journey, which will be fairly quick, as we shall only be stopping one day in the Netherlands with Mr Cockerill in Seraing, otherwise we will be travelling as fast as possible; I long to rest again with you and in the circle of our children. You write nothing to me about Karl and his studies. I hope for the best and that he will become a really industrious young man and make me happy. My warmest greetings to all our acquaintance, Gabains, Schölers[493] etc. Perhaps you will write again to London, a letter from you takes 8 days, and I would be very pleased to learn how it goes with you all and whether my letter has reached you. Farewell, dearest Susanne, kiss the children. Your Schinkel.

Thursday, 20 July

Morning departure from Liverpool by steamboat across to the other bank of the Mersey (the estuary on which Liverpool is situated) where a stage-coach picked us up and took us to Chester. Chester has kept its old appearance completely. The buildings have shops on the street and about 10–12 ft above these is a covered way, behind which are more shops.[494] There is nothing here of English neatness, everything looks old, dilapidated and dirty. The wide city walls allow a pleasant promenade round the whole town. You walk upon a 4 ft wide stone pavement and have views of the suburbs and the wealthy quarter as well as of the town itself. The town is small. There is a racecourse on one side, a beautiful expanse of green, and above is the castle to which a new propylaea[495] (plate 170) has been built, the central section of which has been marred by box-like upper parts. The back of the Castle has walls similar to the Pitti Palace in Florence and are very much in character. – After our arrival in Chester we drove first to Eaton Hall[496] (plate 171), 4–5 English miles from the town, the grand country seat of Lord

[493] General von Schöler, of the Prussian Ministry of War, lived with his family in the same house as the Schinkel family: 4a Unter den Linden (the latter were there 1821–36).
[494] This walkway still survives.
[495] Chester Castle and the Propylaea or gateway were the work of the important Greek Revival architect Thomas Harrison (1744–1829) who had studied in Rome. C.R. Cockerell, the classical scholar and architect, commended his control of masonry, but disliked the mixture of orders in the Chester buildings (Colvin, under Harrison).
[496] Designed by William Porden in a Gothic revival style, in which iron was used both in the construction and in the interior decoration. In 1823–5 Benjamin Gummow added wings to the building. According to a contemporary Porden attempted 'to adapt the rich variety of our ancient ecclesiastical architecture to modern domestic convenience' (Colvin, under Porden).

Grosvenor, all built of fine ashlar in medieval style. The main building alone is 420 feet long, and in addition there is also a courtyard with outhouses. The rooms are most meticulously executed and have the most beautiful view over the park and flower terraces next to the house. The corridors, salons, library and entrance hall allow a view of the whole length of the interior in perspective. Unfortunately, for all the meticulous care with which it has been carried out it is architecturally dull. The library was the last room to be built and is the finest, a soft red, with gold ribs and beading and rich red wall-coverings. – The bookcases are so constructed that a curtain of the same red colour can be let down in front of the books, so that only the architecture stands out against the red background, and all is in harmony with the raised wall-coverings. – After dinner in a very bad Chester tavern we drove on to Holywell (plate 172). Here in a chapel we saw St Winifred's well,[497] with a basin in front of it. People were bathing within this complex of remarkable but not very ancient Gothic architecture, and had many spectators (it was pouring with rain). We bought strong canvas to protect our luggage from the rain on the journey, which was difficult on the post-chaises we have to take here in Wales.

Friday, 21 July

Drive through pleasant hilly region, first to Conway, which we reached by midday. Here is a new suspension bridge[498] (plates 175 and 176) open only 9 days, which goes over an estuary, and the span is 136 paces. A causeway leads across the longer stretch of water to a low rock. The bridge's chain extends on castellated towers to the cliff on which stand the ruins of a well-preserved castle, which together with the old town walls forms a single ancient fortification. We observed closely the construction of the bridge, then the castle, and climbed a hill where I made a drawing of the whole situation.

After lunch we continued on to Bangor, arriving in the evening. The inn lies like a country house alone among trees on the estuary which separates the island of Anglesey from England [*sic*]. We went

[497] St Winifride's Well, Holywell, North Wales. The late Gothic chapel above the well was built at the behest of Lady Margaret Beaufort, mother of Henry VII, about 1500.
[498] Next to Conway Castle, founded in 1284 by Edward I, an iron suspension bridge on castellated supports, designed by Thomas Telford, had been built over the River Conway in 1821–6.

173. *The Menai Bridge*, 1826, pen and pencil

174. Detail of plate 173

175. *Panoramic drawing of Conway with the Castle and Suspension Bridge*, 1826, pen and pencil

176. Detail of plate 175

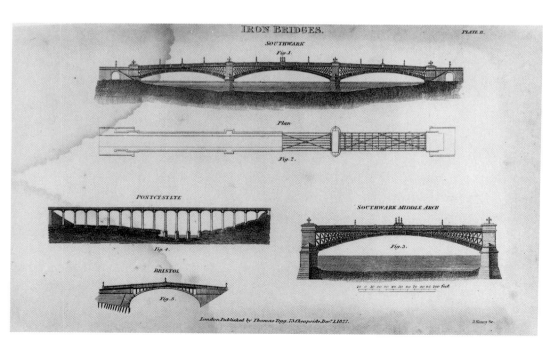

177. J. Shury, *Iron Bridges*, including Pont-y-Cysylltau (fig. 4), 1827, engraving, published by T. Tegg

to the great [Menai] suspension bridge[499] (plates 173 and 174) built by Telford, a wonderful, daring work. The chains are 700 ft long, the span 500 ft, the roadway 100 ft above the water at high tide and 120 ft at low tide. At one end there are 3, at the other 4 arches, each 50 ft wide. No shuddering, which might have been detrimental, as we drove across. We got down where the chains were fixed to the rock. They went into the ground for at least 60 paces, where they were fixed into the rock. I drew the whole scene, to record the hugeness of the thing. We returned late to the inn. Bought an account of the construction.

Saturday, 22 July

We drove back, and from a distance saw the new Penrhyn Castle,[500] park and splendid walls, also an inn belonging to Lord Könering[?]. Then we saw one of the largest slate-quarries[501] in England, fine material, it splits into the finest slates 3–4 ft wide. The workers work in slate huts, the great slate beams are roofed over just as if they are of wood. Many railways. – Soon afterwards we saw the Conway waterfalls in various places, coming in the evening to Llangollen. Walk to the Abbey ruins,[502] it was too late to climb up to the castle. It is a beautiful part of the country, the inn has a small flower garden by the river, where a weir splashes very pleasantly. We had a meal and then went to bed.

Sunday, 23 July

From Llangollen to Shrewsbury. First we saw the Pont-y-Cysylltau[503] (plate 177); it carries a canal across a beautiful valley in iron channels on 19 iron arches, on supports of up to 90 ft high; one part of the canal rests on a bank of earth. A mile away the canal continues on through a mountain and then across another valley, supported by massive arches. – All the work of Mr Telford, whose road construction is so arranged that from the Menai Bridge all his great works can be observed. – The Welsh hills came to an end, the rich English plains began again. We stayed in Shrewsbury, a

[499] The Menai Bridge, spanning the Menai Strait and connecting Anglesey with the Welsh mainland, had only recently been completed. It was designed by Telford 1817–18 and built 1819–26, opening 30 January 1826. It was the first large-scale suspension bridge to be built (580 ft span), and Telford's greatest achievement. Thomas Telford (1757–1834), engineer and bridge-builder, started his work on bridge construction in 1792. He also built canals, including the Ellesmere Canal, and docks.
[500] The medieval Penrhyn Castle had been enlarged and altered in Gothic Revival style by Samuel Wyatt (1737–1807), and finished by 1800. Thomas Hopper (1786–1856) began to remodel the castle in 1827 in the Norman Revival style, of which it is a spectacular example.
[501] The Penrhyn slate quarries were developed by the Pennant family who owned Penrhyn House.
[502] Presumably Valle Crucis Abbey, near Llangollen, founded in 1200 as a Cistercian abbey and dissolved in 1535. It is the most important ruined monastery in North Wales, with main sections dating from the thirteenth century. Schinkel also refers to the ruins of Dinas Bran Castle.
[503] The aqueduct by this name, which carries the Ellesmere Canal across the Dee Valley near Llangollen, was built by Telford 1795–1805. It has 19 stone piers each 120 ft high, connected by cast iron arched structures, and a large channel consisting of a series of iron troughs.

prettily situated town with an old market-hall and a number of old houses, churches and towers in the town walls, and booked outside seats on a coach for the next morning for the Gloucester region. The post-chaises are expensive, extremely uncomfortable for three people, the luggage is repacked at every stage, the toll on the high roads is exorbitant, one never pays less than 1 shilling or 18 pence at any toll-gate. – MacAdam's road surfacing method[504] is now in general use; more than 12,000 miles at least have been treated, and one soon notices whether one is travelling on an old or a new road. In some places a softer stone is used as a underlayer, these stones are also larger; granite, sienite, basalt, hornblende are still the materials used for the actual surface. One never sees ditches at the roadside, but often pavements raised 8 ins., while the road is only gently cambered, almost imperceptably. The road is frequently enclosed by 4 ft high walls, in which about every 4 rods there is a small hole 6 ins square as a gutter for the rain. The walls of quarried stone have pieces of slate along the top which project sharply, making climbing over difficult and giving a good appearance (plate 179).

It appears that clay soil is preferred as a base for this kind of road surfacing. The gravelling is to a regular depth of 6 ins, taking into account the slight camber. During repairs, quite considerable stretches in strips of 15 ins are dug out and piled up alongside each other so that the new material can be mixed with the old. I have not seen rails laid down on any of the roads. The dirt is pushed to the side during heavy rain with wooden sweepers, piled up in heaps and taken away. In the streets of London this was a great business on rainy days, whereas in dry weather the streets were sprayed to such an extent that filth also collected on the roads. Whole streets in London are so flimsily built that the paving damages the buildings when there is vibration caused by heavy traffic, in this respect the high roads are safer because there is less vibration.

Monday, 24 July

Outside on the stagecoach across pleasant hilly countryside, Coalbrookdale, iron bridge,[505] Tewkesbury, Cheltenham, to

[504] John Loudon MacAdam (1757–1836), engineer and road-builder, had invented and introduced vital improvements for road surfacing ('tarmac'). In 1819 he published *A practical essay on the scientific repair and preservation of public roads.*
[505] The first iron bridge in England was built 1777–9 in the industrial area of Coalbrookdale, from a design by Thomas Farnolls Pritchard. It had a span of 30 metres.

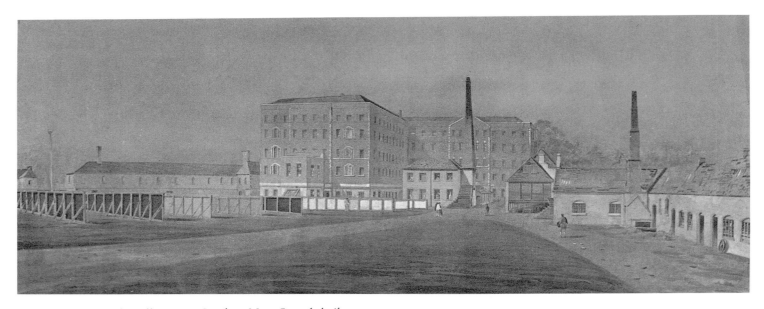

178. Anon., *Cloth Mills, Kings Stanley, Near Stroud, built 1813*, mid–nineteenth century, oil painting. Cowle Museum, Stroud

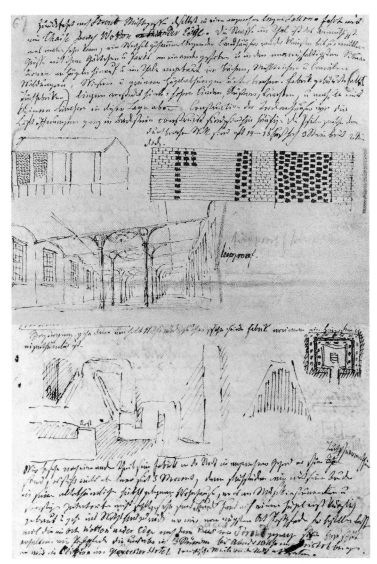

179. *Journal*, p. 66, (middle left) retaining wall on the road near Shrewsbury, (below left) Tewksbury Abbey, (bottom centre) detail of Stanley mills, worked up on next page of *Journal*

180. *Journal*, p. 67, (top) Drying sheds near Stroud or Wotton-Under-Edge, (below middle) Interior of Stanley Mill, with iron columns, inscr.: 'fireproof', (bottom) studies of an oven and outlets, inscr.: 'roast, plan, part of the flue'

[506] Tewkesbury Abbey is one of the most important Romanesque buildings in England (Wegner, 167, fig. 101).

[507] George III visited Cheltenham for the first time in 1788, after which it became a popular summer resort for fashionable London society and rapidly increased in size. Schinkel would have seen the recently completed Montpellier and Lansdown areas.

[508] This must be the Stanley Mill, at King's Stanley near Stroud, a cloth factory built 1812–13. The functional iron pillars and traditional brick construction, and stylish interior made it particularly impressive. No wood was used in its construction, making it fireproof. The factory interior, which Schinkel sketched, is divided by rows of cast iron pillars supporting shallow barrel vaulting above, and iron spandrels that were both decorative and practical. Schinkel's impressions of the building influenced some of his later designs, especially the use of iron in Prince Albrecht's Palace (see *Buildings of England,* D. Verey, *Gloucestershire: The Cotswolds,* 1970, 288 and pl. 90).

Stroud, where we stopped for the night. Beautiful old church in Tewkesbury.[506]

Cheltenham,[507] pleasant place, many handsome ladies and people on the street in their finery. New buildings and new parts of the town, where the nice houses are rendered in light-coloured plaster and have gardens all round, or at least in front, which can be seen through iron railings. Countryside round the town agreeably hilly, with many trees.

Tuesday, 25 July

Beautiful hills near Stroud, dotted with houses and factories. We saw two textile mills, and next to them the fine country houses of the owners, all finely set up; we breakfasted with the last gentleman in the company of 3 ladies, after a visit to the splendid factory. Fireproof building, very solid and better constructed than in Manchester.[508]

Drive back to Stroud, ate there in a pleasant long salon. Drove in a chaise to Wotton under Edge. The road through the valley is the loveliest sight one can imagine: a succession of country houses lying together and ranging from very small to middle-sized with ajoining gardens and parks, set in the most varied positions on slopes and in the valley, interspersed with streams, millponds and canals, woods, meadows and green hillsides. Factories (all textile mills) and small churches alternate, hidden behind tall lime trees, elms, larches. – Construction of the drying-sheds, where the air vents are made solely of brick, are common here (plates 178 and 180). The columns between the incised [iron]work are often 14–16 ft high, 3 bricks wide, 2 bricks thick.

Wednesday, 26 July

We visited early a factory-owner who was not at home, had a little walk, went back at half past ten, saw his factory, which contained an unusual heating system.

We saw another part of his factory just outside the town in pleasant country, where there were fine textile machines; but many have been idle for the last 5 months. Then we ate with his brother in his ancient, prettily situated house, where there was no lack of musical instruments and other pastimes, saw his brother's house on a hill, only recently built, and went back to the inn, where we booked post-horses from the next town because those in Wotton Under Edge had gone to the races in Stroud. The post-horses did not arrive until late, but they got us to Bristol in 3 hours by 10 in the evening, where we booked into the Gloucester Hotel in Clifton, one English mile outside the town.

Thursday, 27 July

In the very pleasant hotel, where I shared a room with Count Danckelmann with a superb view of the high crescents and the river down below, we slept very well, and after breakfast we went into the town. On the way we looked at an old church[509] and a fifteenth-century gate, on the lower half of which there is some late version of early Saxon architecture. These buildings stand in a square containing beautiful tall trees. From there we drove in a hackney to our Consul Watson, and went with him first to a lamp manufacturer who, according to an Austrian writer, produces large amounts of a special kind of wax from the carcases of old animals; we discovered that the whole thing was false, that the man just uses the usual spermaceti. Right next to this man's house is the church of St Mary Redcliffe[510] (plate 181), whose interior is very complete, in the ornate medieval English style, there are 3 paintings over the altar, the Angel at the Tomb, the Ascension and [the Sealing of the Sepulchre], by Hogarth[511] fully English school, modern facial beauty, very little precision in the drawing, and light effects too much sought after. We drove to the workshop of Mr Winwood for the construction of steam-engines[512] (plate 182). Roof construction of simple iron bars joined together. Applied everywhere. 36 ft span, the iron braces 2½ ft apart. The beams are made of iron and tiled over. The roof iron is ¼ in. thick and stands 2 to 3 ins high. 2 men, one at the crank of a drill, the other on the crank of the fly-wheel, were cutting and slotting out half-inch iron.

We drove back across the high plateau[513] on which the town is

[509] This is the Cathedral on College Green, founded in the twelfth century as an Augustine abbey and built mainly in the fourteenth century. Schinkel is referring also to the Abbey house, which is partly Romanesque and partly late fifteenth century.
[510] This spectacular church, begun in the thirteenth century, was altered and extended in Perpendicular style in the fifteenth century.
[511] This celebrated and very large triptych by Hogarth, 1755–56, was removed from the church in the 1850s, and now belongs to Bristol City Art Gallery (see D. Bindman, *Hogarth*, London, 1981, 190–1).
[512] John Winwood & Co., Iron Founders, Steam Engine makers and Wrought Iron Manufacturers, Cheese Lane, St Philip's, Bristol (1826 Bristol Directory).
[513] This is Clifton Down, high up above the Avon, which was probably settled by Britons in pre-Roman times.

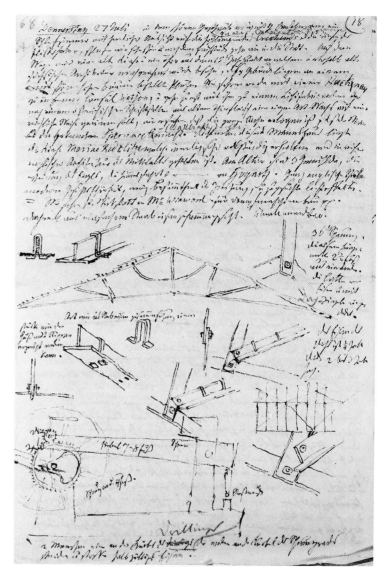

181. James Johnson, *Interior of St Mary Redcliffe, with Hogarth's Altarpiece*, 1828, pencil and watercolour. City of Bristol Museum and Art Gallery

182. *Journal*, p. 68, Winwood workshop, Bristol, studies of iron roof construction and a steam engine. section of roof, with details of iron fastenings, inscr.: 'the way in which the pieces of iron bar are always put together, so the casting can be produced with ribs' (below left) steam-driven trip hammer, inscr.: 'gearwheel. lever 7–8 feet. flywheel 4 feet. cutters. punch'

situated, where there are many new roads and country houses set in gardens all round, the roads are very steep. – The view of the town from the top, where there was originally a Roman *castrum*, into the deep valley of the Avon, the tree-covered cliffs of the river banks and the tree-covered English plains, bordered by blue hills in the distance, is quite superb. The road led down to the river, past the hot-spring baths[514] back to our hotel, behind which two crescents have been built against the hill-slope, one above the other. – We had a good dinner (turtle soup, the epitome of Beuth's earthly bliss), and afterwards walked across the river, which had all but disappeared since it was low tide, only two mud banks remaining. Then we soon returned, found our hackney coachman and hired him to take us one German mile from the town to Kings Weston Inn, a noted beauty-spot.

It is a pleasant road through high-lying uncultivated land and parkland. Kings Weston[515] has a magnificent park with great house and working buildings belonging to a Lord [de Clifford], on a high plateau, where one can see the sea and a delightful panorama. The furthest point of a jutting-out part of the high plateau is marked by a stone sundial, and many people come here to enjoy the view, we saw some ladies on horseback etc. The sunset was magnificent. Steamboats in the distance, superb oaks and elms in the grounds. The landlord of the inn is a German (Schubert from Brunswick), we got back to Clifton very late and tired. – At Kings Weston house the construction of the chimneys was of a series of joined arches, making a kind of arcading on the roof; this makes a fine effect in the distance and in the rural setting, and makes sure that the chimneys, which were exposed to strong winds in that high position, because they were joined together did not get blown down. An old tower on the heath near the park is said to have been built in medieval times against the Danes, but it looked to me of more recent construction.

Friday, 28 July

At 8 we arrived at the coach-office in town in a hackney with our luggage, and travelled outside on a coach to Bath. The

[514] These are the 'hotwells', which constituted a spa in the eighteenth century. This area of Clifton is still known as Hotwells.

[515] King's Weston was designed by Vanbrugh about 1710. It remains one of his most impressive buildings, and the unusual design of the chimneys noted by Schinkel can still be seen (*Buildings of England: North Somerset and Bristol*, 469 and plates 53a & b). In 1826 it belonged to the de Clifford family (I am indebted to Mr Michael Liversidge for his help here).

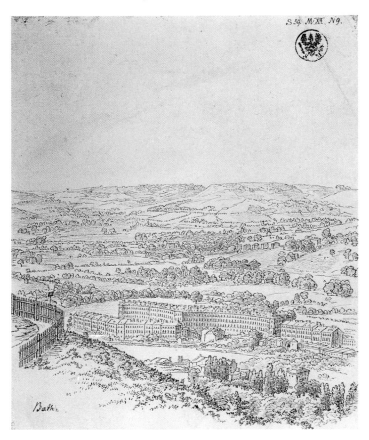

183. *View of Park Crescent, Bath*, 1826, pen and pencil

184. *Bath, street scene*, 1826, pen and pencil

amphitheatre of Bristol looked lovely from the distance, the country around it richly endowed with country houses and beautiful plantations. In 2 hours we were in Bath,[516] where many new things have been built, there is the fine sight of two crescents one above the other against the hill (plate 183). We took rooms in the York Hotel, and Beuth drove off alone in a post-chaise to see some factories in the neighbourhood. Count Danckelmann and I saw the town. We climbed up to the highest part, and I made a sketch of the valley bottom.

The architecture of Bath is very well-thought of in England, but it is rather boring and wholly in the mean English style. The building stone is very fine. The position of the town on hillsides and in valleys, where branches of the width of a single street have been arbitrarily pushed out from the town because of the lack of any cohesion or master plan, is certainly very pleasant and opulent, but it lacks expanses of water or contours of a determined character. The weather was as hot as in Italy, so that we soon had to go back to our hotel, where we waited for Beuth and I made a sketch of the view from the window (plate 184). After a late dinner we had a walk through the town, and observed the high-walled terraces at the back of the houses in the streets going up the hillside. An old church with a forecourt,[517] separated from the street by a propylaeum, the Corinthian oddly running off the medieval building, and a couple of not uninteresting public buildings, one also sees here galleries for shops like those in Paris. On the streets go the sick visiting the baths, carried around in small three-wheeled carts with a device for changing direction, which are pulled or pushed by a man. The loose women on the streets are shameless and importunate even in daytime.

Saturday, 29 July

We left for London at 6 on the outside of a stagecoach, a Spanish officer sat opposite me who had come to England with General Mina,[518] been wounded twice in the chest, and had been taking the waters in Bath, we talked much in French, he cursed all priests and awaited the day for revenge. – We arrived in London at 6; the road

[516] Bath was an important watering-place even in Roman times, developing after 1725 into a fashionable spa. New building in the eighteenth century introduced innovative elements into English architecture. John Wood, senior (1704–54), and his son John Wood, junior (1728–81), with Queen Square (1729–36), South Parade (1743 and later), the Circus (1754 and later) and the Royal Crescent (1761–5) created part of an architectural ensemble of squares and connecting streets (their plans had been even more extensive).
[517] Probably the sixteenth-century Bath Abbey.
[518] Francisco Espoz y Mina (1786–1836), Spanish general who had left Spain and come to England after defeat at the hands of the French army.

was not especially interesting, in some places we saw great Druid tumuli, one particularly large mound, also Druid stones and a village close by which was built entirely of these stones.[519] On two hillocks someone had had the strange idea of laying the image of an English horse into the dark grass of the slope, in a mosaic of white, chalky pieces of flint, of such a size (80 ft long) that it can be seen for miles, as if floating in front of the ridge[520] (plate 185).

Windsor Castle made again an impressive sight in the distance. In London we again found comfortable rooms in St Paul's Hotel.

London and the return to Berlin

(Bruges, Aachen, Cologne, Münster)

London, 30 July 1826

Dearest Susanne. Yesterday we arrived cheerfully back in London, after travelling nearly 1,500 English miles around England and Scotland, as you will have gathered from my letters from Edinburgh and Liverpool, in which last I told you how happy I was to receive your letter from Berlin.

I have seen so many interesting and beautiful things on this journey that we shall have much to talk about for a long time to come, when I am back with you again. I hope that that is now not much further off, as we are only staying in London for 8 days at most, then we go to Calais, from there through the Netherlands to Aachen and, by not stopping long in Westphalia, getting back to Berlin quickly.

You will probably get a letter from me from Aachen, when I should be able to give you the exact day of our return. I hope that you, the children, Mother and Karoline, and Wilhelm are as well as I am and that I shall find you so on my arrival. My best greetings to Rauch, Tieck, Günthers,[521] Schölers, Gabains, Humboldts,[522] Frau Beuth, Langermann[523] etc. I doubt if I shall get another letter from you in London, as I asked in my last letter from Liverpool; I shall

[519] Presumably Avebury.
[520] This is presumably White Horse Hill near Uffington, where there is a huge horse is cut into the side of the hill. It is far larger (112 metres wide) than Schinkel's estimate.
[521] August Günther (died 1842), from 1816 a senior public works official in Berlin, a colleague and friend of Schinkel's in the Public Works Commission.
[522] Wilhelm von Humboldt (1767–1835) and his wife Karoline, *née* von Dachroden (1766–1829). Schinkel had converted Tegel Palace for them in 1822–4.
[523] Privy Chief Medical Counsellor in Berlin, a friend of Schinkel's. His biographer Waagen says of him that 'his impressive, intelligent personality together with his cultured mind, many interests and pleasant ways, had an invigorating and stimulating effect on Schinkel' (G.F. Waagen: *K.F. Schinkel als Mensch und als Künstler*, Berlin, 1844, p. 363).

185. *Journal*, p. 70, (middle) Uffington, White Horse Hill (below centre and bottom left) Meux brewery, storage of large barrels, and section of warehouse

186. Anon., *Exterior view of Meux's Brewery*, watercolour. Museum of London

have anything that arrives here after my departure addressed to Berlin.

You might perhaps be visited by Herr Dannenberger, who left us in Scotland and who came back to Berlin before us; he can bring you a report of our journey into the Highlands.

I have a special request, that you should see to Karl's uninterrupted study and tell him I hope and trust that I shall hear much good of him and that he will behave well and work hard for my sake. Farewell dearest Susanne, I long to be with you, your Schinkel.

Sunday, 30 July

I write my diary and to Berlin, Beuth made various visits. The evening is very pleasant, we take a boat from Southwark Bridge[524] up the Thames to the other side of Vauxhall Bridge, we witness the gorgeous effect of total clarity (no smoke) in a strong evening light, there were particularly beautiful vistas through the varied arches of the bridges, reminiscent of Venice.

Monday, 31 July

We visited Consul Giese and went with him to the large Meux brewery[525] (plate 186). 180 huge horses are kept here, to transport the beer from the factory. The huge barrels, 26–30 ft in diameter, contain beer worth 18,000 pounds sterling. The iron hoops of one of the larger barrels, 36 of them one above the other, 3–4 ins wide, ½ in. thick, make one barrel alone weigh 6,000 hundredweight. Such barrels stand on two levels, in long rows (see plate 185).

The cooling trays very shallow, 8 ins deep, 40–60 ft long, 40 wide, with fans above for cooling. The stores of barley and malt are in a building 120 ft high with 3 ft thick walls, inside this the corn is piled up to a height of 50 ft in separate compartments; the pressure on the outer walls and the joists is not considered. The rough-grinding mill with Archimedean screws which separate the different degrees of coarseness.

[524] Begun 1810/11 by J. Rennie as a stone bridge, but continued 1813–16 by James Walker as a nine-span iron construction.
[525] In Liquorpond Street, probably built by William Robert Laxton (b.1776) c.1804.

I visited the [British] Museum again, looking carefully at every part. – Then I went to the Royal Exhibition in Pall Mall,[526] there are Rembrandts and Teniers here, Ruidaels, Hobbemas, Jan Steen (a scene where a lovely girl is being paid after making love, the behaviour in response to it of the London ladies). Another picture by Steen, a woman stepping out of bed, wonderful tones, gay and classical in colour. Landscape by Both (allegorical landscape by Rubens, and others, portraits with landscape). Landscape by Titian. Rembrandt's Shipbuilder with his Wife, and a Mayor with his Wife at her Toilet, are particularly excellent, as also a man's portrait.

In the evening at 9 I went to Vauxhall[527] (plate 187) with Count Danckelmann. Enormous lower garden space interspersed with fantastic, long, covered galleries, temples, halls, dining rooms, all brightly lit by coloured lamps and at first sight like Armida's magic garden.[528] First there was a concert in a great round salon with boxes, where the foremost singers, male and female, performed a mixture of English, Italian and German music. Between the first and 2nd acts of the concert the whole audience promenaded round the illuminated halls and temples, then watched an entertainment in a theatre formed by the vault of the trees, there were tightrope-walkers and finally a beautiful pantomime ballet. Then there is Janissaries music in an Indian temple, where 4 real Moors played cymbals. Then the second part of the concert was given in the round salon. After that in another place there was a great firework display in front of a wall painted like a tower, which was soon bright with crimson and white fire effects. This ended with the performance of a tightrope-walker, who walked round the tower on a rope 120–130 ft up, lit by Bengal lights. He stood for many minutes on the rope in clouds of thick smoke, with fireworks flying all round, only occasionally visible through the smoke. Finally he came down. – There were over three hundred tables laid for 8 and 12 people in the garden, which were only used after the fireworks; it was 1 o'clock, and we drove home without eating anything at all; for all these amusements you pay 4 shillings (Prussian: 1 thaler, 8 groschen).

[526] These are the exhibition premises of the British Institution in the Shakespeare Gallery, Pall Mall, where works by both contemporary artists and old masters were exhibited annually. The exhibition that Schinkel saw at the British Institution was that of George IV's collection removed from Carlton House; as a result many of the paintings Schinkel remarked upon can be identified:

a. Jan Steen. 'the girl being paid off after lovemaking' is *Scene in a Brothel, with an Old Man giving Money to a Girl.* (C. White, *Dutch paintings in the Collection of H.M. The Queen*, London, 1982, p. 121, no. 187, pl. 162); 'A woman stepping out of bed' is *A Woman at her Toilet* (White, op. cit., p. 122, no. 189, pl. 164).

b. Rubens. The 'allegorical landscape' by Rubens may be conflated with Schinkel's reference to 'portraits with landscape'; in which case he would be referring to the celebrated *Landscape with St George and the Dragon*, with Charles I and Henrietta Maria. (See O. Millar, *The Queen's Pictures*, London, 1977, pl. 33).

c. Titian. Landscape with a flock of sheep is the 'Presumed copy after Titian', *A Landscape with Shepherds and Flocks.* This famous picture had some standing as an early Titian landscape in the nineteenth century, but is now thought to be by a seventeenth century imitator (J. Shearman, *The Early Italian Pictures in the Collection of H.M. The Queen*, London, 1983, pp. 271–3, no. 295).

d. Rembrandt. *The Shipbuilder with his Wife*, 1633 (White, op. cit., p. 104, no. 160, pl. 135).

The 'Mayor with his Wife at her Toilet' is the painting known at the time as 'Portraits of the Burgomaster Pancras, and his Lady at her Toilette'. This is the large painting identified as *Rembrandt and his Wife* which is now attributed to Ferdinand Bol (White, op. cit., p. 24, no. 27, pl. 27).

[527] A pleasure garden popular with London society from *c*.1730 into the early nineteenth century, situated on the south bank of the Thames.

[528] In 1820 Schinkel had designed stage sets for Gluck's opera *Armida* (1778), an episode from Tasso's *Jerusalemme Liberata*, for the Berlin Opera.

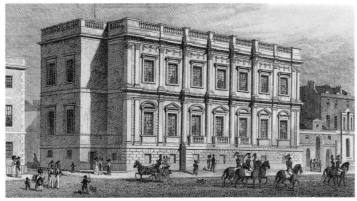

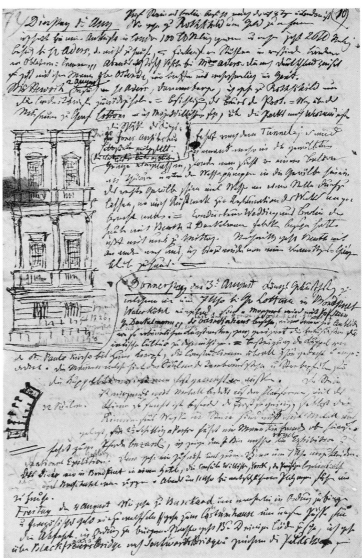

187. A.C. Pugin & T. Rowlandson, *Pavilion in Vauxhall Gardens* from *The Microcosm of London*, 1809, coloured aquatint

188. T.H. Shepherd, *Banqueting House, Whitehall*, from *London in the Nineteenth Century*, 1827, engraving

189. *Journal*, p. 72, (upper left) London, Banqueting House, corner of façade, (below left) St Paul's Cathedral, groundplan of the drum of the dome, inscr.: '36 columns'

Tuesday, 1 August

Prof. Stein[529] from Berlin visited me, he is in London for 8 days. We go to Rothschild to get some money, on my arrival in London I took out 100 pounds sterling and now I took 20 pounds sterling. Visit to Herr Aders who was not at home. – Bought chairs in various shops, also cameo seals etc. – In the evening after supper visited Madame Aders who is travelling to Germany, she is going with her husband via Ostend, we will probably meet up in Ghent.

Wednesday, 2 August

Visits with Herr Aders, Dannenberger, I go to Rothschild to collect the letters of credit. – Inspected the Postal building[530] – Walked via the Museum to Count Lottum's where I saw Major Willisen, then across the parks to Westminster. The royal palaces. Inigo Jones's architecture[531] (plates 188 and 189), widely-spaced half-columns. (The corner-mouldings could have been left out). Drive to the tunnel,[532] no one is any longer allowed into the tunnels; now one looks down into the tunnels from a balcony in the tower beneath the water-pumps. The right tunnel appeared in one place to be letting in a lot of water, and scaffolds had been erected to repair the structure. – Konducteur Wedding[533] from Berlin, who has been looking at factories today with Beuth and Danckelmann, had lunch with us. In the afternoon Beuth went out again with the others, I was too tired from my morning wanderings and stayed in.

Thursday, 3 August

King's birthday,[534] for which we were invited to Count Lottum's at the Wales Hotel, Bond Street at 7. In the morning went with Prof. Stein, Count Danckelmann etc., to see East India House[535] a miserable spectacle of pitiful works of art guaranteed to mortify enthusiasts of Indian culture. Climbed into the dome of St Paul's Church [Cathedral] right up to the lantern, the constructions are everywhere beautifully conceived and executed. The walls behind the columns supporting the drum, which form the buttresses for

[529] This is probably Christian Gottfried Daniel Stein (1771–1830), geographer and teacher at the Gymnasium zum Grauen Kloster in Berlin from 1795. He published, amongst other works, *Reisen nach den vorzüglichsten Hauptstädten von Mitteleuropa*, 1827–9.
[530] The General Post Office, St Martin's-le-Grand, built 1824–9 from a design by Robert Smirke.
[531] The Banqueting House in Whitehall.
[532] Presumably the Thames Tunnel (see p. 97).
[533] This is probably Johann Friedrich Wedding (1759–1830), engineer and architect, Councillor for Mining from 1818. He built iron foundries, mainly in Silesia.
[534] Friedrich Wilhelm III was born on 3 August 1770.
[535] The East India House of 1726, headquarters of the East India Company (founded 1600), had been renovated by Richard Jupp in 1798 under the supervision of Henry Holland who completed it after the former's death. The East India Company Museum or 'Oriental Repository' had been set up as part of the rebuilding at the beginning of the century. The collection was miscellaneous and ill-exhibited, but it had one notorious object: Tippoo's Tiger, the mechanical man-eating tiger captured from Tippo Sahib in 1799, and now in the Victoria and Albert Museum (Altick, *Shows of London*, 299–300).

the dome can hardly be seen from outside. The stone on the exposed surfaces has not any metal covering, because the climate is so mild, as frost is infrequent; even the gutters are of stone and not lined with metal; for 2½ shillings a person a guide takes visitors up 32 columns.

Drive to the horse-market, after which I showed Professor Stein the Royal Exhibition and National Exhibition.[536] Then we went home to dress for the dinner at 7. The dinner was in a hotel in Bond Street, Consuls Willisen and Yorck, the Prussian Legation Consellor [. . .] from Neufchâtel, were present. We drove home at 11 in the evening in a dreadful downpour.

Thursday, London, 3 August 1826

(Letter to Susanne)

Through the kindness of Count Dannenberger from Berlin, you may get this letter before the previous one I wrote from here; he would be able to tell you much about our meetings in Scotland and in other places in England. I did not want to miss this opportunity of sending you some more words. On Saturday we go to Calais, arriving on Saturday evening and then continue our journey to Aachen with all possible speed. If possible I shall write a few lines to you from Aachen. – Perhaps you will also be visited by Professor Stein, Langermann's friend, who came to London for 8 days and returns to Berlin via Hamburg on the same steamboat as Herr Dannenberger. I have seen some things in his company in London, and he will be able to tell you of my good health. I hope to find you all well when I return. Please thank Rauch heartily for his letter, which I received yesterday, just before our departure. I am on the point of driving to Count Lottum's house, he is celebrating the King's birthday with a dinner tonight at half past seven, in place of the Ambassador who has gone to Berlin. Beuth and I were upset to hear that Tieck has been ill; I hope he is now fully recovered, give him my warmest regards.

The longing to be with you will speed us on our way, farewell dearest Susanne. Schinkel.

[536] It is not clear what exhibitions Schinkel is referring to here.

Friday, 4 August

We went to Barckard's to put some things in order and get some French money, went to the Custom House to get our passports sorted out for the departure. Afterwards Beuth and Danckelmann go to see some shops, I go across Blackfriars Bridge to Southwark Bridge and draw St Paul's Cathedral.

We eat, and then promenade through the Temple buildings[537] near Temple Bar, and then through Lincoln's Inn Fields[538] and back to the hotel, and went to bed early.

Saturday, 5 August

After breakfast and after paying our bill we drive with our luggage in two hackney carriages to Tower Stairs, where the Calais steamboat was waiting. Beuth, full of impatience, is not waiting at the waterside for mine and Dankelmann's coach, and has already taken a rowing-boat and gone on board. We, in the narrow streets full of thousands of vehicles, arrived later, and after paying off a number of drivers, porters, boatmen etc. we were able to board the boat, the 'Lord Wellesley', at half past 10. Her two steam-engines together have a horse-power of 80. Our fellow passengers are not unpleasant, and we have a fine trip down the Thames in glorious weather, and said farewell to London, Woolwich, Greenwich etc.

At 5 in the afternoon we reached the last headland of England, and saw Margate through our telescopes, a town situated on low cliffs, shining in the evening sun. The steamboats going to Hamburg, Ostend and Rotterdam, which sailed out with us, on one of which we had seen Herr Professor Stein, Dannenberger etc. a few times in passing, went in different directions at this point and were soon out of sight. The sea was quite rough here, and though I did not feel generally unwell I was sick a few times watching the wash caused by the ship's paddles. We sailed past several stationary guard-ships, which carried three large lamps and whose swaying conveyed very clearly to me the miserable conditions of their crew. We disembarked in Calais at 11 o'clock in the evening, and hurried through the passport controls to M. Dessin's inn.

[537] The Temple buildings (fourteenth to sixteenth century), originally the home of the Order of Knights Templar, also owned by the Crown, became for the most part Inns of Court. Temple Bar was built in 1670 and has often (erroneously) been attributed to Christopher Wren (moved in 1878).
[538] One of the largest squares in London, laid out in the seventeenth century, adjoining Lincoln's Inn.

190. *Journal*, p. 74, (bottom left) Seraing, Cockerill factory, section of a trip hammer

Sunday, 6 August

After we had picked up our carriage again and our luggage had been fetched from the customs, we set off for Dunkirk at 11. The surface of the high road was extremely bumpy in the coupé, and the three of us took it in turns to sit on the box, which was even worse. Drove across the tidal plain behind Dunkirk, the Dutch customs were indulgent. Accommodation for the night in Veurne,[539] a small town with several interesting old buildings, some from the time of the Spaniards.

Monday, 7 August

In Bruges at 11. Pictures in the Academy:[540] van Eyck, Madonna with saints, excellent effect (5 ft square), very strong colours. Hämling [Memling], several paintings and altarpiece wings, beautiful subjects, as big as the van Eyck pictures. Landscape somewhat mannered in the foliage but very fresh in colour. – In the church.[541] – In the monastery masterpieces by Hämling. (St John's Hospital). Memling. Adoration of the Magi, Birth [of Christ], Presentation (Baptism as episode) of the Virgin and child, Donor.[542] In the corridor there are 1 large and 2 small paintings with wings, one of which is completely intact. Wonderful both inside and out, the distances very delicately painted. – The shrine in the church very beautiful but much restored.[543] – Nothing of interest in the town hall.[544] The town hall, public halls with towers and many interesting private houses. Church with 2 pictures. Drove on to Ghent, arrival 9.

Tuesday, 8 August

At 5 in the morning I looked at the van Eyck pictures[545] in the church, then we drove on to Brussels, arriving at 2. Lunch, and then a drive and walk round the town.

[539] Schinkel presumably means: the Town Hall (1596–1612), the Mansion House (1612–28), and the Hooge Wacht (1636). The *Spaansch Paviljoen* dates from the thirteenth and fourteenth centuries. Spanish rule in Flanders (from 1556 onwards) ended in 1714.

[540] The Academy of Arts, founded in 1719, was situated in the former orphanage. Its chapel contained, amongst other things, Jan van Eyck's *Madonna of Canon van der Paele* (1436; painted for the church of St Donatians in Bruges, and Hans Memling's Altar of Christ (1484; from Jacobuskerk).

[541] Presumably the nearby Onze Lieve Vroukerk, dating from the twelfth to the fifteenth century.

[542] Memling's *Adoration of the Magi* (1479), with the *Presentation in the Temple,* and the donor *Jan Floreins.*

[543] The reliquary of St Ursula, one of Memling's most important works, completed in 1489, with six paintings depicting episodes from the life of the saint.

[544] The Town Hall, begun in 1376 and finished in 1420. Above the market halls, the heart of the medieval trading centre, rises the belfry, built in 1280.

[545] This is the Ghent Altarpiece (1420–32) in the Cathedral of St Bavo, the principal work of Jan van Eyck. In 1826 Schinkel saw only the four central panels. The wings were in the possession of Berlin museums at the time (see note 233.)

[546] William Cockerill (1759–1832), inventor and entrepreneur, originally from England, started one of the first factories to produce machines in 1799 in Verviers, Belgium. In 1807 he built a similar factory in Liège, which he handed over to his son John Cockerill (1790–1840) in 1812. The latter built an iron foundry and blast furnace in 1816/17 in Seraing near Liège, which after 1825 was partially owned by the King of the Netherlands (see note 548). According to OHT, 105, Cockerill introduced the coke-furnace in 1823. In 1815 Beuth had invited John Cockerill and his brother William to Berlin, where they directed the building of spinning and cloth factories (in Cottbus, Grünberg and Guben; William Cockerill settled in Guben).

[547] A cast iron statue of a lion was erected on 'Lion's Hill', built 1824–6 by the Dutch government near Waterloo to commemorate the battle.

[548] King William I, from 1815 to 1840 King of the Netherlands, which until 1830 included Belgium (see also note 546).

[549] Johann Peter Cremer (1765–1863), inspector of agriculture in Aachen from 1817. He produced designs for buildings in the new Prussian governmental departments of Aachen and Düsseldorf (including the Aachen government offices and Elberfeld town hall). Schinkel made alterations to some of these (Aachen's municipal theatre and Elise fountain). See also note 550.

[550] This is probably the Aachen building inspector Witfeld. Cremer's design of 1821 for a municipal theatre in Aachen had been altered by Schinkel. It was built 1822–5.

[551] Cremer's design of 1822 for the Elise fountain in Aachen was drastically revised by Schinkel in many of its elements (covered walks, rotunda, proportions). It was built 1825–7 in this new form.

[552] The brothers J.W. and Leopold Bettendorf, friends of the Boisserée brothers, were merchants who had been resident in Aachen since 1814. They owned a large collection of paintings by old masters, which Schinkel had seen in 1816 when he first visited the Rhineland and Brussels and for which he had made tentative offers. He is referring to the version of the *Descent from the Cross* by Rogier van Weyden, which was acquired for the Berlin Museums by the Prussian government in 1830, and which was thought to be the one mentioned by Van Mander. (I am indebted to Dr Lorne Campbell for help with this entry.)

[553] See note 231.

Wednesday, 9 August

Drove from 4 to 5 in the afternoon through Liège to Seraing. Mr Cockerill's factory[546] (plate 190). Splendid lay-out, finer than any in England. Puddling furnaces, hammers, engines, 3 steam-engines for a Dutch East India ship, each of 100 horse-power. Lathes. In the evening the fire of the chimneys, coal mines with air shafts 150 ft high, the mine 800 ft deep.

Thursday, 10 August

In Seraing. Huge iron lion,[547] 16–20 ft long, for Waterloo, garden bridge, canal harbour. Accompanied by King.[548]

Friday, 11 August

With Mr Cockerill through Liège and Chaudefontaine (breakfast) to Aachen. Fine view at Batist, in the English character. In Aachen at 10.

Saturday, 12 August

Steffen the Chief Forester, Herr von Henning, Cremer the Building Inspector,[549] to talk to Wittich[550] on behalf of Cremer's theatre, and Rosler the Water Inspector. Drinking fountain,[551] theatre, new streets, President Reimann, Bettendorf's picture by Rogier von der Weyden[552] highly authentic, the head restored, breakfast with Mr Cockerill and his brother, who accompanied us to the next stage. In Cologne by the evening, where we met Herr and Madame Aders[553] from London.

Sunday, 13 August

At 6 with Building Inspector Ahlert[554] to the Cathedral, restoration going well. Wrote to Cremer in Aachen regarding the construction of the drinking fountain. De Groote.[555] Left at midday. In the evening along a high road past isolated [illegible], Xanten.

Monday, 14 August

From Xanten (the Roman amphitheatre[556] and the Lugsberg) to Cleves. Beuth. Zoo.[557]

Tuesday, 15 August

Cleves. Castle, Roman tower built by Julius Caesar. Surroundings.[558] Visits.

Cleves, 15 August 1826

Dearest Susanne. You have hopefully received my last letter from London via Herr Dannenberger and Professor Stein, and heard from them how we set off from London at the same time. Since then I have travelled safely through Calais, Bruges, Ghent, Brussels, Liège, Aachen, and have now arrived at Cologne, after getting your dear letter in Seraing near Liège which Mamselle Beuth had addressed to Mr Cockerill. We had a very nice and interesting day there and much kindness, Mr Cockerill accompanied us as far as Aachen. In Cologne I spoke to Begasse's wife for a few moments, he had gone out. She told me some news of you, she was ill, by the way, and Begasse[559] himself was in Frankfurt for a week. Hard as we have tried, it is impossible to return to Berlin as speedily as Herr Bürde[560] would wish. I hope however that we shall lose nothing by that, as I would very much like to write up the results of my journey before putting my suggestions to the King,[561] for I have as yet not had the time, and so his absence is very welcome to me, otherwise I would have to

[554] Karl Friedrich Ahlert (1788–1833), in charge of cathedral building from 1822, directed the preservation and restoration of Cologne Cathedral, begun in 1824, which Schinkel had initiated (during visits to Cologne in 1816, 1824, 1826 and 1833; written directions from Berlin, plans for extension 1834).

[555] Eberhard de Groote (1789–1864), lawyer and art-lover in Cologne, friend of the Boisserée brothers, who had accompanied Schinkel on his journey to the Rhine in 1816. Schinkel always visited him when he went to Cologne.

[556] This could be the amphitheatre of Colonia Trajana, with its foundations in Xanten. Colonia Trajana was the second largest town in the Roman province of Germania inferior, after Colonia Agrippina (Cologne). Or it could be the remains of the theatre of the Roman military camp of Vetera Castra, south of Xanten.

[557] In the seventeenth century the Governor of Brandenburg, Johann Moritz von Nassau-Siegen, built the New Zoo at the northern edge of Cleve, from designs by Jacob van Campen. In 1823 Schinkel had given advice on its rebuilding after it had been destroyed during the wars of the French Revolution.

[558] This is the Schwanenburg, a medieval complex of buildings which had been radically altered in the seventeenth and eighteenth centuries. Some parts of Romanesque towers had been preserved, which Schinkel perhaps took for Roman remains.

[559] Karl Begas (1794–1854), painter in Berlin, originally from the Rhineland. Schinkel had had his portrait made by him in 1826 (see plate 1).

[560] Heinrich Bürde (1795–1865), inspector of buildings and head of the planning department in Berlin. He had been collaborating with Schinkel since 1818 (Schauspielhaus, and from 1824 the Museum am Lustgarten).

[561] Schinkel means the new proposals for a more richly ornamented exterior and interior of the Berlin Museum, which he put forward on his return to Berlin. They reflected ideas which he had brought with him from Paris and London (see his report to the King of 24 October 1826, in which he requests additional finance of 58,000 thalers; P.O. Rave, *Schinkelwerk, Berlin I, Bauten für die Kunst*, Berlin 1941, p. 47ff.).

562 Ludwig Friedrich Wilhelm Philipp, Baron von Vincke (1774–1844) had been Lord President of the new Prussian province of Westphalia since 1815.

563 The late Romanesque hall church of St Jacobi had a richly ornamented stepped portal characteristic of thirteenth-century Westphalian buildings.

564 The nave of the Cathedral of St Paulus (thirteenth century) is colossal in its proportions. Schinkel designed a bishop's chair for the cathedral in 1832.

565 One of Schinkel's sketches includes the ground plan of the Liebfrau-Uberwasser-Kirche in Münster (hall church built 1340–46, tower from 1363 to the beginning of the fifteenth century) and the crossing tower of the Church of St Ludgeri (twelfth to early thirteenth century, upper storeys beginning of the fifteenth century). The diary note and the sketch (SM 42.33; see L. Schreiner, *Schinkelwerk, Westphalia*, Munich-Berlin, 1969, Plate 6) are closely connected.

566 On the tower of the town and market parish church of St Lamberti the cages can be seen in which the Anabaptists – a Protestant sect which had established a repressive theocracy in Münster – were incarcerated until their leaders were executed in 1536.

567 In Münster town hall, a major achievement of fourteenth-century secular Gothic architecture, there is the Hall of Peace, the old council room where the Treaty of Westphalia was signed, which put an end to the Thirty Years War.

568 Bernhard Christoph Ludwig Natorp (1774–1846), theologian and pedagogue, consistorial counsellor and educational inspector in Münster since 1816.

569 The palace garden, together with the Prince Bishop's residential palace (built 1767–87), was designed by Johannes Schlaun and laid out 1784–7 in a simpler form. In 1854 it was converted into an English landscape garden at the behest of Friedrich Wilhelm IV.

570 Vice President and the Lord President's representative.

involve myself in very tiring business as soon as I get back, which I would very much like to avoid.

We shall probably continue on to Münster tomorrow morning, perhaps even this evening, where the Lord President von Vincke[562] expects us and where we shall spend 1 to 1½ days, before driving on to Berlin with all possible speed. So I cannot tell you the exact day of my arrival, though it cannot possibly be before Monday, it will probably be one or 2 days later. Please have a big clothes-basket ready, and the two maids, so that my things can be taken out of our trunk and put in it and the trunk can then be put back on the carriage, and Beuth can go home without waiting too long outside our front door. As the post will soon be taking this letter, I shall save everything else until I see you, best wishes to the children and our friends, your Schinkel.

Wednesday, 16 August

Via Bocholt to Borken, in Coesfeld an old Saxon church portal.[563] Dome.

Thursday, 17 August

In Münster at 10, the Lord President not at home. Visited the Cathedral,[564] ancient vaulting of a wide-span [illegible], 2 other churches,[565] on one tower the Anabaptists' cage,[566] town hall recently plastered, good. Hall of the Peace of Westphalia.[567] To Natorp,[568] Chief Counsellor of the Consistory. Promenade in the palace gardens.[569] Gathering with the President Schlechtendal.[570]

[End of the diary, return to Berlin on 22 August]

Schinkel's Itinerary

These handwritten notes constitute a brief and incomplete itinerary of the journey. It contains some details which are not to be found elsewhere and some places Schinkel hoped to visit but was unable to.

16.4.
Berlin
¾ Tag Nacht I
Halle
Naumburg
Mittag 12–2/3

17.4.
Weimar

18.4.
Eisenach
Tag Nacht 5 Uhr morgens—7 Uhr II
Fulda
Mittag 3–5

19.4.
Gelnhausen
Tag Nacht 5 Uhr morgens III
Frankfurt
Ruhetag. Mittag und Nachmittag
Mainz

20.4.
Koblenz
Mittag und Nachmittag

21.4.
Trier
Abend Quednow IV

22.4.
Trier
Mettlach (Kastell) V

23.4.
Mettlach
Abends VI

24.4.
Metz
Mittag VII
Kirche in L'Épine

25.4.
Châlons
Abends. VIII

26.4.
Châlons
Vormittag Römermauern, Kirchen,
    Gewerbeschule
Abends Reims IX

27.4.
Reims
Vormittag Dom, Kirche, St-Remi,
    Triumphbogen römisch
Abends Soissons Dom X

28.4.
Paris

Paris
Abgüsse bei Orzali und Micheli Mouleur, Rue de
    l'Odéon
Conservatoire des Arts et Métiers
Holzbereitung von Roguin, Barrière de la Garre
Jardin des Plantes
Antiquare
Abgüsse im Musée Royale
Bibliothek, Bronzen, Gemmen, Kupferstiche
Charenton, Memby Eisenwerk, englisch Katalog
    von Denon
Bouillon, Zeichnungen auf Stein, Amor e Psyche
Pacho, der Reisende von Cyréne
Beechey (Bitschi), Engländer in London, auch
    über Cyréne
Hittorf, sizilianische Tempel
Ägyptische Sammlung Passalacqua, Rue des filles
    St-Thomas No. 12, auf von 10–4 Uhr
Naviers Kettenbrücke
Börse, Dach Eisen
St-Denis
Kirchen
Cimetière du Père-Lachaise, moderne Monumente
Theater, Bühnenmaschinen
Museum
Spontini
Diorama
Farben, Pinsel pp., l'arbre sec
Cemente, Statuen in Masse

Marquis Sommariva, Privatsammlung von
    modernen Kunstwerken
Belloni, Mosaikfabrik
Lauviers

Rouen
Nacht

Abbeville
Nacht, Tête de Bœuf

Boulogne

Calais
Hôtel Dessin. Bei Tage ankommen

Dover
Wrights Wirtshaus, Ship Inn, ein Commissionair

Canterbury
Fountain Hotel, Kathedrale

London
Gemäldesammlung, Königlich, Buckingham
    House
Marquis Lansdowne, Gemälde und Statuen
Vauxhall
British Museum
Kirchen, Mansion House, Walbrook Church,
    Giese geht mit, St. Paul's
Tower, Rüstungen, Münze Pistrucci, Voigt
    Medailleur
Captain Browne, Fabrik Eisenketten, Kaufmann
    Lindsay
London Docks
London Bridge, Barandon gibt Ketten
East India Dock
West India Dock, eiserne Brücke auf eisernen
    Säulen
Woolwich Militär-Magazine, Kanonen,
    Sägemühlen, Erlaubnis vom Gesandten
Greenwich Hospital, Observatorium, Aussicht auf
    London
Weg unter der Themse, Ackermann bekannt mit
    Brunel
Westminster

Gaswerke in Petersstreet
Maudsley, Maschinenfabrik
Meux, Brauerei
Bramah, Fabrik, Maschinen, neue Ölpresse
Perkins
Wedgwood Niederlage, Portlandvase in Glas
Museum, neues Gebäude, Bibliotheksgebäude,
    Montag, Mittwoch, Freitag 10–2 Uhr
Ägyptische Hall von Bullock, Birmanische
    Wagen, gewebte raffaelische Tapeten
Collins, Glasmaler und Glasfabrikant
Vice-consul Burchard
Hammersmith Bridge, Kette, Ingenieur Architekt
    Clark
Bassin für Westminster
Daniels Zeichner
Horsebazar Westminster
Bazar Piccadilly
Panorama Diorama Regent's Park
Charing Cross, Northumberland House
Carlton House
Brighton, Clam Willan, Ackermanns Werk davon
Buckingham House
Bau des Stadtteils von Lord Grosvenor zwischen
    Hyde Park und Chelsea
Chantry Westmacott, Gießerei Georg III.,
    Bronzestatue, Giese
Taylor Straße Holborn, Architektur,
    Kupferstichhandel
Smithfield Viehmarkt
Treibhaus zu Loddiges
Cook, Kupferstecher für Berliner Kalender
Kupferstecher Exhibition
Exhibition im allgemeinen
Chiswick auf Wege nach Richmond,
    Gemäldegalerie des Herzog Duke Devonshire
Hampton Court
House of Commons, Parlament
Guildhall Lord Mayor, Rathaus
Rondel and Bridges in Ludgatehill, großer
    Juwelier
Transportables Gas
Highgate Higharchsway
Thomson Holzschneider
Tempel, Sitz der Tempelherren, alte Kirche
Kirby Canonstreet, Nähnadeln
Türkische Shawls, vis à vis London Kaffeehaus
Ostindische Tusche, Pinsel bei St. Paul's
Beechey (Bitschi) aus Cyréne kommt heraus bei
    Murray, Albemarle Street
Cemente, Statuen in Masse

Reise in England

Oxford,
Bodleysche Bibliothek, Galerie und Bilder,
    Wirtshaus

Radcliffsche Bibliothek, 2 Kandelaber, antik
    New College, Glasmalereien
St. Mary College, Kartons von Raffael, Stücke aus
    Incendio del Borgo pp.
Kathedrale, altsächsische Fußböden
All Souls College
Christ Church College, Stück Karton von Raffael
Magdalen College, Kapelle mit Glasfenster

Birmingham
Wirtshaus Albion oder Royal Hotel
Herr Thomasson
eiserne Schleuse, Doppelschleuse, Lock oder
    Schloß
Eddington und Henderson, Glasmaler

Dudley
Wirtshaus Dudley Arms
Ruine von einem Kastell, Übersicht der Werke
Oak Iron Works
Horseley Works, Eisenwerke
Newcastle in Staffordshire
Wedgwood Fabrik, Potteries

Leek
Seidenfabrik

Derby
Hospital, Infirmary, Warmluftheizung, Abtritte

Belper
Maschinenfabrik, Herr Strutt, Wasserwerke,
    Gasbehälter

Matlock
Gegend, Bad, Höhle, Herr Maure, Museum von
    Marmor,
Flußspat pp.

Chatsworth
Schloß des Herzogs von Devonshire, Bilder,
    Kunstwerke, antike griechische Vasen

Sheffield
Wentworth Park, Landhaus des Marquis von
    Fitzwilliam, Antiken, Venus, Muse, Dreifuß
    rosso antico, Paris, Raffael, Claude, Guido

York
Kathedrale

Leeds
Herr Fenton Murray, Maschinenfabrik,
    Dampfwagen, Bischoff, Herr Gott,
    Gemäldesammlung, Ruine sehr schön

Manchester
Kirche alt
Dampfmaschinen, Sägemaschinen

Warrington
Stubbs, Handwerkszeug, Mr. Greenig,
    Wireweaver, Drahtweber

Liverpool
Wirtshaus Waterloo Inn
Markt, bedeckt, 240 Schritt lang, 50 breit
Prince's Dock, Prachtschiffe, Ankerketten
Mr. Duncan, flache Ankertaue
eiserne Drehbrücke und Schleusentore
Herculaneum, Pottery
Queen's Dock, eiserne Schuppen für Schiffe
Gibson, Claude, Smith, Leute, die behilflich sind
    Arbeitshaus
12 Stock hohes Haus, feuerfest
Herzog von Bridgewater, der erste Gründer des
    Kanals von Liverpool nach Manchester
Sägemühle von Barygreyson
Architekt Foster, neue gotische Kirchen, eine in
    Stein, eine in Eisen, Grundrisse vom großen
    Badehause
Westmacotts Statue Georg III.
Landhäuser
Rathaus
Botanischer Garten
Work House – Armenhaus
Börse

Ince
Schloß des Mr. Blundell, Antikensammlung, 10
    Meilen von Liverpool

Chester
Kathedrale, Capitelhouse, Stadtmauern, römisch,
    vier Tore der Stadt
Häuser, alte St. John Church, altsächsisch,
    außerhalb der Stadt

Eaton Hall
Schloß, 5 bis 6 deutsche Meilen, ausgenommen
    Sonnabend Sonntag täglich von 12–4 zu sehn,
    Großes modernes gotisches Gebäude Lord
    Grosvenor, eiserne Brücke im Park

Hawarden
Castle alt, Ruine neben dem neuen Gebäude

Holywell
Badeort, Gasbeleuchtungsapparat
Heilquell des St. Bonifatius, Winifride
Kupferwalzwerk, Spinnerei, durch die Quelle
    getrieben
Kirche Mutter Heinrich VII. erbaut, in welcher die
    Quelle entspringt

St. Asaph
Bleierze, Wirtshaus White Lion Inn
Kathedrale, ½ Tagereise

Conway
Kettenbrücke, die Grundbefestigung in der Ruine
    eines alten Schlosses angebracht (im Bau
    begriffen), Ferry

Aberconway
Altes Schloß, alte Stadtmauern, Berge, Felsen

Penrhyn House
Schönes Schloß

Extrapost

Bangor
Ferry, eiserne Waterloobrücke, Kathedrale
Geschäft bei der Kettenbrücke über den Menai

Insel Anglesey
deren Hauptstadt Beaumaris, zu Wasser hin zu
    fahren
Telford Architekt der Kettenbrücke

Chapel Carris
Schöne Gegend, Lord Connery Inn,
    Cermogemavr Inn, komfortabel

Ceiriog
Wasserfall Rhaiadyrywend

Ceiriog-y-druidian
Überreste des Druidendienstes
Römische Verschanzung
Pont-y-glyn
Über einer tiefen Schlucht

Corwen
Römische Festung

Llangollen
Hand Inn
Chirk Aquaedukt

Pont-y-Cysylltau

Über den Pont-y-Cysylltau geht der Kanal von
    Ellesmere weg in Eisenkasten, Fluß Dee, 1007
    Fuß lang, 126 hoch, 12 Fuß breit, 18 Pfeiler, die
    45 Fuß auseinanderstehn

Ceiriog
Fluß und Tal, 10 Pfeiler, 600 Fuß, 65 Fuß hoch,
    auch 750 Fuß unter der Erde

Altes Schloß
Dinas Bran
Alte Steinbrücke von 1346

Valle Crucis Abbey
Ruine vorzüglich, berühmt

Oswestry
Landhäuser

Trevorhall
Stammsitz der Lloyds

Cross Foxe's Inn
Wynnstay
Sir Watkins Wynne, Nachkomme der alten
    wälischen Könige, hat hier ein Schloß, wo
    Pferdezucht kleiner wälischer Pferde getrieben
    wird

Chirk Castle
Ruinen

Shrewsbury

Coalbrookdale

Worcester

Gloucester

Stroud
Tuchfabrikation

Bristol
Kings Weston Inn vor Bristol, schöne Gegend
    (Clifton Terrassen), Kathedrale, 2 große
    Eisenbrücken, Gasanstalt mit eiserner Kuppel,
    Glashütten, Ankerschmiede Acraman

Bath
Bad, Steinbruch Kanal mit 7 Schleusen

Salisbury

Stonehenge

Brighton

Piersfield bei Bristol
Landsitz

Tintern Abbey
Ruine

Fountain Abbey bei York
Hochliegend in einem Park

Bischop Auckland
Landsitz des Bischofs von Durham

Index of Persons

Index of Places